AF497388

THE WORKS

OF THE

EMPEROR JULIAN,

AND

SOME PIECES

OF THE

SOPHIST LIBANIUS,

TRANSLATED FROM THE GREEK.

WITH

NOTES from PETAU, LA BLETERIE, GIBBON, &c.

TO WHICH IS ADDED,

The HISTORY OF THE EMPEROR JOVIAN,

From the French of the Abbé DE LA BLETERIE.

By JOHN DUNCOMBE, M.A.

IN TWO VOLUMES.

THIRD EDITION CORRECTED.

Him Poefy, Philofophy, deplore,
The fcepter'd Patriot, who diftinctions wav'd,
Lord of himfelf, by Pagan rites enflav'd;
Whom all, but Chriftians, held their common friend,
Whofe very errors had a virtuous end.———IRWIN.

VOLUME THE SECOND.

LONDON,

Printed for T. CADELL, in the STRAND.

1798.

[iii]

CONTENTS OF VOL. II.

THE
EPISTLES
OF
JULIAN.

Απαϲαις μεν απαϲας νικων, τα δ'αυϲε τι των ΕΠΙΣΤΟΛΩΝ.

" Superior, as he was, to all men in all his writings, in
" his E PI STL ES he was superior to himself."

LIBANIUS.

VOL. II.   B

⁎ Of the Epistles of Julian, the nine first were printed
in Greek, with other Epistles by various hands, by Aldus,
Rom. 1499, 4to. and afterwards in Greek and Latin, at
Geneva, 1606, folio. The xth was preserved by Socrates
in his History, III. 3. The xith, and those that follow, as
far as the xlviith, were in like manner published among
the Epistles of various writers. The xlixth was taken
from Sozomen, v. 16. The lth, lift, and liid were
first published in Greek by Peter Martinius, together with
the Misopogon, and the other Epistles, illustrated by a
Latin translation, Paris, 1567 and 1583, 8vo. Petau therefore first translated those three, and also the liiid, and the
following, as far as the lviith, which, together with the
Epistle of Gallus to Julian, Bonaventure Vulcanius published at Leyden, 1597, 12mo. at the end of the Epistles
and Problems of Theophylactus Simocatta. The lviiith
and lixth, but doubtfully blended together, were first
published by Nicholas Rigalt, who also added a translation,
at the end of his *Funus Parasiticum*, Paris, 1601, 4to. But
in the edition of Petau, by the advice of Rigalt himself, it
was divided into two, both mutilated, the former having
no conclusion, and the latter no beginning. At length
the former was supplied from a MS. by the learned and
ingenious Lewis Anthony Muratori, in his *Anecdota Græca*,
Padua, 1709, 4to. The lxth and the two following were
first published by Petau, from a copy of an old MS. lent
him by Patricius Junius. The lxiiid, which Martinius
and Petau have given in Greek only, but very imperfect
and incorrect, Ezekiel Spanheim amended and supplied
from the MS. of Allatius, and first added a Latin version.
Muratori has also published three other Epistles of Julian,
the lxivth, lxvth, and lxvith, from the same MS.

FABRICIUS.

For an account of the other Epistles, see the notes.

Epistle I. To * * * * †.

I THOUGHT that you had long ago arrived in Ægypt; and recollecting what I have often said, "Happy," cried I, "are the Ægyptians in "the plenty with which they have long been sup- "plied by the Nile, but happier are they now "in the possession of your Muse, a blessing, in "my opinion, superior even to the Nile : That "river, by flooding, enriches their country ; but "you, by your eloquence, improving the minds "of their youth, endow them with the treasures "of wisdom, like Plato and Pythagoras, their "former visitors."

Such were my reflections, little thinking that you, in the mean time, were not far distant. At the receipt, therefore, of your letter I was at first so much surprised, that I thought it an imposition, and could not believe my eyes. But when I perused the contents, convinced that such elegance could flow from no other pen, how great was my delight! I then entertained hopes of soon seeing you here, and I rejoiced that your own country would soon be blessed with your presence, however short might be your stay. On this subject you seem to have brought a ludicrous charge against

---

† The name of the sage, to whom this Epistle is addressed, is not known. LA BLETERIE.

me.

me. For though I allow that the air is fuch as you reprefent it, that the water is as brackifh as the ocean, and that the bread is made of barley; all which, out of regard to your country, you have by no means exaggerated; yet, my good friend, you are much indebted to her for having furnifhed your mind with philofophy. But beware how you defpife the luxuries of Ægypt. Wife Ulyffes, though he inhabited a fmall and rocky ifland, could not be tempted either by the charms of Calypfo, or the promife of immortality, to prefer them to Ithaca. Nor was any Spartan, I imagine, ever induced by the recollection of his coarfe domeftic fare to complain of Sparta. But I know what has occafioned your bringing this charge againft me. You are fond of money, and in that purfuit being difappointed, you figh with regret, and envy the Nile and the wealth that it produces. This, you fay, makes you defert your country, and renders your perfon as inelegant as that of Chærephon *. But I rather fufpect that you are detained by fome kind nymph, and are fenfible at laft of the power of love. Be this as Venus pleafes! Mean time, farewell; and may I foon hail you the father of a family!

* Chærephon was a writer of tragedies. He celebrated the actions of the Heraclidæ. But being greatly emaciated by his nocturnal lucubrations, he became a vulgar joke. The name of " owl" was alfo given him. See *Erafm. in Chil.* p 685.

He was a difciple of Socrates. His nocturnal ftudies procured him the name of νυκτερις, " bat;" and his palenefs the epithet of πυξινος, " the man of box."   LA BLETERIE.

Epiftle

Epiſtle II. To Prohæresius *.

WHY ſhould I not ſalute the excellent Prohæreſius, a man as exuberant in language
as a river in water, when it overflows its banks;
and in eloquence, the rival of Pericles †, except
that he does not embroil Greece? Be not ſurpriſed
at my adopting the Lacedæmonian brevity. Sages,
like you, may make long and verboſe orations;
but from me to you a little is ſufficient.

A. D.
361.

* One of the Chriſtian profeſſors who ſhut up their
ſchools in conſequence of Julian's edict. [See Epiſtle XLII.]
He taught at Athens, and his reputation extended over
the whole empire. The city of Rome had erected a ſtatue
to him as large as the life, with this inſcription, " The
" queen of cities to the king of orators." He had received from the Emperor Conſtans the honorary title of
" general of the Roman armies." Julian, it is ſaid, exempted him from the general law, and allowed him to retain his ſeat without changing his religion. But Prohæreſius had the delicacy not to avail himſelf of a privilege
which would have rendered his faith ſuſpected. Eunapius,
an admirer and a diſciple of this ſophiſt, but a great enemy
to the Chriſtians, relates this fact differently.
                                        LA BLETERIE.
   On the eloquence of Prohæreſius, Eunapius has fully
enlarged. But Suidas ſays, that Julian, in order to pique
him, preferred Libanius.   PETAU.
   Libanius, in one of his Epiſtles, recommends him to
Maximus, " as an ornament to the world by his eloquence,
a good man, and one to whom both Rome and Athens had
erected a ſtatue of braſs." His death was celebrated in a
remarkable epigram by Nazianzen, preſerved by Muratori
in his *Anecdota Græca*, p. 1.
   † As to the oratory of Pericles, ſee Cicero *de Oratore*,
XXXIV.

                    Know

Know, then, that my affairs are much embarrassed
and distracted. With all the reasons of my return,
if you intend to compile a history, I will most ac-
curately acquaint you by transmitting the original
letters and other authentic evidence. But if you
determine to prosecute your present studies for
the remainder of your life, you shall have no cause
to complain of my silence.

Epistle III. To Libanius *.

A. D.
362.

THOUGH this is now the third day, the philosopher Priscus † is not yet arrived, and a
letter from him seems to intimate that he will defer
his journey. As you have forgotten your promise,
I must remind you of it by demanding my debt.
This debt, you well know, it is no less easy for

* For an account of this sophist, and some of his
epistles, see Vol. I. p. 303.

† A Platonist, whom, at the solicitation of Maximus,
sprung from the same school, the Emperor sent for from
Greece. He was so reserved and mysterious in what he
knew, as even to tax those, who communicated their learning, with prodigality and profaneness. But when he condescended to display his own talents, he discovered a profound knowledge of the systems of the ancients. The court
did not corrupt him, and, instead of becoming a courtier
himself, he endeavoured to render the courtiers philosophers.

He was one of the philosophers that attended Julian to
the Persian war, and with whom he harangued in his last
moments on the nature of the soul. He was called in
question in the reign of the Emperor Valens; but his innocence was immediately acknowledged.   LA BLETERIE.

you

you to difcharge, than it is agreeable to me to receive. Send me therefore your oration, and that divine difcourfe; but, by Mercury and the Mufes, fend them foon. For thefe three days, be affured, you have much wafted me, if what the Sicilian poet fays be true,

   Lovers in one day grow old *.

If this be a fact, as no doubt it is, you, my good friend, have trebled my age.

I have dictated this letter in the midft of bufinefs. I could not write to you myfelf, as my hand is more tardy than my tongue. But my tongue alfo is at prefent tardy and inarticulate through difufe. Farewell, my deareft and beft loved brother!

Epiftle IV.　To Aristomenes †.

IS an invitation neceffary from me to you, and muft friendly offices never be anticipated? Let us take care not to introduce fuch a troublefome cuftom

A. D. 362.

---

* Theocritus, Idyll. xii. by Fawkes.

† This was, without doubt, a man of learning, and perhaps a philofopher. From the conclufion of the Epiftle it may be fuppofed, that he was zealous for the Pagan religion, and perfectly well acquainted with the ceremonies.

This Epiftle feems to have been written by Julian, when he was in Cappadocia; where he ftaid fome time in his way from Conftantinople to Antioch.　　La Bleterie.

In the MS. of Voffius it is addreffed " to Ariftoxenus."
           Petau.

cuſtom as that of expecting a friend to be as ceremonious as a common acquaintance. If I am aſked, " How can you and I be-ſtyled friends, as " we are not yet acquainted ?" I anſwer, Why do we profeſs ourſelves friends to thoſe who were born a thouſand or even two thouſand years ago ? Becauſe they were good and virtuous. We wiſh to reſemble them. And though as to myſelf I am conſcious of being in fact far otherwiſe, in inclination I am certainly not far diſtant.

But to ceaſe trifling, if you come uninvited, you will be cordially welcome ; but if you expect an invitation, you here receive it. Therefore, by Jupiter the Hoſpitable, haſten hither, I intreat you, as ſoon as poſſible, and ſhew us, among the Cappadocians, a true Greek *. For as yet ſome

ſacrifice

The Lxxxixth Latin Epiſtle of Libanius, b. iii. ſeems to confirm the former reading, being addreſſed " to Ariſto- " menes," and much on the ſame ſubject. Being ſhort, I will add it in Engliſh :

" You wiſh, I hear, to be known to me. Be aſſured " that you have gained your wiſh, as I am better acquainted " with nothing than with you. For who can be ignorant " of the ſplendor of ſuch a genius ? Beſides, my love for " you is ſuch, that I love myſelf ſcarce more. Conſe- " quently, command my ſervices, if any thing ſhould offer " in which I can be uſeful."

* Aιδ, α εν Καππαδοκαις καθαρως Ελληνα. " A pure Greek " among the Cappadocians." The reſtorer of the Greek religion could not but be diſpleaſed with Cappadocia. 1. Cæſarea, the capital of the province, was almoſt en- tirely Chriſtian. The temples of Jupiter and Apollo, the tutelar deities of the city, had been long deſtroyed. Even in the reign of Julian, the Chriſtians had juſt pulled down

the

the temple of Fortune, the only one that remained. This prince, not contented with confiscating the effects, moveable and immoveable, of the churches, enrolling the clergy in the most despicable militia, and putting to death those who had assisted in the destruction of the temple of Fortune, erased the town from the number of cities, subjected it to taxation, and made it resume the name of Mazaca, which it bore before Tiberius gave it the name of Cæsarea.

2. In Cappadocia the Pagans themselves could not be agreeable to Julian. Besides his complaining of their want of zeal, their Paganism was apparently blended with the religion of the Magi. Strabo, a native of the province, says, (*Geogr. l. xv.*) that, in his time, " there was a great " number of Magi, called *Pyræthi*, and several temples of " the Gods that were worshipped in Persia. Large in- " closures were seen there, where those Magi kept up the " sacred fire on an altar," &c. The same author seems to say, that those inclosures, called *Pyræthean*, were appendages to the temples of Anaïtis and Oman. The statue of the latter was carried in procession. More than three centuries after Strabo, St. Basil, a Cappadocian also, and contemporary with Julian, being consulted by St. Epiphanius as to the origin of the Magi, and concerning the Magusæi, replied, that " the former were a nation ori- " ginally transplanted from Babylonia into Cappadocia, " and diffused throughout all the country. They wor- " shipped fire, and condemned the killing of animals, " though they scrupled not to eat them when they had " been killed by others. They had neither any law in " their marriages, nor books, nor teachers, nor any rules " but their ancient customs. They were also unsociable " with all men, and incapable of reasoning." The Magusæi could not be very different from the Hypsistarii, a sect in which Gregory, the father of St. Gregory Nazianzen, was born. He informs us, that " the Hypsistarii, " or worshippers of the Most High, professed to adore one " God only. They despised idols, and sacrifice," which must probably be understood with some restriction, as the same St. Gregory elsewhere says, that " his father had " been subjected to the idols of animals. They reverenced " fire and lamps; and though they were not circumcised, " they observed the sabbath and the distinction of meats."

From

3

sacrifice with reluctance, and the few who have zeal, want knowledge *.

Epistle V. To the most honoured THEO-
DORA †.

ALL the books which you sent me, and also your letter, I received with pleasure by the excellent Mygdonius ‡.   And though I have little leisure (the Gods know I do not exaggerate) I return you this acknowledgment.   Farewell, and favour me with more such letters.

From these testimonies it may be inferred, that the tenets and rites of the Persian religion had made a great progress in Cappadocia, but had undergone several alterations. They were certainly adopted, in some degree, even by those who embraced the Greek religion; a mixture highly offensive to Julian, who thought that the re-establishment of Hellenism, in its purity, was the chief purpose of his existence.
LA BLETERIE.

* Εὐελοσίας μεν, ἐκ' εἰδότας δε θύειν, "Willing, but not know-
" ing how, to sacrifice."   Like those Christians, who, St. Paul says, had *a zeal of God, but not according to knowledge.* Rom. x. 2.

† This literary lady I apprehend to be the same who is addressed by Libanius in the following short Epistle (the MCCXCIXth) "We, in return, invite you to come hither,
" and leave the sea.   For it is better that you should live
" soberly with us than that we should feast with you."
By this she appears to have been a person of fortune as well as learning.

‡ This also was a friend of Libanius, as appears from two Epistles to him; the CCCCLXXIst and the DXVIIIth; in the first of which that sophist says, " he was like a pa-
" rent to him at Athens."

Epistle

Epistle VI. To Ecdicius, Præfect of Ægypt *.

THOUGH you write to me on no other subject †, you ought, however, to have written concerning that enemy of the Gods, Athanasius,

---

* It appears from Epistle i, that Ecdicius was very remiss in writing to Julian even on subjects in which he was the most interested.　　　　　LA BLETERIE.

Ecdicius studied oratory at Athens with Libanius, as appears from several of his Epistles.

† After the tumult of Alexandria had subsided, by the massacre of George [see Epistles ix and x], Athanasius, amidst the public acclamations, seated himself on the throne from which his unworthy competitor had been precipitated. Julian, who despised the Christians, honoured Athanasius with his sincere and peculiar hatred . . . . He again banished the archbishop from the city; and he was pleased to suppose, that this act of justice would be highly agreeable to his pious subjects. The pressing solicitations of the people soon convinced him, that the majority of the Alexandrians were Christians; and that the greatest part of the Christians were firmly attached to the cause of their oppressed primate. But the knowledge of their sentiments, instead of persuading him to recall his decree, provoked him to extend to all Ægypt the term of the exile of Athanasius. The zeal of the multitude rendered Julian still more inexorable; he was alarmed by the danger of leaving at the head of a tumultuous city a daring and popular leader; and the language of his resentment discovers the opinion which he entertained of the courage and abilities of Athanasius. The execution of the sentence was still delayed by the caution, or negligence, of Ecdicius, Præfect of Ægypt, who was at length awakened from his lethargy by this severe reprimand.　　　　　GIBBON.

The death of Athanasius was not expressly commanded; but the Præfect of Ægypt understood that it was safer for
him

naſius, eſpecially as you have long been acquainted
with our edicts againſt him.   I now ſwear, by the
great Serapis, that if that enemy of the Gods does
not leave Alexandria, or rather Ægypt, before the
calends of December, the cohort that you command ſhall be fined a hundred pounds of gold *.

him to exceed, than to neglect, the orders of an irritated
maſter. The archbiſhop prudently retired to the monaſteries
of the deſert, and lived to triumph over the aſhes of a
prince, who in words of formidable import had declared his
wiſh, that the whole venom of the Galilean ſchool were contained in the ſingle perſon of Athenaſius.   *Ibid.*

Not contented with baniſhing Athanaſius, the Emperor
gave perhaps ſecret orders to put him to death; or at
leaſt Ecdicius, to ingratiate himſelf with Julian, who ſeemed
diſſatisfied with his negligence, took a reſolution to deliver
Paganiſm for ever from ſo formidable an enemy. Be it as
it may, Athanaſius went up the Nile in order to retire into
the Thebais, when he was informed that he was purſued.
" Fear nothing," ſaid he to the companions of his flight.
" Let us ſhew, that he who protects us is greater than
" he who perſecutes us." Saying this, he made the boat
ſteer back towards Alexandria. They ſoon after met the
aſſaſſin, who aſked them if they had ſeen Athanaſius, and
whether he was far off? He is very near, they replied.
' If you make ever ſo little haſte, you cannot fail to over-
' take him.' The aſſaſſin went on making haſte, in vain.
Athanaſius returned to Alexandria, and there remained
concealed.   LA BLETERIE.

The three Epiſtles of Julian, which explain his intentions and conduct with regard to Athanaſius, ſhould be
diſpoſed in the following chronological order, xxvi, x, vi.
                                                GIBBON.

M. de la Bleterie has, by miſtake, placed the xth before
the xxvith.

* From the excellent diſcourſe of Mr. Greaves on the
denarius, the Roman pound of gold, the uſual method of
reckoning large ſums, may be computed at forty pounds
ſterling.   GIBBON.

4000 pounds ſterling therefore would have been the fine.

You

You know, that, flow as I am in condemning, when
I have once condemned, I am much flower in pardoning *.

P. S. In his own hand.

It grieves me extremely to see all the Gods defpifed by him. None of your tranfactions will
give me fo much pleafure as to hear that the wicked
Athanafius, who has prefumed in my dominions
to perfuade fome Greek women of rank to be bap-
tized, is expelled from all parts of Ægypt †.

Epiftle VII. To Artabius ‡.

BY the Gods, I would neither have the Galileans put to death, nor fcourged, unjuftly,
nor be in any other manner ill-treated. I think it,

A. D.
361.

never-

* Surely this, and the other letters relating to Athanafius, fhew that Julian did not practife that indulgence
and moderation towards the Chriftians which he fometimes
boafted of. For no fault is alleged againft Athanafius,
except that he was " an enemy of the Gods," and made
convicts to Chriftianity from among the Gentiles.
                                        LARDNER.

† Mr. Gibbon tranflates this paffage thus: " Under
" my reign the baptifm of feveral Grecian ladies of the
" higheft rank has been the effect of his perfecutions ;"
and adds, " I have preferved the ambiguous fenfe of the
" laft word (δωκισθαι) the ambiguity of a tyrant who wifhed
" to find, or to create, guilt."

‡ This Artabius, I imagine, is unknown. What is here
given as an Epiftle of Julian is perhaps a fragment of fome
edict. There cannot be a doubt that this prince publifhed
fuch a one at the beginning of his reign, declaring Paganifm the religion of the empire, and at the fame time
                                        forbidding

neverthelefs, highly proper that the worfhippers of the Gods fhould be preferred to them. By the madnefs of the Galileans * the empire was almoft ruined †, but by the goodnefs of the Gods we are now preferved. We ought therefore to honour the Gods, and alfo religious men and ftates.

Epiftle VIII.   To George ‡.

A. D.
362.
" YOU are come, Telemachus §," fays the poet. I have now feen you in your letter. I have there feen your divine mind in miniature, like a large ftatue copied on a fmall feal. For

forbidding the Chriftians to be ill-treated. This therefore muft have been written in 361.   La Bleterie.

This edict fufficiently indicates what treatment the Chriftians were to expect in his reign.   Lardner.

* It was his fancy to call the Chriftians Galileans. In this appellation there was no reafon or argument. But it might anfwer Julian's purpofe to make them appear contemptible in the eyes of weak people.   Ibid.

† It is certain, that the Arian perfecution produced great evils in the ftate. Conftantius, defirous of being a divine, neglected the duties of an emperor. In order to hold councils, he ruined the public carriages, and expended immenfe fums, &c. But it is unjuft to charge the Chriftian religion with faults which it condemns even when committed for its fupport. Of all religions it is beft calculated to render a ftate happy.   La Bleterie.

‡ The procurator, or one of the receivers, of the Cæfar. Epiftle lv is alfo addreffed to him, with the addition of Καθολικω, which the MS. of Voffius has annexed to this.

§ Ηλυθες, Τηλεμαχι. In Odyff. xvi. 23. Ηλθες, κ. τ. λ. the beginning of the welcome of Eumæus to that prince on his return from Pylos.

much

much may be expreſſed in little. The wiſe Phidias * was not only celebrated for his Olympic and Athenian ſtatues, but alſo for compriſing works of real art in ſmall ſculptures. Such, it is ſaid, were his graſshopper and bee, and perhaps his fly †, each of which, though the braſs was formed by nature, ſeemed animated by art. But in theſe, it may be ſaid, the appearances of truth might be owing to the ſmallneſs of the inſects. Obſerve then his Alexander hunting on horſeback ‡, whoſe whole dimenſions do not exceed the ſize of a finger-nail: Each figure, however, is ſo wonderfully executed, that Alexander even wounds the beaſt, and with his looks terrifies the ſpectator. But the horſe refuſing to rear up, even in this

* This excellent Greek ſculptor, in the year of Rome 323, finiſhed the ivory ſtatue of Minerva, ſo much extolled by the ancients, and conſidered as the maſter-piece of his art. He placed it in the citadel of Athens. Afterwards, being baniſhed from that city, he retired into the province of Elis, where he was killed, after finiſhing the ſtatue of Jupiter [of ivory alſo, according to Pliny] which he placed in the temple of Delphi, and which has been reckoned one of the wonders of the world. MORERI.

† Theſe do not occur among the works of this artiſt enumerated by Pliny, in his Natural Hiſtory, xxxiv. 8. though he ſays, that, " in ſmall works Phidias had equal magnificence." Julian does not ſpeak of them as then extant—φασιν is his expreſſion, " it is ſaid." A graſshopper and locuſt of Myron are mentioned by Pliny, as celebrated in the poems of Erinna.

‡ Here Julian ſeems to refer to ſome well-known work then in being, (probably at Rome or Conſtantinople). The expreſſion is Σκοπει, " Behold." A hunting-match of Alexander by Myron, is mentioned alſo by Erinna, as we learn from Pliny.

theft

theft of motion, moves by art. The same im-
pressions, my excellent friend, you have made on
me. For having been often crowned victor in the
lists of eloquent Mercury, your writings, though
few, are excellent, and remind me of the Ulysses
of Homer, who, by only saying who he was, terrified the Phæacians *. Therefore, if my friendship
can be serviceable to you, you may freely command
it. That even the meanest can be useful, princes
may learn from the mouse, whose gratitude preserved the lion †.

* In Odyss. ix. 19. Ulysses tells Alcinous and the
Phæacians who he is, by saying, Ειμ' Οδυσευς Λαερτιαδης,
    Behold Ulysses, fam'd Laërtes' son,
but no terror or confusion, on their part, is mentioned,
nor is his narrative discontinued till b. xi. Perhaps Julian
has substituted by mistake (trusting to his memory) " the
Phæacians" for " the suitors," who are indeed said (xxii.
42) to have trembled at hearing " who Ulysses was."
    ——————— confus'd the suitors stood,
  From their pale cheeks recedes the flying blood.
                        POPE. 53.

  † Alluding to the fable of the mouse, who, having been
preserved by a lion, in return extricated her benefactor from
a net, by gnawing the meshes.
  To this fable Libanius also alludes, in his xlviith
Epistle: " We mice endeavour more to assist you lions, than
" you lions, us ;" and that proverb, which Synesius uses,
" he prefers a mouse to a lion," seems not unknown to the
ancients, applied to those who promise much, but perform
little.   WOLFIUS.

Epistle

Epiftle IX. To Ecdicius, Præfect of Ægypt.

SOME delight in horfes, fome in birds, and others in wild beafts *. I, from my childhood, have always been inflamed with a paffionate love for books †. I think it abfurd to fuffer thefe to fall into the hands of wretches whofe avarice gold alone cannot fatiate, as they are alfo clandeftinely endeavouring to pilfer thefe. You will therefore oblige me extremely by collecting all the books of George ‡: He had many, I know, on philofophical

A. D. 362.

---

* Αλλοι μεν ιππων, αλλοι δε ορνεων, αλλοι θηριων ερωσιν. M. de la Bleterie has tranflated this, *Les hommes naiffent avec des goûts differens*, and fays, " Some delight in horfes, &c. (as in " the original) would have had no grace in French." The Englifh language is not fo faftidioufly delicate. Our affected neighbours might with equal reafon object to that fimilar paffage of the Pfalmift " *Some truft in chariots, and fome in horfes*," &c.

† Thus was truly Julian, what Cicero terms himfelf, *helluo librorum.*

‡ Surnamed, from his parents, or his education, the Cappadocian. He was born at Epiphania in Cilicia, in a fuller's fhop. From this obfcure and fervile origin he raifed himfelf, by the talents of a parafite, firft to a lucrative commiffion, or contract, to fupply the army with bacon, and afterwards, by his profeffion of Arianifm, to the primacy of Ægypt, vacant by the expulfion of Athanafius. His entrance was that of a Barbarian conqueror; and he oppreffed, with an impartial hand, the various inhabitants of his extenfive diocefe. Under the reign of Conftantius, he was expelled by the fury, or rather by the juftice, of the people, and it was not without a violent ftruggle that the civil and military powers of the

phical and rhetorical fubjects, and many on the
doctrine of the impious Galileans.   All thefe I
would have deftroyed *; but left others more
valuable fhould be deftroyed with them, let them
all be carefully examined.   The fecretary of
George may affift you in this difquifition, and if
he acts with fidelity, he fhall be rewarded with
freedom; if not, he may be put to the torture †.

I am

ftate could reftore his authority, and gratify his revenge.
The meffenger who proclaimed at Alexandria the acceffion
of Julian, announced the downfall of the archbifhop.
George, with two of his obfequious minifters, were igno-
minioufly dragged in chains to the public prifon (Nov. 30.
A. D. 361.). At the end of twenty-four days, (Dec. 24.)
the prifon was forced open by the rage of a fuperftitious
multitude, impatient of the tedious forms of legal proceedings.   The enemies of Gods and men expired under
their cruel infults; the lifelefs bodies of the archbifhop
and his affociates were carried in triumph through the
ftreets on the back of a camel; and the inactivity of the
Athanafian party was efteemed a fhining example of evangelical patience.   The remains of thefe guilty wretches
were thrown into the fea.

The meritorious death of the archbifhop obliterated the
memory of his life.   The rival of Athanafius was dear and
facred to the Arians; and the feeming converfion of thofe
fectaries introduced his worfhip into the bofom of the Catholic church.   The odious ftranger, difguifing every circumftance of time and place, affumed the mafk of a martyr,
a faint, and a Chriftian hero; and the infamous George of
Cappadocia has been transformed into the renowned St.
George of England, the patron of arms, of chivalry, and
of the garter.   GIBBON.

* It was mean in Julian to wifh that all Chriftian writings
might be deftroyed.   It was beneath a philofopher to entertain fuch a thought.   LARDNER.

† The deceitful and dangerous experiment of the criminal *queftion* (as it is emphatically ftyled) was admitted,

rather

I am not unacquainted with this library; for when
I was in Cappadocia, George lent me several books
to be transcribed, which I afterwards returned
to him.

Epistle X. To the People of ALEXANDRIA *.

IF you do not revere Alexander, your founder †,
and more especially that great God, the most
holy Serapis ‡; have you no regard for your
country,

A. D.
362.

rather than approved, in the jurisprudence of the Romans.
They applied this sanguinary mode of examination only to
servile bodies, whose sufferings were seldom weighed by
those haughty republicans in the scale of justice or humanity; but they would never consent to violate the sacred
person of a citizen, till they possessed the clearest evidence
of his guilt.   GIBBON.

* This public Epistle [occasioned by the massacre mentioned in a note on the last, p. 17.] affords us a very lively
proof of the partial spirit of Julian's administration. His
reproaches to the citizens of Alexandria are mingled with
expressions of esteem and tenderness. " He suffered his
" friends," (says Ammianus), " to assuage his anger."
                                                           Ibid.

Socrates has transcribed this Epistle, and so has M.
Fleury.

In speaking of George, he did not mention the two
officers who had been massacred with him; because, not
designing to revenge their death, which was most atrocious,
he was ashamed to seem to forgive it. His letter is full of
noble sentiments. I would not affirm, that, after having
written it, he was not in his heart pleased with those who
had furnished him with the subject. The Arians circulated
a report that the partisans of Athanasius were the authors
of the death of George; but the latter need no other
apology than the Epistle of Julian himself, which only accuses the Pagans.   LA BLETERIE.

country, for humanity, for decency? I will add,
for me also, whom all the Gods, particularly the
great Serapis, have thought proper to appoint ruler
of the world *, and who ought to have been informed of the outrage that you have committed?
But anger perhaps has misled you, and rage,
which, subverting reason, often instigates the most
enormous crimes, has, by a sudden impulse, urged
you to perpetrate, as a people, such wickedness as
in others you have justly abhorred and detested.

† Alexander the Great built this city, as one of the most
glorious monuments of his conquests, about 330 years
before Christ. Its situation was most advantageous, between
the sea and one of the arms of the Nile. Alexandria became not only the first city in Africa, after the destruction
of Carthage, but in all the world, next to Rome, as He-
rodian styles it. It is at present subject to the Turks. Selim
subdued it in 1517, with the rest of Ægypt, and the
country which composed the empire of the Mammelus.
The city is almost entirely ruined, and it has no more than
8000 inhabitants. Its haven, however, is very good and
commodious, and it has still some trade.   MORERI.

‡ A false deity which the Ægyptians adored. The
Romans had often forbidden the sacrifices of Serapis to be
celebrated in their cities. The idol of which the Emperor
Hadrian, and afterwards Julian, wished to have a copy,
was composed of all kinds of metals, wood, and precious
stones. The temple and statue were demolished in the
time of Theodosius the Great, A. D. 389, in consequence
of a sedition excited at Alexandria by the Pagans.   Ibid.

* It is observable, that Julian was so addicted to the
idolatry of the Ægyptians, that, though he worshipped so
many Gods of his own country, he professes himself indebted to Serapis alone even for the empire. On this account perhaps he caused himself to be represented on coins,
together with Serapis, or alone, with the name of Serapis
inscribed, as if he were that deity.   BARONIUS.

But

" But tell me, I adjure you, by Serapis, what
were the crimes that incensed you against George?
You will answer, no doubt, " He exasperated
" against us Constantius of blessed memory; he
" brought an army into the holy city; the king
" of Ægypt * seized the most holy temple of
" God, despoiling it of the statues, the offerings
" and ornaments; being justly provoked, on our
" endeavouring to succour the God, or rather to
" prevent his treasures being pillaged, he with
" equal injustice, wickedness, and impiety, dared
" to send against us an armed force, fearing
" George perhaps more than Constantius, if he
" had treated us with lenity, instead of constantly
" acting like a tyrant."

For these reasons therefore, being enraged at
George, the enemy of the Gods, you have again

* Ὁ Βασιλευς της Αιγυπτυ, *rex Ægypti:* so it is expressed in
the edition of F. Petau. He thinks, however, that we
should read στρατηγος, (*dux*) or επαρχος, and M. Spanheim in-
serts that correction in the text. But that is not necessary.
Julian styles Artemius " king," or tyrant, of Ægypt, in
derision, on account of the outrages which he was charged
with having committed, and for which the Emperor had
just caused him to be beheaded.   La Bleterie.

Some months after the tribunal of Chalcedon had been
dissolved, the notary Gaudentius and Artemius, duke of
Ægypt, were executed at Antioch. Artemius had reigned
the cruel and corrupt tyrant of a great province. His
merit, who demolished temples, and was put to death by
an apostate, has tempted the Greek and Latin churches to
honour him as a martyr. But as ecclesiastical history attests
that he was not only a tyrant but an Arian, it is not al-
together easy to justify this indiscreet promotion. Gibbon.

C 3

polluted

polluted the holy city, inftead of bringing him to a legal trial before the judges. In that cafe, there would have been no murder, no crime; by a juft fentence you would have been entirely acquitted, and by punifhing the impious author of thefe incurable evils you would have reftrained all who defpife the laws, all who dare to infult fuch flourifhing ftates and cities, and think that their own ufurped power is aggrandifed by cruelty.

Compare with this epiftle that which I fent you not long ago; obferve the difference, and recollect how much I then commended you. But now, though I would gladly praife you, by the Gods I cannot, fo heinous is your guilt. For the people have dared, like dogs, to worry a man, without being abafhed, nor have kept their hands pure to approach the Gods, the purifiers of blood. But " George," you allege, " deferved fuch a " punifhment." Allowed, and one even more fevere. " And for us," you fay. This alfo I will grant, but not by you. For you have laws, which you all ought to obey and revere; and though fome individuals tranfgrefs them, yet ftill the republic fhould be well governed, you fhould obey the laws yourfelves, and not violate thofe which have hitherto been conftantly well adminiftered.

This is nobly done by you, men of Alexandria, in my reign, who, from my reverence towards God, and from a regard to my grandfather *, and

* Conftantius-Chlorus.

my uncle and namesake *, who governed Ægypt
and your city, esteem you with a brotherly
affection. The undespised authority of a good
and strict government will never suffer the abandoned wickedness of its subjects to pass unpunished.
A desperate disease must be cured by rough pre-
scriptions. For the reasons above-mentioned I ad-
minister to you, however, the mildest, this epistle
and reprimand, which I hope will have the more
effect †, as you are by origin Greeks, and the
laudable and illustrious stamp of that noble descent
still remains in your sentiments and actions.

*Let this be communicated to my citizens of Alex-
andria.*

* Julian, afterwards Count of the East. See Epistle
XIII. Note *.

† I cannot suppose that he flattered himself with correcting the Alexandrians merely by reprimands. Their
tumults, which generally arose in the theatre, were so
frequent, that the government hardly deigned to take
notice of them. It found, no doubt, that they did themselves sufficient justice, for there was always some blood
spilt. They were as foolish as the inhabitants of Antioch,
and much more wicked. LA BLETERIE.

Epistle

Epiſtle XI. To the BYZANTINES .

ALL your ſenators we have reſtored to you, and alſo thoſe of ſenatorial families, whether they have attached themſelves to the Galilean religion,

* This title ſeems to me faulty. I do not think that any Emperor, eſpecially in a law, has given the name of Byzantium to the city of Conſtantinople. But this is not my only reaſon for thinking that this law of Julian was not addreſſed to the inhabitants of New Rome. Whatever was the city to which Julian wrote, he declares to the citizens that he admits into their ſenate thoſe who by birth, or any other means, obliged to take their ſeats there, ſhould allege ſome exemptions and privileges, by way of excuſe. I have often mentioned the zeal of Julian to fill up the council of the cities. But that he had occaſion to employ his ſovereign authority to retain in the ſenate of Conſtantinople, or to recall to it, thoſe who ought to have been members of it, cannot be conceived. I know, that, at leaſt, till the reign of Theodoſius the Great, this ſenate was not in all reſpects equal to that of Rome, without being able to aſcertain in what that inequality confiſted. But it was, without doubt, a very auguſt aſſembly, eſpe-cially when Conſtantius and Julian had augmented its pre-rogatives. With regard to the Eaſt, it was confidered as the public council of the Roman nation. It there held in the political order the ſame rank which that of Rome held in the Weſt. The ſame titles were given to both ſenates. The Emperors gloried in being members and chiefs of both, &c. Thus, though the place of ſenator, even in the two capitals, was attended with very great expences, it muſt have been the object of the ambition of individuals ; and we ſee that one of the methods which was employed to eſcape municipal dignities, obſcure and ruinous honours, was to obtain, when they could, the place or title of ſenator
either

ligion, or have taken any other method of absenting themselves from the senate, such as have filled any public office in the metropolis * excepted.

either of Rome or Constantinople. One law of Constantius had suffered ecclesiastics, in certain cases and on certain conditions, to quit the *curiæ*, or municipal senates; and it is probable that Julian, as well from hatred to Christianity, as from zeal for the *curia*, was desirous to make the ecclesiastics sit there again; as we see by one of his laws, XII *cod. Theod. tit.* I. *De decurionibus l.* 51. *Decuriones, qui ut Christiani declinant munia, revocentur.* But who can be persuaded that he wanted to force them to be senators of Constantinople? That would have been a strange kind of persecution. I could add many other reflections, were I not apprehensive that they would make this note degenerate into a dissertation, perhaps curious, but certainly misplaced. I think I have said enough to prove, that the word Βυζαιτιοις, which appears in the title of this Epistle, has been put by mistake, instead of some other similar word, which I will not endeavour to restore, because I should only advance very uncertain conjectures.   LA BLETERIE.

From this Epistle it should seem that the place of senator was considered as a burthen rather than as an honour; but the Abbé de la Bleterie has shewn that this Epistle could not relate to Constantinople. Might we not read, instead of the celebrated name of Βυζαιτιοις, the obscure but more probable word Βισαιθηνοις? Bisanthe, now Rhodosto, was a small maritime city of Thrace.   GIBSON.

* Εν τη μητροπολι. I suppose Rome and Constantinople.
          LA BLETERIE.

Epistle XII. To Basil *.

A. D.
361,
or 362.

"YOU do not declare war †," says the proverb. But I add, from the comedy, "O
" meſſenger of golden words !" Come then, ex-
emplify this, and haſten hither. You will come a
friend to a friend. Conſtant attendance on public
buſineſs is fatiguing to thoſe who diſcharge it negli-
gently; but thoſe with whom I act are diligent and
induſtrious, and in every reſpect deſerving. I embrace therefore this opportunity, without neglecting public buſineſs, to take ſome relaxation. For
being ſtrangers to the courtly hypocriſy (which
you perhaps have experienced) of loading with

* There is not a word in this Epiſtle which can autho-
riſe the ſuppoſition of its being addreſſed to Baſil the Great.
The name of Baſil was not uncommon. Who this was is
unknown. As to the Epiſtles of Julian to St. Baſil, and
from St. Baſil to Julian, which are printed with the works
of that father, they are unworthy of either, both as to
their ſtyle and matter. Their ſpuriouſneſs is viſible at the
firſt glance. La Bleterie.

† Ου πολεμον αγγελλης. A common ſaying, when any one
brings good news to a town, as war is the moſt calamitous
of all things: and yet with the rumour of it many people
at preſent are delighted; namely, thoſe who feed on the
miſeries of mankind. Julian has doubled the proverb; as the
following expreſſion, χρυσον αγγειλας επων, taken from the
Plutus of Ariſtophanes, is alſo proverbial. They are the
words of the old men, who ſupply the chorus, to Carion,
who had informed them of the approach of Plutus. They
are alſo adopted by Plato in his Phædrus; and again in his
IIId book _De Legibus_. Erasmus.

praiſes

praises thofe whom it really detefts, with mutual freedom we accufe, when neceffary, and blame each other, yet are as cordial as the greateft friends. Hence it happens, envy apart, that I find ftudy a relaxation, and thus ftudious as I am, I feel no anxiety, and fleep ferenely; as when I have watched, I have watched not for myfelf alone, but alfo for others. Thus far perhaps I have been trifling with you through mere idlenefs, and, like Aftydamas *, I have praifed myfelf. But I fend this to inform you, that the company of a fage like you will be highly ferviceable to me. Haften therefore, as I have faid before, making ufe of a public carriage †, and when you have ftayed here as long as you pleafe, you fhall be conveyed wherever you think proper.

Epiftle XIII. To his Uncle Julian ‡.

IT is now the third hour of the night, and having no fecretary, as they are all employed, I with difficulty write you this. I am living, thanks

A. D. 361.

to

---

* An actor who, being ordered a ftatue in the theatre, for his excellent performance of Parthenopæus, infcribed his own elogium; whence the proverb, *Aftydamas fe ipfum laudat.* See Erafmus *in Chiliad.* p. 627. It is alfo ufed by Julian, in his LIXth Epiftle, and by Libanius.

† The government furnifhed carriages to thofe who travelled by order of the prince; and thefe were then called public carriages. La Bleterie.

‡ Afterwards Count of the Eaft, the Emperor's maternal uncle. He had alfo been præfect of Ægypt. (See Epiftle X.)

to the Gods, and have been preserved from doing
or suffering incurable evils.   The sun, whose affist-
ance I particularly requested, and also royal Jupiter, can attest, that I never wished the death of
Constantius, but that I rather wished the contrary.
Why then did I wage war? Because the Gods
expressly commanded me, promising me safety if
I obeyed, but, if I hesitated, that which all the
Gods avert! By appearing openly in arms I
thought I might intimidate him, and thus accom-
modate matters more easily; or, if a battle should
prove inevitable, I determined to rely on Fortune
and the Gods, and to wait whatever their goodness should determine.

Epistle XIV.   To Libanius *.

I READ yesterday most part of your oration †
before dinner; and after dinner, without in-
termission, I finished the remainder. How happy

At his request, being also an apostate, and hating the
Christians with less distinction than his nephew, Julian
pardoned the Pagan murderers of George at Alexandria.
As soon as Julian had heard in Illyricum of the death of
Constantius, he wrote this Epistle to his uncle by the
messenger whom he dispatched with the news of that interesting event.   La Bleterie.

 * One MS. adds Σοφιση και Κοιαιςωρι, "Sophist and
Quæstor." See the first note on Epistle XXVII, which is so
superscribed.

 † Perhaps this was the oration in praise of Julian, which
is mentioned by Suidas; or perhaps one of the two that
are published.   Baronius.
                                          are

are you to be able thus to fpeak, or rather, thus
to think! What a difcourfe! what judgment!
what an underftanding! what wifdom! what arguments! what an arrangement! what ftrength!
what language! what harmony! what compofition!

Epiftle XV. To the Philofopher MAXIMUS *.

ALEXANDER of Macedon is faid to have
flept upon the poems of Homer, that, night
and day, he might be converfant with his martial
inftructions.

A. D.
361.

* The boldeft and moft fkilful mafter of the Theurgic
fcience, by whofe hands Julian (after having imbibed the
firft rudiments of the Platonic doctrines from Edefius) was
fecretly initiated at Ephefus, in the twentieth year of his
age.

As foon as Julian had taken poffeffion of the palace of
Conftantinople, he difpatched an honourable and preffing
invitation to Maximus; who then refided at Sardis, in
Lydia, with Chryfanthius, the affociate of his art and
ftudies. . . . His journey through the cities of Afia difplayed the triumphs of philofophic vanity; and the magiftrates vied with each other in the honourable reception
which they prepared for the friend of their fovereign.
Julian was pronouncing an oration before the fenate, when
he was informed of the arrival of Maximus. The Emperor immediately interrupted his difcourfe, advanced to
meet him, and, after a tender embrace, conducted him by
the hand into the midft of the affembly; where he publickly acknowledged the benefits which he had received
from the inftructions of the philofopher. Maximus, who
foon acquired the confidence, and influenced the councils,
of Julian, was infenfibly corrupted by the temptations of
a court. His drefs became more fplendid, his demeanour
more lofty, and he was expofed, under a fucceeding reign,
to an enquiry into the means, by which the difciple of

Plato

inftructions *.   But I fleep with your epiftles as fo
many Pæonian medicines, and am no more weary
of perufing them, than if they were new and juft
received. To give me therefore in your corre-
fpondence a picture of yourfelf, write, I intreat
you, and fail not to write frequently. Or rather
come, with aufpicious omens; and be affured that,
during your abfence, I cannot be faid to enjoy life,
except while I am reading your letters.

Plato had accumulated, in the fhort duration of his favour,
a very fcandalous proportion of wealth. Three other
Epiftles (xvi, xxxviii, and xxxix.) in the fame ftyle of
frendfhip and confidence, are addreffed to this philofopher.
                                                    GIBBON.

  Maximus and other philofophers accompanied Julian in
his Perfian expedition; and, when he was mortally wounded,
fome of his laft words were a metaphyfical argument with
Maximus and Prifcus on the nature of the foul, having
Socrates no doubt in view. See Ammianus, xxx. 5. He
was fined and imprifoned in the reign of Valens, and at
laft beheaded for magic by Feftus, pro-conful of Afia, in
374.
  Though Maximus was greatly refpected, and much
admired by the Emperor Julian, and many learned Heathens,
as a great philofopher, and was alfo reputed to have commerce with the Gods, I do not think he was a wife man.
                                                    LARDNER.

  * Of all the remains of antiquity, Alexander had the
greateft efteem for Homer, who, he thought, was the only
writer who had perfectly defcribed that wifdom by which
empires fubfift; and fuch was his paffion for him, that he
was ftyled " Homer's lover." He ufed to carry his works
always with him; and even when he went to bed, he put
them and his fword under his pillow, calling them his
" military viaticum, and the elements of martial virtue."
                                                FREINSHEMIUS.

Epiftle

Epiftle XVI. To the fame.

THE fable fuppofes, that the eagle, when he
would try his genuine brood, carries them
unfledged into the air, and expofes them to the
rays of the fun, that by the teftimony of that God
he may diftinguifh the true from the fpurious off-
fpring. But I offer my writings to you as to
eloquent Mercury: and if they can bear your
penetrating ray *, you will judge whether they
are fit to be publifhed. If not, throw them away,
as ftrangers to the Mufes; or plunge them, as
fpurious, in the river. Thus the Rhine, the decent avenger of adultery, does juftice to the
Celts †, by overwhelming illegitimate infants with
his

* Τηι σην ακἰυα in one MS. which feems preferable to
ακοην (" hearing") the common hearing, as it continues the
metaphor.

† On examining all the paffages in which Julian has ufed
the word *Celtes*, I have obferved that he makes it fometimes
fignify the Gauls, fometimes the Germans, and at other
times both of them. I think that it is employed in this
latter fenfe here. Claudian (*in Rufin. l.* 11.) reckons
among the Gauls thofe to whom he afcribes the cuftom of
making their infants undergo the trial of water, by plung-
ing them in the Rhine:

Thus the fierce Gauls with yellow locks proceed,
Whom the fwift Rhone or flower Arar breed,
Or whom, new-born, the Rhine's deep current try'd,
Or whom Garumna wafhes with his tide,
When fwell'd with torrents from the troubled main,
The refluent river floats the cover'd plain.

JABEZ HUGHES.
But

But this poet does not afcribe to them this cuftom exclufively of the Germans. The nations fettled on the two
banks of the Rhine muft have had nearly the fame manners
and the fame cuftoms, becaufe many of thofe who inhabited the left fide of that river were of German origin.
We know alfo that the Germans plunged their children in
cold water as foon as they were born, to afcertain whether
they were ftrong, and to inure them to the cold, as did
many other nations, and as, it is faid, feveral in America
do at prefent.

As to the intention of proving the legitimacy of infants,
it is probably a fable invented by the Romans. Seeing them
plunge in the Rhine thofe children of whom fome perifhed
through weaknefs of conftitution, or by the mifmanagement of thofe who bathed them; and judging, by their own
corruption, of that of other nations, they imputed to the
Germans fome views which they had not, and an anxiety
from which the prudence of the women fufficiently preferved
their hufbands. Be that as it may, the moft ancient authors who mention this motive are Julian, Gregory Nazianzen, and Libanius; but many have mentioned it fince;
among others, Nonnus, Theophylactus, Euftathius, &c.
I know not whether Claudian fhould be added, as he does
not mention the object of the trial. According to the
author of a Greek epigram, quoted by Cluvier (*German.
l. i.*) infants were expofed on the Rhine in a buckler.
When a fable is once invented, circumftances never fail to
be added. I fhall obferve, however, that Julian, who in
two paffages mentions this trial, fpeaks of it as a report
in his fecond Panegyric on Conftantius; inftead of which,
in this Epiftle to Maximus, fubfequent to that difcourfe,
he expreffes himfelf in an affirmative manner: a difference
the more remarkable, as in the fame Epiftle he takes care
to relate only as a fable what he fays of the eagle and his
young ones. Ο μιν μυθος ποιει τον αετον, κ. τ. λ. *Fabula fingit
aquilam,* &c. But, after all, it is probable that Julian was
really certain of the fact, that he had feen the nations
bordering on the Rhine plunge their children in that river,
but that he was miftaken as to the motive. La Bleterie.

The other paffage, to which M. de la Bleterie alludes, is
the following, in the iiid Oration: " It is faid, that,
" among the Germans, there is a river, which is an in
" fallible judge of chaftity, which neither fighing mothers,

                                         " nor

his flood; but such as he acknowledges to be of a pure origin he supports above the water, and again delivers into the hands of the trembling mother, rewarding her with the safety of her child, as a testimony of her uncorrupt and irreproachable nuptials.

Epiftle XVII. To Oribasius *.

WE are told by the divine Homer, that there are two gates of dreams, and that their credit, as to future events, is different †. I think

you

" nor fathers dreading the event for their wives and chil-
" dren, can persuade to conceal their shame, being always
" true and sincere."

That in those days of darkness and ignorance such a superstition might prevail, may easily be believed, when we consider, that in much later times female chastity was as absurdly subjected to the test of another element; and that even in our own country, polished as it is, and in our own memory, the aged of the same sex have been exposed to a trial similar to that above-mentioned, and drowning has been deemed the only method of exculpating them from the charge of witchcraft.

* Of Pergamus. He was physician to Julian, and one of the four domestics whom Constantius allowed him to retain when Cæsar. (See the Epiftle to the Athenians, p. 78.) Oribasius attended him to the Persian war, and in his last moments tried in vain all the resources of medicine. This letter must have been written in Gaul.

The Christian Emperors afterwards stripped him of all his fortune, and banished him among cruel Barbarians, by whom and their kings he was much esteemed, probably for his skill in physic or surgery. He was then recalled to his native country, had his estate restored to him, and married

you have had a clear infight into futurity ‡.   And

a wife with a large fortune.   This we learn from his life,
among thofe of the fophifts, by Eunapius, who mentions
him as living when he wrote, which was about the year 400,
above forty years after his going into Gaul with Julian.
Suidas fays, that Oribafius was of Sardis, and both he and
Photius mention feveral of his works, particularly thefe
four : I. " An abridgment of the works of Galen," in feveral books.   II. " The fentiments of other phyficians,
" as well as Galen," in feventy books. Both infcribed to
the Emperor Julian. III. " An abridgment of the other
" two," in nine books, to his fon Euftathius. IV. " Another
" compendious reprefentation of the principles of medi-
" cine," in four books, infcribed to Eunapius (probably his
biographer), at whofe defire it was compofed. LARDNER.

The Cæfar had rejected with abhorrence a mandate for
the levy of an extraordinary tax; a new fuperdiction, which
the præfect [Florentius] had offered for his fignature ; and
the faithful picture of the public mifery, by which he had
been obliged to juftify his refufal, offended the court of
Conftantius.   We may enjoy the pleafure of reading the
fentiments of Julian, as he expreffes them with warmth
and freedom in a letter [the above] to one of his moft
intimate friends.   GIBBON.

† Odyff. XIX. 562.
　　Immur'd within the filent bower of fleep,
　　Two portals firm the various phantoms keep;
　　Of iv'ry one, whence flit, to mock the brain,
　　Of winged lies a light fantaftic train :
　　The gate oppos'd pellucid valves adorn,
　　And columns fair incas'd with polifh'd horn,
　　Where images of truth for paffage wait,
　　With vifions manifeft of future fate.   FENTON.
Virgil has imitated this in Æneid VI. 893.

‡ It is obfervable, that Julian ufes this language to an
intimate friend. Can his belief then in dreams be doubted ?
In what remains of his books againft the Chriftian religion,
he affirms that " Æfculapius often cured him by remedies
" which he had difclofed to him." The Pagans believed
that that God appeared to them in their fleep.
                                            LA BLETERIE.
                                                      the

the fame I myfelf alfo have had to-day *. A lofty tree † grew, I thought, in a fpacious room, with its branches bending down to the ground, and from its root fprouted another, fmall and young, and very flourifhing. For this plant I was very anxious, fearing left it fhould be rooted up, together with the tree. Approaching nearer, I faw the large one fallen to the ground, but the fmall one not only erect, but raifed into the air. Seeing this, I exclaimed, with much concern, " What a " downfall is this! The root, I fear, will perifh " alfo." One, who was a ftranger to me, then faid, " Obferve with attention, and be not afraid! " For as the root ftill remains in the ground, " the plant is unhurt, and will fix more firm- " ly ‡." Such was my dream; what it portends God knows.

* Even in his fleep the mind of the Cæfar muft have been agitated by the hopes and fears of his fortune. Zofimus relates a fubfequent dream.   GIBBON.

† This tree is Conftantius, and the fhoot Julian himfelf.
                                                    LA BLETERIE.

‡ He here plainly intimates, that he fhould fucceed Conftantius. To the fame purpofe is the following paffage of Ammianus, xxi. 2. " As Cæfar Julian was brandifhing " a buckler, which he was exercifing with various motions " in the field, the pegs, by which it was faftened to- " gether, being fhaken out, the handle alone remained, " which he grafped hard in his hand. And all that " were prefent being terrified by the bad omen," ' Let " ' no one,' he faid, ' be alarmed: I grafp firmly what " I held!'

As to that wicked and effeminate wretch *, I am very desirous to learn, when he thus discoursed concerning me, whether before we met, or since: inform me as far as you are able. He well knows, that frequently, when he oppressed the provincials, I was more silent than I ought; not hearing some things, not admitting others, not crediting a few, and imputing many to his friends and favourites. But when he thought proper to endeavour to brand me with infamy by sending me base and scandalous memorials to sign †, what was the proper step for me to take? To be silent, or to revolt? The former was foolish, mean, and odious; the latter was just, manly, and liberal, but, on account of some present circumstances, inconvenient. How then did I act? In the presence of many, who, I knew, would acquaint him with it, I said, " He will " certainly alter his plan, its injustice is so ap- " parent." Hearing this, instead of acting with discretion, he did what, by heaven, a common tyrant would have scrupled, and that almost before my eyes. In such a situation, what conduct could one, who is a zealous observer of the precepts of

---

* Τν μιαρν ανδρογυνν. He means Florentius, præfect of Gaul.   LA BLETERIE.

See the Epistle to the Athenians, p. 92. Petau and others understand this of the eunuch Eusebius.

† A scheme to augment the capitation.   *Ibid.*

This, in the reign of Constantius, was in Gaul twenty-five pieces of gold, annually, for every head. The humane policy of his successor reduced the capitation to seven pieces.   GIBBON.

Aristotle

Ariftotle and Plato *, with propriety adopt? Should I abandon the wretched people to the mercy of thefe extortioners, or fhould I not, to the utmoft of my power, protect them, reduced as they are, by that profligate crew, to the laft gafp †? Shall I punifh a military tribune, when he deferts his poft, with immediate death, and not deem him worthy even of interment; and fhall I abandon my own ftation, when I am called upon to defend the oppreffed; a ftation, in which I was placed by God himfelf? If difgrace muft be my portion, a pure confcience is no fmall confolation. Would to heaven, that I were ftill bleffed with fuch an excellent friend as Salluft! ‡ If, on this account, I fhould be fuperfeded, I fhall not be concerned; as a fhort time

* It is plain that his illuftrious actions proceeded from pedantry at leaft, as much as from virtue. LA BLETERIE.

† In the original, Τὸ κυκνεῖον ᾄδουσι, "they fing the fong "of fwans." Julian here adopts the ancient poetical idea of the dying melody of this bird. And the fame expreffion of the "fwan-fong" is proverbially ufed to this day, in the fame fenfe, in Sweden. Yet even among the ancients it was doubted by Ælian, denied by Pliny, and ridiculed by Lucian, and by modern naturalifts it is generally exploded. Some, however, have fupported it. Mr. Judrell, in his elaborate illuftrations of Euripides, after employing thirty-four 8vo pages on the fubject, recapitulates the modern evidence on both fides; and a late writer in the Gentleman's Magazine (for 1782, p. 420.) wifhes "Mr. Hunter "would afcertain the capabilities of this common bird for "fuch enchanting melody," as he has thofe of the Ouran-Outang for fpeech; and queries "whether it may not re-"fide, like that of bees and other flying infects, in the "motion of the wings."

‡ An officer of great merit, by nation a Gaul. See the Confolatory Oration on his departure, or recall, in Vol. I.

 well

well spent is preferable to a long course of evil *. The Peripatetic philosophy is not, as some think, more pusillanimous than that of the Stoics. In this only, I apprehend, they differ; the former is more sanguine and less systematical; the latter more cool and prudent, urging a tenacious adherence to opinions.

Epistle XVIII. To the Philosopher Eugenius †.

DÆDALUS, it is said, formed waxen wings for Icarus ‡; and endeavoured by art to surpass nature. Though I admire his art, I cannot commend his prudence, in venturing to trust the safety of his son to dissoluble wax. But if I had the power, according to the wish of the Teian lyric, to be changed into a bird §, I would not fly to Olympus, or on any amorous pursuit, but to

---

* Such a conduct almost justifies the encomium of Mamertinus: *Ita illi anni spatia divisa sunt, ut aut Barbaros domitet, aut civibus jura restituat; perpetuum professus aut contra hostem, aut contra vitia, certamen.*   GIBBON.

† There is great reason to suppose that this Eugenius was the father of Themistius. For he also was a philosopher, and of no small reputation, if the testimony of his son may be credited. See the IId oration of Themistius.   PETAU.

‡ See Ovid. Metam. VIII. Fab. 3.

§ No such passage occurs in any of the Odes of Anacreon that are known to us, or so styled. See a note on the Misopogon, p. 291. The idea is, certainly, Anacreontic.

the

the tops of your mountains, that, as Sappho says,

Thee, my care, I might embrace *.

Nature, however, having confined me in the prison of a human body, and not allowing me to elevate even my words on high, with such wings as I have I pursue you, with my writings, thus endeavouring to be with you as much as possible. Homer styles words " winged †," because they can fly any where, like the swiftest birds, and make what excursions they please. But do you, my friend, write also. For you have an equal, if not a larger, share of the wings of words, to enable you to reach your friends, and, as if you were present, every where to afford them delight.

Epistle XIX. To Ecebolus ‡.

PINDAR thinks that the Muses are of silver §, comparing the clearness and splendor of their art to the most splendid of all substances. The

wise

----

* Ἱνα σε, το μελημα τεμον, περιπλυξωμαι.
This also must be in some Ode of Sappho that has not been preserved.

† Επεα πτεροεντα, Il. I. 201. II. 7. and innumerable other places. Thus also Virgil,

——————— *verbis,*

Quæ tuto tibi magna volant. Æn. XI. 380.

‡ The preceptor of Julian, a sophist, whose conscience was so supple, that he was constantly of the religion of the sovereign, and perhaps, in reality, of none. Under Constantius he inveighed against the Gods of the Pagans. Afterwards he declaimed for them, when his pupil Julian

 had

wise Homer styles silver " shining *," and water " silvery †," as glittering by the bright rays of the sun, and by its own splendid form. Fair Sappho calls the moon " silvery," and says, " on this account all the other stars are obscured ‡." Some therefore may suppose that the Gods abound with silver more than gold. For that silver is more fit for the use of mankind, and better than gold, as being more easily attainable, and much more pleasing and commodious, is not my idea, but that of the ancients.

had opened the temples again. And as soon as he heard of the death of that prince, he acted the part of a penitent by prostrating himself at the doors of a church, and, in a lamentable tone, exclaiming to the faithful, " Trample me " under foot : I am like salt that has lost its favour."

He made Julian promise, with the most dreadful imprecations, never to be the disciple of Libanius ; precautions likely to give Julian a greater taste for that sophist.

La Bleterie.

§ Pindar, in his VIIIth Isthmian, styles the Muse " golden," (χρυσιαν); but I do not find that the epithet " silver" is so applied in any of his works now extant.

* Αιγληεντα.

† Αργυριον. Neither of these epithets are to be found so applied in the Index of Homer by Seberus. They must therefore be in some work that has not reached us. Water indeed is often styled " splendid," (αγλαον) both in the Iliad and Odyssey.

‡ This also must be taken from some poem of Sappho that is lost. The only passage in which the moon is mentioned in her few remaining works is in a fragment, and that without the epithet, which the translator has added:

Δεδυκε μεν α σιλαινα,
Και Πλειαδες, κ. τ. λ.
The Pleiads now no more are seen,
Nor shines the [silver] moon serene.   Fawkes.

— There-

Therefore, if for a piece of gold, prefented by you, I return filver, as of equal value, think not the favour lefs, nor imagine, as in the cafe of Glaucus, that the exchange of armour is difadvantageous to you; and even Diomed perhaps exchanged his filver * arms for gold, becaufe he thought thofe much more ufeful and more proper, like lead, to blunt the point of fpears.

What you wrote has occafioned this jocularity. But if you would fend me gifts more valuable than gold, write, and fail not to write inceffantly. For a letter from you, however fhort, will be preferred by me to the moft coftly prefents.

Epiftle XX. To Eustochius †.

THE wife Hefiod thinks, that our neighbours ‡ fhould be invited to entertainments, that they may feaft and rejoice together, as well as lament and mourn together, when they meet with any unexpected misfortune. But I think, that our friends, not our neighbours only, fhould be

A. D.
362.

-----

* *Αργυρα χρυσων.* In Homer the arms of Diomed areof brafs: *χρυσια χαλκεων.* Il. vi. 236.

M. de la Bleterie has not tranflated this Epiftle.

† A native of Paleftine, an eloquent orator, mentioned by Libanius in feveral of his Epiftles. In one of them he fays, " Euftochius, by his manners, conciliates every one; " they render thofe who are fierce gentle," &c.

‡ Works and Days, I. 340.
No friends forget, nor entertain thy foe,
Nor let thy neighbour uninvited go.　　Cooke, 457.

invited;

invited; becaufe a neighbour may be an enemy; but a friend cannot, any more than white can be black, or hot cold. That you are my friend, not only now, but have long been fo, and that your regard for me has never varied, if there were no other evidence, my love and efteem for you would fufficiently prove. Come then, and partake the confular feftivity *. The public road will convey you, and you may command one carriage, and a fupernumerary horfe †. To complete your wifhes, I have invited the friendly Enodia and Enodius to meet you.

* It was a cuftom for the confuls elect to invite their friends to the confulfhip, which was on the calends of January; this was called *rogare ad confulatum.* And fometimes the confuls elect not only invited their friends by their own letters, but alfo by the letters of the prince himfelf caufed them to be afked to their confulfhip by his agent; which honour, Libanius, in his oration on his own life, p. 67, fpeaking of the conful Richomeres, fays, was firft offered to him. Be that as it may, that the cuftom was frequent in thofe times we learn from the 5th and 6th books of the Epiftles of Symmachus. And of the fame kind is this Epiftle of Julian. VALOIS.

Julian invited Euftochius both as prince and conful, which he was the fucceeding year. Salluft the fecond was his collegue.

† This παριπτος I interpret to be a fingle horfe, a third, in addition to the two that drew the carriage, which horfe, for the greater expedition, king Theodoric, in an Epiftle preferved by Caffiodorus, forbade to carry more than an hundred pounds weight. The fame indulgence is granted by Julian to Ætius, in Epiftle xxxi. PETAU.

This is alfo omitted by M. de la Bleterie.

Epistle XXI. To CALLIXENE *, Priestess of Ceres.

TIME alone evinces men to be juſt, So we were taught of old. Let me add, pious and religious. But you ſay, the love of Penelope for her huſband was alſo thus demonſtrated. To this I anſwer, who can prefer, in a woman, conjugal love to piety, without being thought to have ſwallowed large draughts of mandragora † ? And who that

---

* It is plain, by this Epiſtle, that Callixene had been moleſted, on account of her religion, for twenty years, that is, during almoſt the whole reign of Conſtantius. The date of it may evidently be fixed to the time of the journey which Julian took to Peſſinus. LA BLETERIE.

See note * next page.

The enthuſiaſm of Julian prompted him to embrace the friends of Jupiter as his perſonal friends and brethren ; and though he partially overlooked the merit of Chriſtian conſtancy, he admired and rewarded the noble perſeverance of thoſe Gentiles who had preferred the favour of the Gods to that of the Emperor. Thus he praiſes and rewards the fidelity of this prieſteſs, and thus, in Epiſtle XXVII, he applauds the firmneſs of Sopater of Hierapolis. GIBBON.

† Mandragora has ſuch a ſoporific quality, that, if we credit Pliny, (xxv. 11.) large draughts of it are fatal. It is alſo called Circean, becauſe its root is ſuppoſed to be uſeful in love-philtres. Therefore thoſe who neglect their duty, and fall aſleep, are ſaid " to have drunk much man-" dragora." ERASMUS.

Thus Shakſpeare, in Othello:

—— Not poppy, nor mandragora,
Nor all the drowſy ſyrups of the world,
Shall ever medicine thee to that ſweet ſleep
Which thou hadſt yeſterday.   Act III.

considers

considers the times, and compares Penelope, though
praifed almoft univerfally for her conjugal fidelity,
with the pious matrons who lately hazarded their
lives, and, in addition to thefe evils, twice the
length of time, can juftly put Penelope in competition with you?

Difregard not thefe praifes. All the Gods will
reward you. We, for our part, will honour you
with a double priefthood, and to that, which you
had before, of the moft holy Goddefs Ceres, we add
the priefthood of the great Mother, the Phrygian
Goddefs at facred Peffinus *.

* The ftatue of Cybele had been removed from this
temple to Rome by Scipio Nafica many centuries before.
See Livy, xxix. 10. and Pliny, v. 32. When Julian arrived
on the confines of Galatia, in his way to Antioch, he quitted his route to vifit Peffinus. And probably he compofed
there, in honour of the Mother of the Gods, that hafty
difcourfe which is ftill extant, as " it coft him," he fays,
" not a whole night," εν βραχει νυκτος μερει, after venting
his anger on two Chriftians, one of whom had pulled down
the altar of the Goddefs.

The Peffinuntians had fuch an indifference for the
Mother of the Gods, their ancient protectrefs, that it is
no wonder that this priefthood was vacant. Julian confers
it as Sovereign Pontiff, the head of the Pagan religion.

                                        LA BLETERIE.

Epiſtle XXII. To Leontius.

THE Thurian hiſtorian ſays, that " mens ears
" are leſs faithful than their eyes *." But
as to you I diſſent, and my eyes are leſs faithful than my ears. For though I were to ſee you
ten times, I ſhould never truſt my eyes ſo much as
I now truſt my ears; having heard, from one of
unimpeached veracity, that, as you excell others
in every thing elſe, you excell yourſelf in acting,
as Homer expreſſes it, both " with hands and
" feet †." Allowing you, therefore, the uſe of
arms, we have ſent you a complete ſuit of armour
proper for the foot, being lighter than that of the

* Thus Horace, in his Epiſtle to the Piſos,

———————— What we hear

More ſlowly moves the heart than what we ſee.

Julian ſtyles Herodotus, the author of this ſaying, " the
" Thurian," becauſe he lived and died at Thurium, in
Magna Grecia. It is taken from his Clio, ſpeaking of
the queen of Candaules, whom he wiſhed to ſhew naked
to his friend Gyges.

† When we mean to expreſs our utmoſt endeavours, we
ſay, " with hands and feet." For by the " hands" is declared induſtry in performing, and by the " feet" ſwift-
neſs in forwarding, an undertaking. Thus Hom. Il. XX.
360. ERASMUS.

horſe;

horse; and have enrolled you among our domestic guards, who consist of such as have borne arms, and served in the army *.

Epistle XXIII. To HERMOGENES, formerly Præfect of Ægypt.

A. D.
361.

ALLOW me to say, with the poets,

> How bless'd beyond my hopes am I!

How much beyond my hopes have I heard of my escape from that many-headed Hydra †! I do not mean my brother Constantius (whatever he was), but the wild beasts who surrounded him, whose eyes nothing could elude, and who made him more severe, who in his own disposition was not the mildest, though he seemed so to many. But he is no more. On him therefore, as the saying is, light lie the earth! As to them, I would not have them, Jupiter knows, treated with the least injustice; but as many charges are brought against them, I allow them a trial ‡. In order to be present,

---

* Symmachus, Epist. 67. l. iii. "For to such veterans "a prerogative is due, that they may have the rank of "guards, as a reward for their long services." PETAU.
This Epistle is omitted by M. de la Bleterie.

† Πολυκεφαλοι [in one MS. τρικεφαλοι] υδραν. Hermogenes was, like himself, conversant with the Greek poets.
GIBBON.

‡ To conduct this enquiry, Julian named six judges of the highest rank in the state and army; and as he wished to escape the reproach of condemning his personal enemies,

prefent, haften hither, my dear friend, even beyond your ftrength ; for, by the Gods, I have long wifhed to fee you : and as I have had the great fatisfaction of hearing that you are well, I now command you to come.

Epiftle XXIV. To the moft excellent SERAPION *.

SOME prefent their friends with panegyrics; but I, as a delicious repaft, have fent you a hundred of our long-ftalked, dried figs † ; a gift whofe beauty far exceeds its value. Ariftophanes fays, that " dried figs are the fweeteft of all things, " except honey;" and he is afterwards of opinion that not even honey is fweeter ‡. The hiftorian Herodotus thought that a true folitude was fufficiently defcribed by faying, " it has neither figs,

he fixed this extraordinary tribunal at Chalcedon, on the Afiatic fide of the Bofphorus, and transferred to the commiffioners an abfolute power to pronounce and execute their final fentence, without delay, and without appeal. They were a fecond Salluft, Præfect of the Eaft, Prefident ; the eloquent Mamertinus, one of the confuls elect, and four generals, Nevitta, Agilo, Jovinus, and Arbetio.   *Ibid.*

* A fenator, probably, of Conftantinople.

† Pliny (*l.* xv. *c.* 18.) mentions, among the various kinds of figs [twenty-nine in all], thofe of a purple colour (*porphyritides*) with very long ftalks.   PETAU.

‡ The only two paffages in which Ariftophanes mentions figs, are in his Knights, act II. fc. 2. and his Acharnians, act. III. fc. 3. and in neither of thefe are they compared with honey. Julian muft therefore refer to fome play, or

" nor any thing else that is good *." As if no fruit
excelled figs, and where there were figs, nothing
good could be wanting. Homer praises other
fruits for their size, their colour, or their beauty;
but to the fig alone he gives the appellation of
" sweetness †." Honey he calls " new ‡," fearing
lest he should inadvertently style that sweet which
often happens to be bitter: on the fig alone he

* Herodotus, in the first book of his histories, thus
proves the excellence of figs: " You are preparing to
" make war, O king, against men who wear breeches,
" and other garments, of leather, who feed, not on what
" they like, but on what they have, inhabiting a rugged
" country; they have no wine, by Jove, but are water-
" drinkers; nor have they figs to eat, *nor any thing else*
" *that is good.*"   ATHENÆUS.
The above is part of the speech of Sandanis, a Lydian,
who in vain attempted to dissuade Crœsus from invading
Persia.

† In the garden of Alcinöus, Odyss. VII. 117. Συκαι τε
γλυκεραι. κ. λ. τ.
The blushing fig with luscious juice o'erflows. POPE, 148.
And again, XI. 589. among the fruits that torment Tan-
talus, where though the line in the original is the same,
Broome drops the epithet, and substitutes two of his own:
——Figs sky-dy'd a purple hue disclose.
" Homer's epithets," says Eustathius, " are excellent.
" For it is observable, that the poet gives every tree an
" epithet suited to its peculiar nature. Thus the apple is
" " beautiful," and its fruit, as he expresses it, " splendid"
" (αγλαος) he therefore styles the apple a " splendid-fruited
" tree" (αγλαοκαρπος); among the autumnal fruits, the fig,
" by way of eminence, " sweet," and the olive " verdant."

‡ Μελι χλωρον, part of the entertainment given by Nestor,
in Il. XI. 630. and by Circe in Odyss. X. 234. Pope renders it in one place by " fresh," and in the other by
" new-pressed." The Latin translator of Julian has made
it *flavum.*

bestows

beſtows this peculiar praiſe, as on nectar, becauſe of all things the fig only is ſweet. "Honey," ſays Hippocrates, "is ſweet to the taſte, but quite "bitter when digeſted *:" and I am of his opinion; for that it breeds bile is generally allowed, and gives the humours a different ſavour; which ſhews that it is in its nature rather bitter than ſweet. For it would never change to bitter, if it were not ſo originally, and afterwards became the reverſe.

But the fig is not only ſweet to the taſte, but eaſy of digeſtion. It is ſo uſeful to mankind, that Ariſtotle deems it an antidote againſt all poiſons, and ſays, that "for no other reaſon it is introduced at "the beginning and cloſe of meals; as, in pre "ference to every thing elſe, affording a ſacred re "medy againſt the injuries of food." That the fig is conſecrated to the Gods, and in all ſacrifices is placed on the altar, and is better for perfumes than any frankincenſe, is not merely my opinion; but all who are acquainted with its uſe know that ſuch alſo is the opinion of that ſage the Hie

* Hippocrates ſays this, though not in theſe words, in ſubſtance, in his work *de internis affectionibus*, but of honey boiled : "Boiled honey is heating, and adheres to the " belly; but after it is digeſted, it ferments, and the belly " ſuddenly ſwells, and burns, and ſeems as if it would " burſt." Galen alſo, in his iiid book *de facultate alimentorum*, ſays, that "honey, in its nature, is ſubtle, and by " its acrimony ſwells the belly before it can be digeſted, ſo " as to be voided. Therefore by correcting this we render "it fitter for digeſtion and concoction." And this is done by mixing it with water, and boiling both together. For then, being clarified, it digeſts eaſily. PETAU.

rophant *. The excellent Theophrastus †, in his precepts of husbandry, explaining what kinds of trees can be grafted on others, and the manner of engrafting them, commends, I think, above all, the fig-tree as capable of admitting various sorts, and as being singular in easily bearing at the same time grafts of every kind, if you split any of its boughs, and engraft upon them the shoots of other trees; so that it often resembles a whole orchard, diffusing, like a beautiful garden, the variegated splendor of different kinds of fruit. And while the fruits of other trees continue but a short time, and attain no age, the fig alone survives the year, and accompanies the growth of the succeeding fruit ‡. Homer therefore says, that, in the garden

of

* Ανδρος σοφου και ιεροφαντου. I suppose that Julian here means the Eleusinian pontiff, peculiarly styled *Hierophantes*, or a revealer of sacred things. He was obliged to devote himself to the divine service, and lead a chaste and single life. He was attended by three officers, a torch-bearer, a herald, and one who assisted at the altar. (See Epictetus, *l.* III. *c.* 21. and Potter's Greek Antiquities, vol. I. c. 20.) This pontiff was supposed to be more profound even than Maximus in the science of Theurgy. And Julian must have been well acquainted with his sentiments, as he initiated him in the mysteries at Eleusis, and was afterwards invited by that prince to the court of Gaul, to perfect his sanctification. I am not confident, however, that the interpretation which I have given is the true one.

† Theophrastus has treated on figs, and on the grafting of them in the 11d book of his *Hist. Plant. c.* 1. and 7. and also in his 1st book *de Causis, c.* VI.   Petau.

‡ Theophrastus also mentions some wild fig-trees which bore twice, and others thrice, in a year, as in the island of Ceos. The late Mr. Markland, in an ingenious illustration

of Alcinöus, some fruits grew old upon others *; which, as to other fruits, perhaps may seem a poetical fiction, but, as to the fig, is consistent with truth, because of all fruits it is the most lasting.

Such, I think, is the nature of the fig in general; but of all figs ours is far the best; as that is superior to all other fruits, ours is superior to all other figs, and though it excells every other kind of fruit, it is, in its turn, excelled by ours. And, to continue the comparison, it not only surpasses, as is fit, all others, but even in those particulars, where it seems inferior, it really excells. Nor is this undeservedly our peculiar lot. For it was just, I think, that the true city of Jupiter, and the eye of the whole East, I mean the holy and most spacious Damascus, as she is pre-eminent in every thing else, in the elegance of her sacred rites, the magnificence of her temples, the happy temperature of her climate, the beauty of her fountains, the number of her rivers, and the fertility

tration of Mark xi. 13. adopted from Bishop Kidder, refers " those who will not be convinced that the tree should " have figs on it at the time of the Passover," to the above passage of Julian. See Bowyer's Critical Conjectures and Observations on the New Testament, 4to, p. 65.

* Odyss. VII. 117.
    Each dropping pear a following pear supplies,
    On apples apples, figs on figs arise:
    The same mild season gives the blooms to blow,
    The buds to harden, and the fruits to grow.
                    POPE, 154.

of her foil *, fhould alfo be unrivalled in this wonderful fruit.

This tree will not bear tranfplanting, nor will it leave its native foil, difdaining, like an indigenous plant, to grow any where but in the colony. Gold and filver are probably produced in various places; but our country is fingular in giving birth to a plant which will not flourifh in any other. As the wares of India, and the filks of Perfia, and all the valuable productions of Æthiopia, by the law of commerce are exported to all other parts of the world, fo this our native fig is tranfmitted by us into all other countries; nor is there a city, or an ifland, to which its admirable flavour is unknown. It graces even royal banquets; of every entertainment it is the boaft and ornament; nor is there any cake, or wafer, or conferve, or any other kind of confectionary, that is comparable to it in fweetnefs, fo much does it excell all other dainties. Other figs are eaten in the autumn, or are dried for that purpofe; ours alone are fit for either purpofe; they are good on the tree, and when they are dried they are ftill better. And were

* Damafcus is fituated in a very fertile plain at the foot of Mount Libanus, being furrounded by hills in the manner of a triumphal arch. It is bounded by a river which the ancients named Chryforrhoas, as if it flowed with gold, and it is divided into feveral canals. Damafcus has ftill a great number of fountains, which render it extremely agreeable. Its fertile and delightful meadows, covered with fruits and flowers, contribute alfo to its fame.

MORERI.

5

you

you to obſerve their beauty when growing, how they hang from every bough by long ſtalks, like ſo many cups, and ſurround the tree in a circular form, thus exhibiting various charms, you would ſay, that what a necklace is to the neck, ſuch is this appendage to the tree. In the art of preſerving them, there is alſo no leſs ingenuity than there is pleaſure in eating them. For they are not, like other figs, thrown together in heaps, and promiſcuouſly dried in the ſun; but, firſt, they are gathered carefully from the trees, and then they are hung againſt a wall, by briars or twigs, that they may be bleached by the action of the pure rays of the ſun, and may alſo be ſecured from the attacks of animals and birds, being protected by the prickles as by ſo many guards.

In the praiſe of their origin, flavour, beauty, confection, and uſe, my epiſtle has been ſportive. Let me now inform you, that the number a hundred is more honourable than any other, and contains in itſelf the perfection of all numbers. I know indeed that the ancient ſages preferred an odd to an even number *..... Homer ſeems to

me

---

* Thus Virgil, *Ecl.* viii. 75.—*Numero Deus impare gaudet.* Some paragraphs that follow in the original, being only a trifling play on the number a hundred, I have omitted, " as affording," in the words of M. de la Bleterie, " neither " entertainment nor inſtruction." The French tranſlator indeed has omitted the whole Epiſtle, and reprobates it in his preface, as one of thoſe " which turn on mere trifles." " I would ſuppoſe," he adds, " that this piece is only a

E 3

" proſti-

me to have given in his poem, not lightly or inconfiderately, a hundred-folded fhield to Jupiter *; as he meant by this obfcurely to intimate either that he appropriated the moft perfect number, and that which would moft honour him, to the moft perfect God, or perhaps becaufe, as no number but a hundred defcribes the world, which, on account of its rotundity, is difplayed in the circular form of a fhield, that intelligence which is fo apparent in the world is alfo expreffed by a century of circles. For the fame reafon, hundred-handed Briareus is placed near Jupiter, and contends with the Father to give an idea of his perfect ftrength by a perfect number. Pindar alfo the Theban,

" proftitution of wit and learning, and perhaps a criti-
" cifm; for it appears, by the Letter itfelf, that fuch
" elogiums were fafhionable." Wit and learning, however, are never more difplayed than by giving importance and charms to trifles.

* The paffage alluded to is in Iliad II. 447.
    The dreadful Ægis, Jove's immortal fhield,
    Blaz'd on her † arm, and lighten'd all the field :
    Round the vaft orb a hundred ferpents roll'd,
    Form'd the bright fringe, and feem'd to burn in gold.
POPE, 526.

    This fnaky Ægis, but without the number, is defcribed alfo in Il. V. 738.

    But to make amends (which I wonder Julian fhould omit) the helmet of the Goddefs is defcribed as ἑκατον πο- λιων πρυλεισ᾽ αραρυια, either, as Euftathius fays, " becaufe " it could cover a hundred warriors, or becaufe it had the warriors of a hundred cities engraved upon it." Pope adopts the latter, but amplifies the idea :
    So vaft, the broad circumference contains
    A hundred armies on a hundred plains.   920.

† Minerva.

when

when he celebrates the slaughter of Typhœus in a
triumphal song, and ascribes the strength of this
greatest of giants to the greatest king of the Gods *,
bestows such extravagant applause on him, for no
other reason than his being able to destroy this
hundred-headed monster with one blow; as if no
giant was able to contend with Jupiter but he
alone whom his mother had armed with a hundred
heads, and as if no God but Jupiter was worthy
of the conquest and destruction of such a giant.
Simonides, the Lyric poet, thinks it a sufficient
commendation of Apollo to style him Εκαλον, and,
in preference to any other title, adorns his name
with this sacred distinction, because he slew the
serpent Python, it is said, with a hundred arrows;
and he delights rather to be styled Εκαλον than
Pythius, being distinguished by that as by a sur-
name †.   The island Crete, the nurse of Jupiter,
as a reward for his birth and education, is now
honoured with a hundred cities ‡.   Homer styles
                                        Thebes

* This must probably be in one of the Olympics that
are lost, as no such passage, or " triumphal song", is
extant.

† This seems a forced construction. Apollo's name
Εκαλος is naturally derived from his shooting at a distance,
like εκηβολος, so often applied to him by Homer, and I do
not recollect his being any where styled Εκαλον. The above-
mentioned passage of Simonides is not in his few remaining
fragments collected by Henry Stephens.

‡ Il. II. 649.
Crete's hundred cities pour forth all her sons. POPE, 790.
It is observable, that in the Odyssey, XIX. 174, only
— Ninety cities crown the sea-born isle. FENTON, 197.

Thebes " hundred-gated *," but gives this praise
to no other, because there is a wonderful beauty
in a hundred gates. I say nothing of the hecatombs † offered to the Gods, of the temples a
hundred feet wide ‡, the altars with a hundred
bases, the hundred rooms, the hundred-acred fields,
and other things, divine and human, which are included in the appellation of this number. This
number adorns the establishments both of war §
and peace ||, it exhilarates the military centuries,
and with its addition honours the title of the
judges.

on which Euftathius remarks : " Crete is ' ninety-citied,'
" in the Odyssey, which is ' a hundred-citied' in the
" Iliad, from an accidental circumstance ; for it is said
" that ten cities were destroyed by Idomeneus, at his re-
" turn from Troy, when Leucus possessed it, whom, being
" his son by adoption, he left guardian of the kingdom,
" " a fostered snake," as Lycophron styles him ; but those
" ten cities are said to have been rebuilt after the Trojan
" war. Others understand ' hundred-citied' here not in
" a determinate sense, but merely as ' many-citied.' For
" ' a hundred' was sometimes so used on account of the
" distinction of that perfect number, like ' a hundred
" fringes,' and the warriors of ' a hundred' cities. Thus
" ' hundred-citied' Crete is ' many-citied." Virgil has
followed the Iliad : *Centum urbes habitant magnas.* Æn,
III. 106.

 * Εκατομπυλοι. Il. IX. 383.
  That pours her heroes through a hundred gates.
POPE, 503.

 † The sacrifice of a hundred oxen.
 ‡ Εκατοιπατιδος. Such, as appears from Plutarch, was the
temple of Minerva, in the citadel of Athens. SPANHEIM.
 § Centurions, captains over a hundred foot each.
 || *Centumviri*, judges chosen, three out of every tribe,
to hear and determine certain civil causes.

I could

I could add more, did not the rules of epistolary composition forbid. Pardon me, if I have said too much. Should it, in your opinion, attain mediocrity, the laudable attempt shall be communicated to others, such is my confidence in your judgment. But if another hand should be necessary to make it answer its intention, who better than you can polish this epistle so as to enable it to delight its readers?

Epistle XXV. To the COMMUNITY of the JEWS *.

FORMER times were not so grievous to you on account of the yoke of slavery, as on that of your being oppressed by surreptitious decrees, and

A. D. 362.

* We are informed by some or all our ecclesiastical historians, who write of Julian, that he sent for some of the chief men of the Jewish nation, and enquired of them, why they did not now sacrifice, as the law of Moses directed. They told him, that "they were not to sacrifice "at any place, except Jerusalem; and the temple being "destroyed, they were obliged to forbear that part of "worship." He thereupon promised to rebuild the temple at Jerusalem. And we still have a letter of Julian, inscribed, "To the Community of the Jews," which, however extraordinary, must be reckoned genuine. For Sozomen expresly says, that "Julian wrote to the patriarchs "and rulers of the Jews, and to their whole nation, de- "siring them to pray for him, and for the prosperity of "his reign." That is an exact description of the letter which is inscribed (as above). It was writ in the year 362, as Bleterie supposeth; in the beginning of that year, say Tillemont and the bishop of Gloucester. LARDNER.

Aldus

and obliged to pay large sums into the treasury;
of which I saw much with my own eyes, and have
learned more from the edicts which were preserved

Aldus (*Venet.* 1499.) has branded this Epistle with an
ου γνησιος; but this stigma is justly removed by the subsequent editors, Petavius and Spanheim. It is mentioned
by Sozomen (v. 22.) and the purport of it is confirmed by
Gregory (*Orat.* iv. *p.* 111.) and by Julian himself, Fragment, p. 295.   GIBBON.

What Gregory Nazienzen, in his second invective, tells
us of the conference that followed this letter, plainly shews
it to be genuine. " Julian," he says, " assured the leaders
" of the Jews, that he had discovered from their sacred
" books, that the time of their restoration was at hand."
It is not a mere curiosity to enquire what prophecy it was
that Julian perverted; because it tends to confirm the truth
of Nazianzen's relation. I have sometimes thought it
might possibly be the words of the Septuagint in Dan. ix.
27. Συντελεια δοθησεται επι την ερημωσιν, the ambiguity of which
Julian took the advantage of (against hellenistic Jews, who,
it is probable, knew no more of the original than himself),
signifying *the tribute shall be given to the desolate*, instead of
the consummation shall be poured upon the desolate. For the
letter in question tells us he had remitted their tribute, and
by so doing, we see, was for passing himself upon them
for a second Cyrus.   WARBURTON.

It seems that the Jews, after the destruction of Jerusalem,
preserved a sort of monarchy till the beginning of the Vth
century. They had in Palestine an Ethnarch, or chief of
their nation, who, by the toleration of the Romans, was
invested with great power. He styled himself also Patriarch.
His place was hereditary, and descended from father to son.
All the synagogues of the East and West paid him tribute,
under the pretence of contributing to the support of the
Rabbins, who applied themselves in Judea to the study of
the law. Those whom he commissioned to levy this tax
were styled *Apostles* or *Envoys*. These patriarchs, who had
made themselves very odious by their extortions and rapines,
did not exist in 429. See M. de Tillemont's *Histoire des
Empereurs*, tome I.   LA BLETERIE.

against you. The tribute again ready to be levied upon you I have revoked; this infamous impiety * I have restrained; and the decrees against you remaining in my offices I have destroyed, that none may be able to circulate such an impious report. Of these great oppressions the memorable Constantius, my brother, was less guilty than some men, barbarous in their understandings and wicked in their minds, who frequented his table; whom, arrested by my own hands, and thrown into dungeons, I put to death, that no memorial of their destruction might remain among us †.

Desirous

---

* Ασιβημα. Julian, desirous of flattering the Jews, considers them as a sacred nation, who could not be injured without impiety. La Bleterie.

† From this part it appears to have been written early in his reign, on his first coming to Constantinople, when he purged the city and palace of spies and informers, and the like pests of a corrupted court. Warburton.

The chamber of justice, created by Julian, proceeded against the favourites and ministers of Constantius with the utmost rigour. But that Julian thrust any of them into dungeons " with his own hands," no where appears, and is not even probable. It must therefore be deemed a most extravagant exaggeration; or we must suppose, that the words εν χερσιν εμαις λαβομενος were added by some Jew. Though with Messrs de Tillemont and Fleury, I have made use of this Epistle in the Life of Julian, I own nevertheless, that this passage makes me in some measure suspect it, and strikes me much more than the style of the Epistle, which seems to me written with much less purity than the others; for, after all, it is not necessary for it to have been dictated by Julian himself, or that all his secretaries should have been pure writers. It might also, as well as some others, have been written in Latin. La Bleterie.

In

Defirous to fhew you ftill greater favours, I have
urged my brother Julus *, your moft venerable
patriarch, to forbid the tax which you ftyle
apoftlefhip, and no one fhall opprefs you by ex-
acting fuch for the future, that you may enjoy
eafe and fafety in all my dominions, and may be
ftill more fervent in your prayers for my empire to
the moft excellent God, the creator of all things †,

who

In the ftrange boaft of his perfonal atchievement in
thrufting down the delators into dungeons " with his own
" hands" the Imperial character is fo little preferved, that
the learned M. de la Bleterie is almoft tempted, on this
fingle circumftance, to give up the letter as a forgery.
But he here forgets what he himfelf had before mentioned
of the ftrange efcapes of this fantaftic monarch: " St.
" Gregory Nazianzen fays, that Julian drove away with
" cuffs and kicks the poor who came to folicit favours from
" him." *Life of Julian*, b. IV. Warburton.

* Julian in this refcript forbids the affeffments and
tributes which the patriarchs of the Jews ufed to exact by
apoftles. Of the Jewifh patriarchs, fee *lib.* xvi. *Cod.*
Theod. tit. 8. Petau.

† This language of Julian is by no means a proof that
the letter is forged. We fhall fee, in the conclufion, that
he believed that the God of the Jews was the *Demiurgus*,
who had created, or rather arranged, the univerfe. The
Demiurgus, or Λογος, proceeded eternally, fubftantially, and of
himfelf, from the firft God, named The Being, the One and
the Good. Whether the Platonifts admitted a diftinction of
nature between The Being and the *Demiurgus*, or whether
they only acknowledged a diftinction of perfons, or laftly,
whether they confidered the *Demiurgus* as an attribute of The
Being, it is certain that they gave even the *Theurgus* the name
of the firft, the Supreme God. It was the *Theurgus* whom
Julian worfhipped under the name of the Sun-King, meaning
not the orb which ftrikes our eyes, but an intelligence which

pre-

who has condescended to crown me with his own
pure hand. Those who labour under any anxiety
must necessarily be timid and dispirited, and cannot elevate their hands with confidence in prayer;
but those who are utterly free from care rejoice
with their whole hearts, and more frequently and
more effectually offer their devout supplications to
God that the state may be governed in the best manner agreeably to my wishes. In this also you are
deeply interested; that, after having happily terminated the Persian war, I may dwell in the holy city
Jerusalem *, which you have long desired to see
inhabited;

presides over that orb, and holds the same rank in the intelligent world which the material sun holds in the sensible.

La Bleterie.

* Julian did not wait so long before he gave the Jews
some proofs of his affection, or rather of his hatred to the
Christians, by the project which he formed of re-building
the temple of Jerusalem; a project, which, as Pagan writers
themselves attest, was confounded by one of the most astonish-
ing and best attested miracles mentioned in history. *Ibid.*

On this remarkable event Mr. (afterwards Bishop) Warburton, published, in 1750, his Discourse, entitled, Julian,
&c. (occasioned by Dr. Middleton's Free Enquiry into the
miraculous Powers) written, it is generally thought, with
temper and candour, though Mr. Gibbon brands it " with all
" the peculiarities which are imputed to the Warburtonian
" school," and charges the author with " revealing the
" secret intentions of Julian, and, with the authority of a
" theologian, prescribing the motives and conduct of the
" Supreme Being."

Dr. Lardner, however, (Jewish and Heathen Testimonies, vol. IV. p. 47—71.) doubts the truth of this
miracle. His reasons are drawn from Julian's own writings
(the

inhabited, and in that, reſtored by my labours, may with you glorify the Moſt High *.

(the above paſſage in particular, which intimates his intention of re-building Jeruſalem after his return from the Perſian war, which never happened), the improbability of his allotting money for ſuch an expenſive work when he was juſt ſetting out for Perſia, the credulity, in other inſtances, of Ammianus, the incredible miracles, or pretended miracles, with which the hiſtory of this event is loaded by Chriſtian writers, there being no occaſion, at that time, for ſuch a miraculous interpoſition to hinder that undertaking, and the ſilence of ſeveral Chriſtian contemporary writers, particularly Jerom, Prudentius, and Oroſius. He concludes thus: " Let not any be offended " that I heſitate about this point. I think we ought not " too eaſily to receive accounts of miraculous interpoſitions " which are not becoming the divine Being. There are " many things ſaid of Julian, which all wiſe and good " men do not believe." But let us hear another excellent writer.

The interpoſition certainly was as providential as the attempt was impious. . . There are indeed many witneſſes to the truth of the fact, whom an able critic † hath well drawn together, and ranged in this order: " Ammianus Mar" cellinus an Heathen, Zemuch David a Jew, who confeſ" ſes that Julian was *divinitus impeditus*, ' hindered by God, " in this attempt,' Nazianzen and Chryſoſtom among the " Greeks, St. Ambroſe and Ruffinus among the Latins, who " flouriſhed at the very time when this was done; Theo" doret and Sozomen, orthodox hiſtorians, Philoſtorgius an " Arian, Socrates a favourer of the Novatians, who wrote " the ſtory within the ſpace of fifty years after the thing " was done, and whilſt the eye-witneſſes of the fact " were yet ſurviving." But the public hath been obliged with the beſt and fulleſt account of this whole tranſaction in Dr. Warburton's Julian, where the evidence for the miracle is ſet in the ſtrongeſt light, and all objections are clearly refuted, to the triumph of faith and the confuſion of infidelity.   Biſhop NEWTON.

* The blind ſuperſtition and abject ſlavery of theſe unfortunate exiles muſt excite the contempt of a philoſophic

† Whitby's general Preface, p. xxviii.

Emperor;

To THE PRINCIPAL PHYSICIANS. An Edict *. 12 June, 362.
That the medical art is salutary to mankind, experience clearly demonstrates. The philosophers therefore justly teach that it came down from heaven; for the weakness of our nature, and the frequent disorders to which we are liable, are by that corrected. Therefore, as reason and justice require, and according to the example of former princes †, we, from our benevolence, exempt you, for the future, from the senatorial functions.

Dated at Constantinople, on the 4th of the ides of May, in the consulship of Mamertinus and Nevitta.

Epistle

Emperor; but they deserved the friendship of Julian by their implacable hatred of the Christian name. GIBBON.

* This law was, without doubt, written originally in Latin. An abridgement of it is found, with the title and date, in the Theodosian Code, XIII. t. 3. *de medicis et professoribus*. It is addressed *ad archiatros*. The title of *archiatri* was given to the physicians of the Emperor, and to those who practised physic in the two capitals. It is therefore to the physicians of the court, and to those of Rome and Constantinople, that this law of Julian is addressed. LA BLETERIE.

† The Imperial laws exempted the principal physicians from every public office. They could not be obliged to be members of the council, nor to exercise the magistracies in the municipal towns. If they became senators of Rome or Constantinople, they enjoyed some honours and privileges annexed to that office, without being required to discharge its functions, or to bear its burthens, &c. See the Theodocian Code, at the title just quoted, and the notes of Godefroi. These privileges were as early as the reign of Augustus. They had been confirmed by a great number of Emperors, and very recently by Constantine, whose laws are still in being. But it is well known that Julian was the declared enemy of exemptions, and that he loved to undo what Constantine had done. The physicians therefore were uneasy. Julian, however, maintained them

Epistle XXVI.   To the ALEXANDRIANS.
An Edict *.

A. D.
362.

ONE who had been banished by so many Imperial decrees should have waited at least for one edict † before he returned home, instead of contumeliously insulting the laws, as if there were none in being. For we have not allowed the Galileans, who were banished by Constantius, of

in their privileges. The Latin text seems to give them more than is granted to them in the Greek. *Securi à molestiis munerum omnium publicorum reliquum tempus ætatis jugiter agitabitis.* The Greek only says, τωι Βελτιδικων λειδυργημάων. It is remarkable that the exemptions of the professors, though they were the same as those of the physicians, and though Constantine had confirmed them by two laws, were not attacked. It was notorious that Julian's love of literature, and of those who taught it, exceeded his hatred of exemptions, and even of Constantine.   LA BLETERIE.

* Athanasius had been banished once by Constantine, and twice by Constantius. He was in his third exile when Julian recalled all those whom Constantius had banished on account of religion. Prudence did not allow Athanasius to avail himself of this recall while his see was occupied by George of Cappadocia. But soon after the death of the usurper (see p. 18.) he returned to his church, where the Pagans did not suffer him to remain long in quiet. They represented to the Emperor that Athanasius would pervert the whole city, and that, if he continued there, not a single Heathen would soon be found there. Their complaints determined Julian to issue this edict.   *Ibid.*

† This was not necessary, as Julian had, without distinction, recalled all those whom Constantius had banished for the " madness" of the Galileans.   *Ibid.*

blessed

essed memory, to return to their churches *, but only to their countries. Yet I hear that the most audacious Athanasius, with his usual insolence, has again usurped what they call the episcopal throne; and that this has not a little displeased the people of Alexandria †. We therefore command him to depart from the city on the very day that he shall receive the letter of our clemency; and if he remain there, he may expect a much severer punishment.

Epistle XXVII. To the Sophist and Quæstor Libanius ‡.

ON my arrival at Litarbe §, a town in Chlcis, I found a road where were some remains of the Antiochian winter camp. One part of it was; morassy;

March, 363.

---

* Whether Julian thought of this distinction at first, or whether it was an after-stroke, that this prince employed it only against Athanasius is glorious to that prelate.
La Bleterie.

This explication seems evasive, and perhaps was now first thought of. Lardner.

† This was the "pious" people who tore "men in pieces "as if they had been dogs." [See Epistle X.]
La Bleterie.

‡ It appears that Julian had given Libanius the honorary title of Quæstor. But Eunapius reports, that Libanius refused the honorary rank of Prætorian Præfect, which one of the successors of Julian would have given him, as less illustrious than the title of Sophist (*in vita Sophist.* p. 135.) The critics have observed a similar sentiment in one of the Epistles (xviii. *edit. Wolf.*) of Libanius himself.

moraffy; the other hilly, and extremely fteep; over the morafs loofe ftones were placed by chance, and not artfully cemented, as roads are in a manner built in other places, where, inftead of fand, the ftones are laid in mortar, as in a wall. Paffing this with fome difficulty, I reached my firft ftage *, about the ninth hour, where I faw in the hall the principal part of your fenate †. Of the fubject of our converfation, though perhaps you may have heaïd it already, if the Gods permit, I will inform you. From Litarbe I proceeded to Berea ‡, where Ju-

In this Epiftle Julian gives the journal of his march from Antioch to Hierapolis.   La Bleterie.

He informed Libanius of his progrefs in an elegant Epiftle, which difplays the fertility of his genius, and his tender regard for the fophift of Antioch.   Gibbon.

§ This place Euagrius mentions, *l.* v. *c.* 12. and fays, it was three hundred ftadia from Antioch.   Petau.

* It is fingular that the Romans fhould have neglected the great communication between Antioch and the Euphrates.   Gibbon.

† The martial impatience of Julian urged him to take the field in the beginning of the fpring; and he difmiffed, with contempt and reproach, the fenate of Antioch, who accompanied him beyond the limits of their own territory, to which he was refolved never to return.   *Ibid.*

‡ Now Aleppo. The inhabitants of this place are recorded with honour in the *Acts of the Apoftles,* ch. xvii. for the *readinefs of mind* with which *they received the word,* preached by Paul, *and fearched the fcriptures daily whether thofe things were fo.* By Julian's account, they ftill adhered to their Chriftian principles, receiving, as Mr. Gibbon expreffes it, " with cold and formal demonftrations of re-" fpect, the eloquent fermon of the Apoftle of Paganifm."

St. Bafil has addreffed two Epiftles to the inhabitants of Berea, applauding their piety. See his works, vol. III. p. 1026.

piter, by the cleareſt omens, declared all things
auſpicious. Staying there a whole day, I viſited
the caſtle, and royally ſacrificed to Jupiter a whit:
bull *. With the ſenate I converſed a little on
matters of religion, but though they all praiſed
my diſcourſe †, a few only were convinced by it;
however, they were ſuch as, before I ſpoke, I
thought ſenſible; the others aſſumed a kind of
licence, and ſeemed totally deſtitute of ſhame.
Men are apt to be extremely abaſhed at qualities
that are laudable, ſuch as fortitude of mind and

* He was more a ſuperſtitious than a legal obſerver of
ſacred rites, ſacrificing innumerable cattle without parſi-
mony, ſo that it was thought, if he had returned from
Perſia, oxen would have been wanting; like Marcus Cæſar,
of whom, we are told, it was ſaid, " White bulls to Marcus
" Cæſar:" ' If you conquer, we periſh.'   AMMIANUS.
To Capitoline Jupiter white victims only were ſacrificed
in triumph. See *Turneb. l.* 29. 26.

† The ſon of one of the moſt illuſtrious citizens of
Berea, who had embraced, either from intereſt or conſcience, the religion of the Emperor, had been diſinherited
by his angry parent. The father and the ſon were invited
to the Imperial table. Julian, placing himſelf between them,
attempted, without ſucceſs, to inculcate the leſſon and
example of toleration; ſupported, with affected calmneſs,
the indiſcreet zeal of the aged Chriſtian, who ſeemed to
forget the ſentiments of nature, and the duty of a ſubject;
and at length, turning towards the afflicted youth, " Since
" you have loſt a father," ſaid he, " for my ſake, it is
" incumbent on me to ſupply his place."
Julian alludes to this incident [above]; which is more
diſtinctly related by Theodoret (*l.* III. *c.* 22) The intolerant ſpirit of the father is applauded by Tillemont,
(*Hiſt. des Empereurs, tom.* IV. *p.* 534.) and even by La
Bleterie (*Vie de Julien, p.* 413.)   GIBBON.

                    piety;

piety; but in the baseft actions and fentiments *,
in facrilege and pufillanimity, they have the confidence to glory.

Batnæ next received me, a place to which I never
faw any fimilar but Daphne †. But though Batnæ
may now vie with Daphne, not long ago, when
the temple and the image were in being, I fhould,
without fcruple, not only have compared Daphne
to Offa, Pelion, Olympus, and Theffalian Tempe,
but even have preferred it to them all. The place
above-mentioned is dedicated to Olympic Jupiter
and Pythian Apollo. But on the fubject of
Daphne you have compofed an oration ‡, fuch as
no other mortal,

Of thofe who live in thefe degenerate days §,
with his utmoft efforts, could have written, and, I
think, not many of the ancients. Why therefore
fhould I enlarge upon what has fo elegantly been
defcribed by you? Far be that idea!

---

* Μαλακια γνωμης και σωματος. It is not furprifing, that by
the Pagans that abftraction and contempt of the world, with
which the gofpel infpires every true Chriftian, fhould be
deemed meannefs of fpirit. But why is not Julian afhamed
to blame in the Chriftians thofe virtues whofe very fhadow
he adored in the philofophers? See his Epiftle to Themiftius.   LA BLETERIE.

† See an elegant defcription of Daphne by Mr. Gibbon,
in a note on the Mifopogon, Vol. I. p. 280.

‡ This lamentation is ftill extant in the works of Libanius, and compofes his IXth Oration. It is entitled, " A
" Monody on the Temple of Apollo at Daphne, confumed
" by fire, or, as it is faid, by lightning." It is tranflated
in this volume.

§ Hom. Il. V. 304.

I

At Batnæ (though the name is barbarous, the town is Greek) we inhaled the fumes of incense from all the adjacent country, and saw victims every where prepared. This, though it much pleased me, seemed rather too fervent and foreign to religion *. For sacrifices should be offered in private, far from all public roads and paffengers, and all that is required is a fupply of victims and offerings. But this by proper care may be eafily corrected.

Batnæ is fituated on a plain fkirted by a grove of cyprefles, none of which were old or decayed, but all were equally young and flourifhing. My palace was by no means magnificent, being conftructed of clay and boards, and having nothing ornamental. Nor could the garden vie with that of Alcinöus †, but rather refembled that of Laërtes ‡. There was alfo a fmall grove of cyprefles, and a row of thofe trees was planted along the walls: in the middle were pot-herbs and fruit-trees of every kind. I facrificed there in the evening, and again early in the morning, as was my conftant cuftom every day; and as the rites were aufpicious, we proceeded to Hiera-

* He too clearly difcerned that the fmoke which arofe from their altars was the incenfe of flattery, rather than of devotion.   GIBBON.

† Odyff. VII. 112.

‡ Ibid. XXIV. 204.—Laërtes cultivated land.
    The ground himfelf had purchas'd with his pain,
    And labour made the rugged foil a plain.
                                      POPE, 235.

F 3

polis,

polis *, where we were met by the citizens, and I was received as a guest by one whom, though I had scarce ever seen him before, I had long esteemed. Though you are well acquainted with the reason, I cannot deny myself the pleasure of repeating it; for to hear and speak of these persons is always nectar to me. Sopater, the father-in-law of this, was a disciple of the most divine Jamblichus †. Did I not love all that were connected with him, I should deem myself guilty of the

---

* Hierapolis, situate almost on the banks of the Euphrates, had been appointed for the general rendezvous of the Roman army, who there passed the great river on a bridge of boats, which was previously constructed.

GIBBON.

The ancient and magnificent temple, which had sanctified, for so many ages, the city of Hierapolis, no longer subsisted; and the consecrated wealth, which afforded a liberal maintenance to more than three hundred priests, might hasten its downfall. *Ibid.*

† Of Chalcis, a Pythagorean philosopher, the disciple of Porphyry, and uncle to the philosopher of the same name, to whom Julian has addressed six subsequent Epistles, and whom M. de la Bleterie supposes to have been here meant; but as I understand that the father-in-law of this Sopater (then dead) had been his disciple, it seems rather more applicable to the elder Jamblichus. The elder Sopater was probably that Platonic philosopher who was put to death by Constantine the Great, being styled, by Suidas and others, " a disciple of Jamblichus."

The French translator also styles this Sopater of Hierapolis the " son-in-law" (as well as " pupil") of Jamblichus, for which I can see no authority in the original, or in any other author. Let the reader judge. Ιαμβλιχε τυ διδασκαλε το γραμμα Σωπατρος, τυλυ ανδισης εξ οτυ. In the French, *Sopatre est l'eleve et le gendre du divin Jamblique*, meaning the younger of these philosophers, then living.

worst

worst of crimes. But there is another reason still more cogent. Having often entertained at his house my cousin and my brother *, and, as might well be supposed, being strongly urged by them to apostatise from the Gods, he had the great merit of never being infected with that contagion.

These particulars, immediately relating to myself, I now communicate to you from Hierapolis. As to military and civil transactions, you should be present to see and observe them yourself. For, be assured, if they were distinctly related, they could not be comprised in a letter of twice the length of this. But, as I am writing, I will briefly mention them. I have sent an embassy to the Saracens †, urging them, if they are so inclined, to join us. This is the first article. Next, I have dispatched, as was proper, some observant spies, lest any deserter should acquaint the enemy with our motions. Add to these, I have decided a military dispute ‡, I am persuaded, with lenity and justice.

---

* Constantius and Gallus.

† A wandering people in the deserts of Arabia [who stretched from the confines of Assyria to the cataracts of the Nile], warlike and self-interested, dangerous enemies and burthensome friends. *Nec amici nobis unquam nec hostes optandi*, are the words of Ammianus. The love of rapine and war allured several of them to the imperial standard, though Julian sternly refused the payment of the accustomed subsidies. La Bleterie.

‡ Στρατιωτικης δικην. M. de Tillemont suspects that this relates to a fact mentioned by St. Chrysostom. Being

ready

justice. I have procured excellent horses and mules, and my army is assembled. The boats are filled with corn, or rather with biscuit and vinegar. What a long letter would it require to tell you how each of these points was accomplished! What was said on every subject you may easily guess. As to the happy omens *, having recorded them in many letters and books, which I every where carry with me, why should I trouble you with the repetition?

ready to pass the Euphrates, Julian made an attempt to gain such of his soldiers as were still Christians. Some suffered themselves to be seduced, but the rest refused, and the Emperor did not dare to cashier them, for fear of weakening his army.   *Ibid.*

* Infatuated with his expedition, he saw every thing in the best light, and only kept a register of what he considered as happy presages. He passes over in silence the fatal accident which happened when he made his entry into Hierapolis. Fifty soldiers were crushed to death by the fall of a portico, and many more wounded. Ammianus xxiii. 2.
Ibid.

Another bad omen is mentioned by Ammianus at Batnæ in Osdroëna (after the date indeed of this letter), fifty men being also killed there by the fall of a stack of straw.

Julian stayed three days only at Hierapolis, and then proceeded to Carrhæ in Mesopotamia, fourscore miles distant.

This is the last Epistle of his writing that is extant.

Epistle XXVIII. To Duke Gregory *.

A SHORT letter from you is sufficient to give me great pleasure. Being much delighted therefore with what you have written, I return you many thanks. The love of our friends should be measured, not by the length of their epistles, but by the extent of their affection.

Epistle XXIX. To Alypius †, the Brother of Cæsarius.

SYLOSON ‡, it is said, came to Darius, reminded him of a cloak which he had formerly given him, and in return requested Samos. Darius

A. D.
361,
or 362.

---

* Though the military Counts and Dukes are frequently mentioned both in history and the codes, we must have recourse to the *Notitia* for the exact knowledge of their number and stations. The second of those appellations is only a corruption of the Latin word, which was indiscriminately applied to any military chief. All these provincial generals were therefore dukes. GIBBON.

The Greek word is ηγεμων, which M. de la Bleterie translates *Commandant des troupes*.

† Among the friends of the Emperor (if the names of Emperor and of friend are not incompatible) the first place was assigned by Julian himself to the virtuous and learned Alypius. The humanity of Alypius was tempered by severe justice and manly fortitude; and while he exercised

his

Darius afterwards was much elated, thinking that
he had returned a great present for a small one.

But

his abilities in the civil administration of Britain, he imitated,
in his poetical compositions, the harmony and softness of
the odes of Sappho. [See the next Epistle.]   GIBBON.

This minister, who is styled by Ammianus "a man of an
amiable character," and who, like himself, was a native of
Antioch, afterwards received from his master, just before
he set out for the Persian war, the extraordinary commission to rebuild, in conjunction with the governor of the
province, the temple of Jerusalem. But the attempt was
defeated, as Ammianus, a Heathen and a contemporary,
relates (xxiii. 1.), by a miraculous interposition, "dread-
"full balls of fire (*metuendi globi flammarum*), breaking out
"frequently near the foundations, and rendering the place
"inaccessible to the scorched and blasted workmen." The
truth of this miracle Mr. Gibbon questions, and even Dr.
Lardner has doubted. The reasons adduced by the latter
have been briefly mentioned, p. 62. "A philosopher
(says Mr. G.) "may still require the original evidence of
"impartial and intelligent spectators." But Ammianus
also was "a philosopher," and therefore, no doubt,
"required" and had the "original evidence" of his
fellow soldiers, of his friend and countryman Alypius,
in particular; and would not rashly have named him, and
related a fact, which, if false, must have been immediately contradicted. In the reign of Valens, after having
been long in a private station, Alypius and his son
Hierocles, a youth of an excellent disposition, were both
apprehended on a charge of poisoning. Alypius was deprived of his estate, and banished. And the son, when he
was leading to execution, was happily saved. How is not
mentioned. Amm. xxix. 1. Yet Libanius (Ep. xxv. &c.)
mentions this Hierocles as perishing in the earthquake at
Nicomedia, in 358.

‡ Syloson was the brother of Polycrates, tyrant of
Samos. See Herodotus, *l.* iii. *c.* 140. and Ælian. *Var.
Hist. l.* iv. *c.* 5. He gave his cloak at Memphis to Darius,
when that prince was only one of the guards of Cambyses.
Julian relates the same story in his IIId Oration.

"The

But Syloson found it a woeful gift *.   Compare
my conduct with that of this prince.   In one respect I have the advantage.   I did not want to be
reminded, but retained the remembrance of you
unimpaired, and on the first opportunity that God
gave me I ranked you, not among my second but
my first friends.   So much for the past.

As to the future, will you allow me (for I am a
prophet) to predict? We shall be more successful,
I doubt not, if Nemesis be propitious.   For you
need not a prince to assist you in destroying a city,
but I require the assistance of many in re-building
those that have been destroyed †.   Such is the
pleasantry of my Gallic and barbarous Muse ‡.
Come with the auspices of the Gods.

P. S.   *In his own hand-writing.*

" The cloak of Syloson," (ἡ Συλοσῶντος χλαμύς) is adduced
by Erasmus (*Chil.* p. 352.) as a proverb applied to " those
" who boast and pride themselves on their dress." And (he
adds) " it may be properly said of those to whom a small
" gift, seasonably bestowed, returns with large interest ;"
and then relates, as the origin of it, the above story from
Herodotus.

* Syloson was put in possession of Samos, but the city
being taken, it was pillaged by the Persians, so that he
only reigned over a desert.   LA BLETERIE.

† This perhaps may allude to the forty cities in Gaul,
which, Zosimus says, the Barbarians destroyed, and Julian
rebuilt.   See the Epistle to the Athenians, Vol. I. p. 84.

‡ Julian somewhere says, [Ep. LIV.] that his residence
in Gaul had made him a Barbarian, so that he had almost
forgotten Greek.   He would have been sorry to have been
taken at his word.   LA BLETERIE.

There

There is ready for you plenty of game, goats and sheep *, which we hunt in our winter-quarters. Come to a friend who loved you before he knew your worth.

————————

Epiſtle XXX. To the ſame †.

I WAS juſt recovering from an indiſpoſition, when I received the geography ‡ that you ſent me, nor was the book leſs acceptable for coming from you. For it contains not only better deſcriptions than any book of the kind, but you have

* Ἀφις εριφων και της εν τοις χειμαδιοις θηρας των προβατειων.

This paſſage is obſcure and perhaps corrupted. Does Julian mean to ſay that the winter did not allow hunting; and that there was nothing at his table but butcher's meat? But Julian was not fond of dainties, nor, as I recollect, of hunting. No more might Alypius. The meaning is, that the troops of Julian made incurſions, during the winter, on the territories of the enemy, and carried off flocks and herds. If ſo, this Epiſtle muſt have been written in the Gauls before the abſolute rupture between Julian and Conſtantius. Alypius might be then in Britain, where, we know, he was employed before the reign of Julian. *Britannias curaverat pro præfectis*, ſays Ammianus Marcellinus. LA BLETERIE.

Vice-præfect therefore, or vicar, was his proper title, Britain being one of the dioceſes that were governed by a magiſtrate ſo named, ſubordinate to the Præfect of the Gauls.

† La Bleterie has neglected to tranſlate this Epiſtle. It was probably addreſſed to Alypius, while he was governor of Britain.   GIBBON.

‡ This geography ſeems to have been the compoſition of Alypius. Moreri ſays, " another geographical work " is alſo aſcribed to him, which was a deſcription of the " old world."

also embellished it with Iämbics, not " singing a Bupalian * war," as the Cyrenean poet † expresses it, but such as fair Sappho would have thought worthy of adapting to her hymns. Such a work it may be proper perhaps for you to give, but certainly it is most agreeable to me to receive. With your administration of affairs, as you study to act, on all occasions, both with diligence and mildness, I am highly satisfied. For to blend lenity and moderation with fortitude and resolution, and to exert those in encouraging the good, and these in correcting the wicked, requires, I am confident, no small degree of genius and virtue.

May you have these objects always in view, and make both subservient to your own honour! The wisest of the ancients justly thought that this should be the end proposed by every virtue ‡. May health and happiness be your portion as long as possible, my most esteemed and beloved brother § !.

Epistle

* Bupalus, a statuary, made the image of the poet Hipponax, who was very deformed in person, in ridicule; which he resenting, wrote such severe Iämbics against him, that he hanged himself. This was the common report, which Horace (Epod. v. 14.) seems to confirm. But Pliny (xxxvi. 5.) says, that report was false. Hipponax is reprobated by Julian in his Duties of a Priest, Vol. I. p. 132.

† Probably Callimachus, born, as Strabo says (*l.* xvii.) at Cyrene in Africa, in the reign of Ptolemy Philadelphus. Thence he is often styled " the Libyan bard." His hymns were translated by Dr. Dodd.

‡ Thus they made the entrance to the temple of Virtue the passage to that of Honour.

§ Little did Alypius imagine, while he was exercising his poetical and political talents in Britain, among a people

---

Epiſtle XXXI.   To Biſhop Ætius *.

ALL the reſt who were baniſhed by the late
Conſtantius, on account of the madneſs of
the Galileans, I have recalled.   As to you, I not
only remit your baniſhment, but, mindful of our
old acquaintance, I alſo invite you hither.   Uſe a
public vehicle as far as my camp, and one ſuper-
numerary horſe †.

as inſenſible to the charms of his poetry as their rocks and
foreſts, that, in a diſtant age, when the Britons could have
reliſhed his verſes, he would not have been known as a
poet, and ſcarcely as a governor, eminent as he was in both
thoſe characters, had not this accidental billet been happily
reſcued from the gulph of time.

* A celebrated Arian prelate, who had been ſent by
Gallus to his brother Julian, while he was reader in the
church of Nicomedia, to ſtrengthen him in the Chriſtian
religion.   See the Epiſtle from Gallus to Julian, Vol. I.
p. 1.

The death of Gallus had been followed by the exile
of Ætius, his divine and confident.   He was made reſponſible for ſome of the faults of that unfortunate prince,
and the demi-Arians accuſed him to Conſtantius as a
very dangerous hereſiarch.   The rank of biſhop, which
is given him in the title of the above Epiſtle, muſt have
been added by the tranſcribers.   Ætius was not a biſhop
when Julian wrote to him.   But he was ſoon after ordained by the biſhops of his party, who then came to an
open rupture with the demi-Arians.   The credit which
Ætius had with the Emperor, who preſented him with an
eſtate in the iſland of Leſbos, no doubt inſpired the Ano-
means, or pure Arians, with the boldneſs to complete their
ſchiſm.   It does not appear that Ætius, though a biſhop,
was ever fixed to any ſee.   La Bleterie.

† See note † on Epiſtle XX. p. 44.

Epiſtle XXXII. To the Sophiſt Lucian.

I WRITE, that I may be entitled to an anſwer. If I offend you by the frequency of my letters, give me, I intreat you, the ſame offence *.

Epiſtle XXXIII. To Dositheus †.

I COULD ſcarce refrain from tears, and with reaſon, when I heard your name mentioned, recollecting your ‡ beloved, noble, and in every reſpect excellent father; whom if you imitate, you will be happy, and, like him, render your life honourable; but if you are indolent, you will grieve me, and diſgrace yourſelf, for being uſeleſs to the world.

* The length of this letter could not offend. Many ſcraps, equally inſignificant, from Pope, were treaſured up by his friend Richardſon. But, *le jeu ne vaut pas la chandelle.*

† Doſitheus is mentioned by Libanius, in his cxxxiſt Epiſtle, and a ſhort Epiſtle to him from that ſophiſt is preſerved (in Latin) by Zambicari.

‡ In the printed editions it is ημων, a miſtake ſurely for υμων. Julian could ſcarce remember his own father.

Epiftle XXXIV.   To the Philofopher Jamblichus *.

IT was fufficient for Ulyffes to fay to his fon, in order to check his high opinion of him,

No God am I; for heaven referve that name †.

But I cannot think myfelf a man, as the faying is, while I am abfent from Jamblichus. I will allow myfelf, however, to be your admirer, like that father of Telemachus, and though fome perhaps may think it unbecoming, that fhall not prevent my loving you. For I know that many who have

---

* This Jamblichus muft not be confounded with another of the fame name, who was more ancient (fee p. 70. note †.) This was the difciple of Edefius. Julian has addreffed fix Epiftles to him, [xxxiv, xl, xli, liii, lx, lxi.] which I have not tranflated. To thefe Epiftles in particular may be applied what M. Fleury fays, in general, of thofe which are addreffed to the fophifts, *Elles font pleines des louanges outrées, et d'un empreffement qui marque plus de légereté que d'affection.*   La Bletreie.

Mr. Dodwell (*Exerc. de Pythag. ætate*) fufpects the authenticity of thefe Epiftles, " becaufe they treat on very " trifling fubjects, more worthy of a fophift than a prince, " and fhew a greater attention to ftyle than becomes even " a philofopher." As to his argument drawn from a miftake in chronology, in regard to Sopater, that may eafily be obviated by fuppofing there were alfo two of that name, as Julian feems to intimate   See note †. on Ep. xxvii. p. 70. Libanius has addreffed feven Epiftles to this younger Jamblichus, of which one is preferved by Fabricius, Bibliotheca Græca, vol. IV. p. 384.

† Odyff. xvi. 187. Broome, 222.

admired

admired fine ftatues, far from detracting from the
praife of the artift, have by their paffion for them
added fresh honour to the work.   As to your
humoroufly ranking me among the ancient fages,
that I am far diftant from them is as certain as that
you are one of them.   But you unite not only
Pindar, and Democritus, and the moft ancient
Orpheus, but almoft all the Greeks, who are faid
to have gained the fummit of philofophy, as the
various notes of vocal and inftrumental mufic
combine in a perfect concert.   And as Argus, who
guarded Io, is defcribed by the poets as furrounded
with eyes, fo you, the genuine guardian of virtue,
are enlightened by eloquence with the pure eyes
of learning.   It is faid, that Proteus, the Ægyptian,
affumed various forms, fearing left he fhould inadvertently appear wife to thofe who queftioned
him *.   But as Proteus was really wife, and, as
Homer fays, had much knowledge, I praife him
for his knowledge; but I do not admire his
virtue, as he acted not like a benevolent being,
but an impoftor, in concealing himfelf to avoid
being ufeful to mankind.   But who, my noble
friend, does not admire you, not only for equalling Proteus in wifdom, but alfo for never in-
vidioufly withholding from any one that virtue
and perfect knowledge, which you poffefs, of all
things excellent? Thus, like the fplendid fun, the
radiance of your wifdom enlightens all, both by

* See Virg. Georg. IV. and Ovid. Metam. XI.

inſtructing the preſent, and by your writings, as far as poſſible, improving the abſent. In this you excell even the illuſtrious Orpheus, ſince he waſted his muſic in the ſolace of brutes, but you, as if born for the good of mankind, imitate the hand of Æſculapius, and every where diffuſe your eloquent and ſalutary precepts. So that Homer, I think, if he were to return to life, might with much more reaſon apply that line to you,

— One ſtill living traverſes the world *.

For to thoſe who are of ancient ſtamp, to us in particular, a certain ſacred ſpark, as it were, of true and fertile learning is by you alone rekindled and revived. And, O Jupiter the Preſerver, and eloquent Mercury, grant, in return, that, for the general good of mankind, the life of the excellent Jamblichus may be prolonged to the utmoſt extent! If for Homer, Plato †, and all that are worthy of their ſociety, juſt vows were of old ſuc-

---

* Homer. Odyſſ. iv. 198. Proteus ſpeaking of Ulyſſes to Menelaus,

Εις δ' ἔτι τυ ζωος κατερυκεται ευρω ποντει,

Otherwiſe, ευρεϊ κοσμω.

Not ſo well. For the word κοσμος does not occur in Homer in that ſenſe.   CLARKE.

This various reading may perhaps reſt on no better foundation than the above paſſage of Julian, in which his inſertion of κοσμω may be accidental, by his quoting (as uſual) from memory, or intentional, as better ſuiting his purpoſe.

† The Latin tranſlator has added " Socrates," but without any authority from the original; and indeed Julian would hardly have mentioned him on this occaſion, as his life, though in an advanced age, was ſhortened by violence, and the prayers of the virtuous were therefore in that reſpect unſucceſsful.

                                        cefsfully

cefsfully offered, and their lives were thus prolonged, why fhould not a contemporary of ours,
their equal both in virtue and eloquence, be tranfmitted by fimilar vows to the extremeft old age,
and endowed with every blefling?

Epiftle XXXV. For the Argives *.

IN favour of the city of the Argives much may
be faid by any one who would celebrate their
actions ancient and modern. Of the glory acquired at Troy they are juftly entitled to the
greateft fhare †, as are the Lacedæmonians and
Athe-

* The Argives being oppreffed by the Corinthians, and
fubjected to new exactions, contrary to law, Julian recommends them, as I imagine, to the Pro-conful, faying it
was unjuft that a city, fo flourifhing of old, and, on account of the expence of the facred games, exempted from
taxes, fhould pay a tribute to Corinth towards the amphi-
theatral fports. Corinth was made a Roman colony by
Auguftus, who, at the defire of Julius Cæfar, raifed that
city from ruins. Under this title fhe claimed authority
over feveral cities that were not colonies. That this was
not an edict of the Emperor, but a petition of Julian, then
a private man, appears by an obfervation made in a fubfequent note. PETAU.

This Epiftle, which illuftrates the declining ftate of
Greece, is omitted by the Abbé de la Bleterie.

The eloquence of Julian was interpofed, moft probably
with fuccefs, in behalf of a city which had been the royal
feat of Agamemnon, and had given to Macedonia a race
of kings and conquerors. GIBBON.

† It feems ftrange that he fhould afcribe the greateft
fhare in the Trojan war to the Argives, in the fame manner
as he does afterwards to the Lacedemonians and Athenians.

Athenians afterwards. For though both thofe
wars were waged by all Greece, of praife, as well
as of cares and labours, the generals may claim a
large proportion. But thefe are of ancient date.
After the return of the Heraclidæ, the birth-right
taken from the eldeft *, the colony fent from thence
into Macedonia, and the conftant prefervation of the
city, free and independent, from the neighbouring
Lacedæmonians, were proofs of no moderate or

For they attempted nothing afterwards againft the Tro-
jans ; but by the appellation of " Trojan" he means fome
other expeditions which were undertaken by the Greeks
againft the Perfians, as if Τρωικα were the fame as Βαρβαρικα.

PETAU.

Agamemnon, the " king of men," was king of Argos
(in Achaia), as well as of Mycenæ, but is not fo ftyled by
Homer in his catalogue of the fhips, the troops of Argos
being there fubdivided from thofe of Mycenæ, and led by
Diomed, acting as their general under Agamemnon. " Di-
" omed" (as Mr. Wodhull obferves, in his notes on the
Oreftes of Euripides), " though he derived his title of
" king from Ætolia, never poffeffed that throne, but re-
" fided chiefly at Argos (about fix miles only from My-
" cenæ), till he fettled in Italy. Euripides, it has been
" obferved, perpetually confounds thofe two cities."

* Temenus. The origin of the Macedonian kingdom
was derived from the Argives by Caranus (their firft king),
brother to Phidon, king of the Argives. On which account, he fays, the anceftors of Philip and Alexander
fprung from Argos. PETAU.

This pedigree from Temenus and Hercules may be fufpicious, yet it was allowed, after a ftrict enquiry, by the
judges of the Olympic games (Herod. *l.* v. *c.* 22.) at a
time when the Macedonian kings were obfcure and un-
popular in Greece. When the Achaian league was declared
againft Philip, it was thought decent that the deputies of
Argos fhould retire. GIBBON.

common

common fortitude. Actions similar to those of the Macedonians against the Persians may also be ascribed to this city; as this was the country of the latter ancestors of Philip and Alexander. In later times it obeyed the Romans, not as a vassal, but rather as an ally; and, I think, partook with the rest of the freedom and other privileges which the Emperors have always indulged to the cities of Greece. But now the Corinthians *, prone to oppression, compell that city, which is annexed to theirs (for thus it should properly be expressed) by the reigning city †, to be tributary to them; and this innovation, it is said, they have now

* Argos, he says, was made tributary to Corinth by the authority of the reigning city, because when the Achaians were subdued by Mummius, and Corinth destroyed, all Greece, being assessed under the name of Achaia, received a magistrate from the Romans, who, under the Emperors, was styled a Pro-consul, and resided at Corinth, which was therefore the metropolis of Achaia, nay of Peloponnesus, and consequently of all Greece. See Pausanias, *in Achaicis*, *p.* 222. and Pliny, *Ep. ult. I.* VIII. Seven years before Julian wrote this Epistle, the Corinthians had begun to exact a tribute from the Argives towards their wild beasts and hunting-matches. PETAU.

† Rome. Julian gives her the same appellation in his 1st Oration, p. 5. Eunapius, who flourished after the death of Julian, styles her η βασιλευσα Ρωμη, in his Prohæresius. Themistius, though he was ambassador from Constantinople to Constantius at Rome, in his IId Oration, p. 41. styles the one " the queen of cities," and the other " the " second." For the same reason, Rome is represented on ancient coins, and those struck even under Constantine or his sons, as a woman sitting, and holding a globe in her right hand. SPANHEIM.

 practised

practised for seven years, not considering that Delphi and Elis are by agreement exempted from tribute on account of their celebrating the sacred games. For since there are, as is well known, four great and most illustrious games in Greece, the Eleans furnish and direct the Olympic, the Delphians the Pythian, the Corinthians the Isthmian, and the Argives the Nemean. Why then should those retain the exemptions formerly granted, and these, who, on account of the like expences, were formerly exempted, or perhaps not taxed originally, now be deprived of a privilege with which they were once honoured? Besides, Elis and Delphi *, for those highly celebrated games every fifth year, are used to contribute only once; but at Argos there are two Nemean, as there are two Isthmian at Corinth. And at this time also two other games

* The Olympic and Pythian games were celebrated once in five years; the Nemean and Isthmian twice. For the Nemean were kept at the beginning of the first, and, in like manner, at the close of the third year; the one being in winter, and the other in summer. Besides the two Nemean, the Herean also were defrayed by the Argives. Four solemnities therefore, in the whole, were exhibited by them, on which account they ought justly to have been exempted from tribute.   PETAU.

The first institutor of the Olympic games is unknown, though it is generally supposed to have been Pelops. They were consecrated to Jupiter, and were performed in the neighbourhood of Olympia, in the district of Pisa. The Pythian were celebrated at Delphi in honour of Apollo; the Nemean at Nemea, in Peloponnesus, in honour of Hercules; and the Isthmian in the Isthmus of Corinth, in honour of Neptune.

are

are added to thofe at Argos, fo that there are four games in four years. Is it proper then that thofe who exhibit them only once fhould be exempted, and that thefe who exhibit them four times at home fhould be obliged to contribute to others, efpecially as they are not ancient nor accuftomed in Greece? For the Corinthians do not require thefe large fums for the fupport of gymnaftic or mufical performances; but for hunting-matches, which they often exhibit in the theatres, purchafing, for that purpofe, bears and panthers; an expence which they eafily defray by means of their wealth and large revenues; and as many others contribute alfo towards it, they reap the advantage of their own inftitution. But do not the Argives, who are extremely indigent, by thus being made to contribute to a foreign entertainment in another country, fuffer unjuftly and illegally, and in a manner unfuitable to the ancient power and glory of their city? And as they are neighbours, they ought on that account to be more efteemed, if that faying be true,

"———— Bad muft be your neighbours,

" If an ox perifh *."

But

* Ουδ' αν βες απολοιΐο, ει μη δια κακιαν γειΐονων.
Taken from one of the moral maxims of Hefiod,
Ουδ αν βως απολοιΐ, ει μη γειΐων κακος ειη.
Works and Days, ver. 346.
A correfponding Latin proverb occurs in Plautus:
— *Verum illud verbum effe experior vetus,*
Aliquid mali effe propter vicinum mal m.
Mercator, Act. IV. Sc. 4. 31.
Juvenal

But the Argives do not bring this charge against
the Corinthians through their folicitude for one
ox only, but for many and great expences with
which they are unjuftly burthened. The Corinthians might alfo be afked, whether they would
choofe to adhere to the ancient laws of Greece, or
adopt thofe which they have fince received from
the reigning city? For if they approve the majefty of the ancient laws, the Argives are no more
bound to pay tribute to the Corinthians, than the
Corinthians are to pay it to the Argives. But if the
Corinthians adopt the modern laws, and, becaufe
they are made a Roman colony, contend that they

Juvenal, in his xvith Satire, ver. 36. expreffes his apprehenfion of fimilar dangers from bad neighbours;

——— *Convallem ruris aviti*
Improbus, aut campum mibi fi vicinus ademit,
Et facrum effodit medio de limite faxum.

If any rogue vexatious fuits advance
Againft me for my known inheritance,
Enter by violence my fruitful grounds,
Or take my facred land-mark from my bounds.
                                        DRYDEN.

Many other parallel paffages might be adduced both
from the Latin and Greek writers.

I am indebted for this note to a writer in the Gentleman's
Magazine for 1783, p. 215.

Similar humanity to animals and good neighbourhood
are inculcated in the Levitical law. *Thou fhalt not fee thy
brother's ox or his fheep go aftray, and hide thy felf from them:
thou fhalt in any cafe bring them again unto thy brother. Thou
fhalt not fee thy brother's afs or his ox fall down by the way,
and hide thyfelf from them: thou fhalt furely help him to lift
them up again.* Deut. xxii. 1, 4. &c.

have

have the dominion over Argos, we will humbly intreat them not to be more assuming than their fathers, nor to new model, or subvert, to the detriment of their neighbours, those customs which their ancestors with sound judgement observed; relying on the decree which they lately obtained, and meanly taking advantage of the ignorance of the advocate who pleaded for the Argives *. For if this cause had been removed out of Greece, the Corinthians would have had much less influence, and its merits, discussed by many skilful advocates, would have been more apparent; on which account it is probable, that the judge, abashed by the established dignity of Argos, would have made a just decree. Concerning the rights of the city, if you will only hear the orators, and they may be allowed to speak, you shall be acquainted with the cause from the beginning, and, from their arguments may form a judgement of the whole. On what is said, that we ought not to credit those who are sent hither as petitioners †, it may now be proper to add a few words.

---

* In the reign of Constantius this dispute between the Corinthians and Argives had been litigated, and the latter lost their cause through the inexperience of their advocate in law-affairs.   PETAU.

† It appears from this passage that Julian, then a private man, had been requested by the Argives to use his interest with the pro-consul of Achaia in their behalf: otherwise he would have commanded with authority, instead of presenting a petition; as he himself would have put an end to the dispute.   Ibid.

If there are any philofophers in thefe times,
Diogenes and Lamprias are fuch. They decline
the legiflative and lucrative offices of the ftate;
but if their country wants their affiftance, they
ferve her to the utmoft of their abilities; when
the city is in any emergency, they plead caufes,
affift in the government, engage in embaffies, and
liberally expend their money, thus confuting by
their conduct the fcandalous afperfions on philofophy, and difproving that vulgar notion, that
thofe who ftudy philofophy, are ufelefs to their
country. For their country employs them in thofe
functions, and they endeavour to defend the caufe
of juftice by our affiftance; but we employ yours.

All that remains for the defence and fafety of
the oppreffed is the appointment of a judge both
willing and able to make a juft decree. If either
of thefe be wanting, if he be either miftaken or
unfaithful, juftice muft abfolutely perifh. But
though we fhould have a judge agreeable to our
wifhes, we have not the liberty of fpeaking *, as
we have not appealed; this, they requeft, may
firft be allowed them, and that the indolence of
him who then pleaded for the city, and managed
her caufe, may not entail fuch a burthen on pofterity. Nor can there be any impropriety in granting a new trial. It is fometimes expedient to forego

* The advocate of the Argives, when he loft the former
caufe, neclected to appeal; therefore the city could not
bring a new action, nor demand another trial.   PETAU.

fome

some present advantages and opportunities, for the
sake of future security.   And as life is short, they
wish to pass that short space with tranquillity. But
that the cause should sink before the judgement-
seat, and be transmitted to posterity undetermined,
is dreadful; so that, the hazard being so great,
it seems better to accept half the advantage, than,
by contending, to lose the whole.   But those immortal cities, unless a just decree be made, and
their mutual animosities terminated, must neceffarily be at perpetual variance.   For enmity gains
strength by time.

I have said *, as the orators express themselves.   May justice direct your determination!

* Εἴρηταί μοι λόγος, analogous to *Dixi*, in Latin.

Epiſtle XXXVI.   To PORPHYRY *.

A. D.
364.

THE library of George was large and copious †. It was ſtocked with books of philoſophy of all kinds, and with many of hiſtory;
on other ſubjects not a few; and with various
writings of the Galileans.   Examine therefore
carefully the whole, and ſend it to Antioch.   Be
aſſured, that, unleſs you make a diligent ſcru-
tiny, you ſhall be ſeverely fined; and as to thoſe
who are in the leaſt ſuſpected of having ſecreted
any of theſe books, if you cannot induce them, by
all kinds of arguments, and adjurations, and in
particular by putting their ſlaves to the torture,
let them be compelled by force to reſtore them all ‡.

* Treaſurer-general of Ægypt.   Libanius mentions him
in one of his Epiſtles as an excellent friend; and ſays, that
he was caluminated and oppreſſed by two Ægyptians,
a race " more ſavage than all the wild beaſts of Libya."

† See Epiſtles IX. and X.

‡ This is by no means an inſtance of cruelty in Julian.
A conſiderable robbery had been committed, and of pro-
perty much more valuable than it is at preſent.   The Romans, on the ſlighteſt ſuſpicions, put their ſlaves to the
torture.   LA BLETERIE.

Epiſtle XXXVII.   To Amerius *.

YOUR letter, in which you mention the death of your wife, and expreſs your extreme affliction, filled my eyes with tears. Painful would it have been to hear that any wife, young, chaſte, and engaging, and alſo an excellent mother, was prematurely ſnatched away; but that you have ſuſtained ſuch a loſs gives me peculiar concern. For, of all my friends, Amerius leaſt deſerved ſuch a calamity; a man whoſe underſtanding is ſuperior to moſt, a man whom I highly eſteem.

If I were writing on this ſubject to any other perſon, I ſhould be more prolix in telling him that ſuch is the lot of human nature, that ſubmiſſion

---

* I know not that this man of letters, apparently a ſophiſt and a Pagan, is elſewhere mentioned. One MS. ſtyles him "Himerius." We are acquainted with a celebrated profeſſor of that name, the rival and the colleague of Prohæreſius, and who, like him, taught eloquence at Athens when Julian was there. Himerius left ſome diſcourſes, of which there are ſome extracts in the Bibliotheca of Photius. It might be ſuppoſed that this Epiſtle was addreſſed to him, if the MS did not ſtyle him "Præfect of Ægypt."

In the reign of Julian that province was governed by Eedicius; and this Epiſtle is certainly written to one who was a teacher: but it might not be impoſſible for the title of Præfect to be here no more than an honorary title. In thoſe times honorary titles of the greateſt employments were ſometimes given to men of letters. I would not venture, however, to aſſert, they had that of governor of any particular province.   La Bleterie.

is neceffary, that the moft poignant grief admits of confolation *, and, in fhort, fhould ufe, as to a novice, all the arguments that are likely to alleviate affli&ion. But as I am afhamed of employing to one who inftru&s others thofe arguments which are ufed to teach and improve the ignorant, waving every thing elfe, I will relate to you a fable, or rather a true ftory, of a certain wife man, not new perhaps to you, but probably unknown to many, whofe only medicine, mirth, you will find as effe&ual a remedy for forrow as that cup † which the fair Lacedæmonian is fuppofed, on a fimilar occafion, to have given to Telemachus.

It is reported, that Democritus ‡ of Abdera, finding nothing that he faid could confole Darius

for

---

* Thus the three remedies which Pliny prefcribes are, " Length of time, the neceffity of fubmiffion, and fatiety " of grief."

† In the IVth book of the Odyffey, ver. 220, &c. when Menelaus gives an entertainment to Telemachus, Helen puts into the wine a drug which had the virtue to induce an oblivion of the moft cruel anxieties.   LA BLETERIE.

Julian refers to the fame paffage in his Confolatory Oration, Vol. I. p. 32, where it is quoted in the notes.

‡ Demonax comforted Herod the philofopher under affli&ion by a fimilar fable, as Lucian relates in his life.   PETAU.

This ftory is no where found. Though Democritus had travelled into Perfia, and was acquainted with the fecrets of magifm, his difcourfe with Darius has all the appearance of being only a philofophical novel. At the time of the death of Darius, the fon of Hyftafpes, Democritus was, at moft, 28 years old; perhaps he was no more than

for the loss of a beautiful wife, promised to restore her to life, if the king would supply him
with all things necessary for the purpose. Darius
ordered him to spare no expence, but to take whatever was requisite to perform his promise. Soon
after, Democritus told him, that " every thing was
" ready for the completion of the work, one only
" excepted, which he knew not how to procure;
" but that Darius, as he was king of all Asia,
" would perhaps find no difficulty in providing
" it." On his asking what this important matter
was, Democritus is said to have replied, " If you
" will inscribe on the tomb of your wife the names
" of three who have never known affliction, she
" shall immediately return to life, this ceremony
" being irresistible *." Darius hesitating, and not
being able to recollect any one who had not experienced some sorrow, Democritus laughed, as
usual, and said to him, " And are not you, the ab-
" surdest of men, ashamed still to lament, as if

23, or even nine. This philosopher was on his return to
Greece, when Darius II. surnamed Nothus, ascended the
throne, in the year before Christ, 423. LA BLETERIE.
See Vol. I. p. 21. note †.

* It is in the Greek Ευθυς αυτην αναβιωσεσθαι τω της τελευτης
νομω δυσωπομενην, which Martinius has translated thus: *Illam
ab inferis esse redituram; fore enim ut ejus mortis consuetudine
erubesceret.* I think that it may be restored by leaving out a
single letter. Instead of της τελευτης, we should read της
τελετης, and translate it, *fore ut statim revivisceret, ejus ceremo-
niæ ritu exorata.* The word δυσωπεισθαι signifies not only
" to blush, to be ashamed," but also, " to suffer oneself
" to be persuaded, to be moved."   *Ibid.*

" you

" you alone were involved in such distress, when
" you cannot find one that ever lived exempt from
" some domestic misfortune?"

That Darius, an illiterate Barbarian, a slave both to joy and grief, should be told this, was highly proper; but you, a Greek, who cultivate true literature, should learn from yourself to govern your passions. For it is shameful that reason should not anticipate the certain effects of time *.

Epistle XXXVIII. To the Philosopher Maximus †.

A. D. 360.

MY ideas crowd so fast upon me, that they choak my utterance, some hindering the passage of others. Whether this be frigidity, or any thing else, you will determine. But let me now arrange them in order, and first return my

* If Julian had read the Latin authors (and why should he not have read, at least, some of them?) I should say that he has copied this passage of the letter of Servius Sulpicius to Cicero: *Nullus dolor est quem non longinquitas temporis minuat atque molliat. Hoc te expectare tempus turpe est, ac non ei rei tuâ sapientiâ te occurrere.* La Bleterie.

† This Epistle was written in Illyricum at the time when Julian was preparing to march against Constantius.
Ibid.

Among the philosophers, Maximus obtained an eminent rank in the friendship of his royal disciple, who communicated, with unreserved confidence, his actions, his sentiments, and his religious designs, during the anxious suspence of the civil war. Gibbon.

See the first note on Epistle XV. p. 29.

        thanks

thanks to the Gods, whofe goodnefs ftill allows me to write *, and perhaps will permit us to meet.

When I was firft made Emperor (the Gods know, and I, as far as poffible, declared to them, with what reluctance), I was waging war againft the Barbarians. After paffing three months in that fervice, as I was returning to Gaul, I looked round, and enquired of thofe who came from thence whether any philofopher, any fcholar, or any one clad in a woollen coat or cloak, had arrived there. At length I approached Vefontio †. This fmall town, now rebuilt, was formerly a large city, adorned with magnificent temples, and fortified both by ftrong walls and its natural fituation, being furrounded by the river Dubis ‡, and elevated, as if in the fea, on a high rock, almoft inacceffible even to the birds, except where an ifthmus joins it to the continent. Near this town I met a Cynic philofopher, with his cloak and ftaff.

---

* It is probable that Julian, after his taking the title of Auguftus, wrote feldom to Maximus, for fear of embroiling that philofopher, who dwelt in Iönia, or Greece, and confequently under the dominion of Conftantius.

La Bleterie.

† Now Befançon, the capital of Franche-Comtè. Julian paffed through this town, which had fuffered feverely from the fury of the Barbarians, after his fourth expedition beyond the Rhine, A. D. 360, in his way to Vienne, where he fixed his head-quarters for the enfuing winter. See Ammianus, xx. 10. Of the citadel of Vefontio, on a high mountain, fee Cæfar, de bell. Gall. *l.* 1. F. Martinius tranflates it " *Danubius.*"

‡ Now the Doux.

At

At a diftance I thought it was you *, and on his
nearer approach I imagined that he came from you.
He proved to be alfo a friend of mine, but not
fuch as I hoped and expected. He was ufeful to
me therefore in one inftance only, that of giving
me reafon to conclude that your anxiety on my account had prevented your leaving Greece. Witnefs
Jupiter, witnefs great Sun, witnefs Minerva, and
all ye Gods and Goddeffes, how much, in my return from Illyricum to Gaul, I trembled for you!
And I enquired of the Gods, not that I dared
myfelf (for I was not able † to fee or hear any
thing of the fituation in which you then might be),
but I entrufted that office to others. The Gods
clearly fhewed, that fome troubles would befall
you, but that nothing terrible fhould enfue, nor
any wicked device prevail.

I omit, you obferve, many important events.
You are chiefly interefted to know how foon we
experienced the manifeft affiftance of the Gods, and

---

* This clearly fhews that Maximus was of the fect of
the Cynics. A Cynic was as vain of his ftaff and cloak as
if he had been decked with all the ornaments of drefs.
But this Maximus muft be diftinguifhed from another Cynic
of the fame name, under the Emperor Theodofius, who was
of Alexandria.   BARONIUS.

† He means the danger to which Maximus was expofed under Conftantius, and affirms, that he did not
venture himfelf to confult the Gods concerning him, left
he fhould be compelled to hear fome inaufpicious tidings,
as was highly probable.   PETAU.

After this, can there be a doubt of Julian's belief in
theurgy?   LA BLETERIE.

escaped

efcaped fuch a multitude of traitors, killing none and fpoiling none, but only imprifoning thofe who were apprehended in the very fact *.

Thefe things perhaps it might have been better to fpeak than to write. I am certain, however, that they will give you pleafure. We worfhip the Gods publickly, and all the troops that are returning with me profefs the true religion. We openly facrifice oxen. We have made our grateful acknowledgments to the Gods in feveral hecatombs †. They command me to reftore their worfhip with the utmoft purity ‡. Moft willingly I obey them. They promife me great rewards, if I am not remifs. Euägrius § is arrived.

* Soon after Julian was proclaimed Auguftus, an eunuch, fuborned by the partifans of Conftantius, attempted to affaffinate him. Julian pardoned him. We learn from hence, that this was not the only confpiracy which threatened his life. *Ibid.*

† The legions of Gaul devoted themfelves to the faith, as well as to the fortunes, of their victorious leader; and, even before the death of Conftantius, he had the fatiffaction of announcing to his friends, that they affifted, with fervent devotion, and voracious appetite, at the facrifices, which were repeatedly offered in his camp, of whole hecatombs of fat oxen. " So that the foldiers," fays Ammianus (XXII. 12.) " living grofsly on fat meat, and " greedy of drink, were carried through the ftreets on the " fhoulders of paffers-by, from the public-houfes .... " to their quarters." The devout prince and the indignant hiftorian defcribe the fame fcene; and in Illyricum, or Antioch, fimilar caufes muft have produced fimilar effects. GIBBON.

‡ He had no doubt of his being raifed up by the Gods to be the reftorer of Paganifm. LA BLETERIE.

§ See the firft note on Epiftle XLVI.

 Epiftle

Epistle XXXIX.   To the same.

A. D.
361.

WELCOME the coming, speed the parting guest *.
Such is the law of the wife Homer. But our
friendship is superior to that of hospitality, being
founded on learning and religion. So that no one
could juftly charge me with tranfgreffing this law
of Homer, if I fhould think proper to detain you
longer with me. But as, I fee, your diminutive
frame † requires more attention, I allow you to
go into your own country ‡, and have provided
for the convenience of your journey, by giving
you the ufe of a public carriage. May Æfculapius, and all the Gods, conduct you, and bring
you fafely back to us again!

* This is faid by Menelaus (Odyff. xv. 74.) when Telemachus, after vifiting him at Lacedæmon, was going to
take his leave.   LA BLETERIE.
   Pope, 84. He has adopted this line in his imitation of
the 2d fatire of the 1ft book of Horace. Thus alfo Theocritus, Idyll. xvi. 27. as tranflated by Fawkes:
   With prudent hofpitality they fpend,
   And kindly greeting fpeed the parting friend.
   † Σωμάτιον, corpufculum. As from ανθρωπισκος, homuncio,
applied to Athanafius in Epiftle LI. it has been inferred,
that the primate of Ægypt was a little man, the fame conclufion perhaps may be drawn from the above expreffion
in regard to Maximus; though, in this inftance, the diminutive is a term of affection, and, in the other, of contempt.
   ‡ Ephefus. Maximus probably took this journey while
the Emperor was at Conftantinople.   LA BLETERIE.

Epiftle

Epistle XL.   To Jamblichus *.

I AM so sensible of the good-nature with which
you blame me, that I think myself equally honoured by your letters, and instructed by your re-
proofs. But were I conscious of the least failure of
attention to you, I would certainly endeavour, if possible, to palliate the fault, or I would not scruple to
ask your pardon, especially as I know that, whenever
your friends indiscreetly violate the laws of friendship, you are not implacable. Now then (since
negligence, or indolence, generally prevents my
accomplishing what I ardently desire), ascend, as
it were, a tribunal, while I plead my cause before
you, and shew that I did not treat you with impropriety, or act with tardiness or neglect.

Three years ago I left Pannonia †, with difficulty escaping those snares and dangers of which
you are well apprised. But when I had crossed the
Chalcedonian strait ‡, and approached the city of
Nicomedia §, to you first, as to the God of my
country, I paid due offerings for my safety, by
sending you a message as a token of my approach,

A. D.
363.

* See the first note on Epistle **XXXIV**.
† Now Hungary.
‡ Now the Bosphorus.
§ This city was then in ruins by an earthquake, which
happened in 358. See a note on an epistle of Libanius,
vol. I. p. 304. and his Monody on that event, in this vol.

H 3

or

or a kind of facred prefent. The letter was configned to the care of one of the Imperial guards,
by name Julian, the fon of Bacchylus, a native of
Apamea *, to whom I the more readily entrufted
it, as he was going thither, and declared that he
knew you perfectly well. After this, I received,
as from Apollo, a facred epiftle from you, expreffing that you had heard with pleafure of my
arrival. Wife Jamblichus, and a letter from Jamblichus, were to me a happy omen, and the dawn-
ing of good hopes. Need I fay how much I rejoiced, and how greatly I was affected by your
letter? For if you have received what I wrote on
that fubject (which was fent to you by one of the
letter-carriers that came from thence), you certainly know the great fatisfaction that it gave me.
And again, when the man who nurfed my children † returned home, I fent you another letter,

in

* The metropolis of Phrygia.

† Τὴ τροφέως τῶν ἐμαυτῦ παίδων. M. de Tillemont, who
takes in its moft rigorous fenfe that fufpicious paffage in the
Mifopogon (p. 244.) in which Julian ironically urges the
reproach of the people of Antioch, that " he *almoft always*
(ως επιπαν) lay alone," and confiders it as a confeffion that
Julian himfelf makes of his incontinence, obferves, in order
to ftrengthen this pretended confeffion, that Julian, in
this Epiftle (which is one of thofe that I have not tranflated), fpeaks of " the man who had nurfed his children."
" Now," fays M. de Tillemont, " he never had any le-
" gitimate, except a fon who perifhed by the wickednefs
" of the midwife, whom the Emprefs Eufebia, the wife of
" Conftantius, had fuborned. The fact is certain: there-
" fore he had fome illegitimate."

But

in which I expressed my acknowledgments for your former, and also requested a repetition of the favour. Afterwards the distinguished Sopater * came to us on an embassy, and, as I knew him, I instantly sprung forward to embrace him, and shed

But we must not conclude from this passage, as M. de Tillemont does, that there was actually a man who was charged with the care of the children of Julian. Helena had a son. After her first lying-in, she never went her full time. But at every pregnancy a nurse was provided. The same perhaps was frequently chosen. It was probably the husband of that nurse whom Julian styles "the nurse "of his children." I say probably, because a number of other plausible reasons may be supposed for Julian's having given some one that name. Who knows, for instance, but that it was a man whom he had destined for the care of the children that he hoped to have? Whether he did not cause some children that did not belong to him to be educated with the tenderness of a father? Or whether it was not a joke which Jamblichus perfectly understood?
LA BLETERIE.

When Julian speaks of "the tutor of his children," who is not named, the expression must be understood figuratively. For Julian had no children, legitimate or illegitimate. Historians are quite silent about them, excepting that one which he had by his wife Helena, who was not suffered to live. If Julian had any children out of lawful marriage, and therefore illegitimate, can it be supposed that Christian writers would have been silent about it? By no means. Eumenius, in his Panegyric, recommends to Constantine not only his five children of whom he was the parent, but his other children likewise, as he calls them, whom he had educated for the bar or the court. In some such figurative sense Julian must be understood. He intends some young persons under his special care.   LARDNER.

* See Epistle XXVII. p. 70. note †. That this was the same Sopater who entertained Julian afterwards at Hierapolis, though probable, I cannot affirm.

H 4

tears

tears of joy, dreaming of nothing but you and a
letter from you. As soon as I received it, I kissed
it, held it to my eyes, and strained it close, as if
I had feared, that, while I was reading it, the
features of your face should secretly escape me.
I immediately wrote an answer, not only to you,
but to the excellent Sopater, his son, telling him,
in joke, that I had accepted a common friend from
Apamea as an hostage for your absence.

From that time to the date of my present writing,
I have received no letter from you, but that in
which you seem to chide me. If by this appearance of a charge you mean only to urge me to
write, I accept the whole charge with the utmost
joy, and the very letter which I have now received
I deem the highest favour. But, if you really
accuse me of having given you the least offence,
who can be more miserable than I in having been
prevented by the negligence of letter-carriers from
giving you the satisfaction that I wish? However,
though I were not to write very frequently, I might
justly claim your indulgence, not on account of
the business in which I am engaged (for I am not
such a wretch as not to prefer you, as Pindar says,
to all my affairs *); but, because there is more

* Ασχολιας απασης το καλα σε κρειτιον ηγεισθαι. The sense, but
not the words, of Pindar.
—— Τον τεον, χρυσασπι Θηβα,
Πραγμα και ασχολιας υπερτερον
Θησομαι ——   Isthm. I. 1.
Your business, golden-shielded Thebes,
To all my own I willingly prefer.

wisdom

wisdom in being loth to write to such a man as you,
who cannot be recollected without veneration, than
in being too presumptuous. For as those who venture to gaze stedfastly on the light of the sun,
unless they are in a manner divine, and can behold
his rays like the genuine off-spring of eagles *,
cannot see what is unlawful to be seen †, and the
more they endeavour it, the weaker are their
efforts; so he, who presumes to write to you,
clearly shews that the bolder he is, the more he
ought to fear. But you, distinguished sage, who,
I may say, were created for the total preservation
of Gentilism, judged right in sending me frequent
letters, and thus, as far as possible, checking my
indolence. For as the sun (again to compare you
with that deity), when he shines perfectly bright
with full radiance, is regardless whether all the
objects that he illuminates perform their respective functions with propriety ‡; you, in like
manner, should liberally diffuse the light of your
knowledge among all the Gentiles, and not secrete it because fear or modesty prevents your
hearers from making a reply. Æsculapius does
not heal diseases from interested motives, but
every where displays his humanity, like a kind of
doctrine. You, being the physician of noble souls,

* See Epistle XVI. p. 31.

† Ουκ α μη θεμις οφθηναι. Not unlike St. Paul, α υκ εξον
ανθρωπω λαλησαι, *not lawful for a man to utter.* 2 Cor. xii. 4.

‡ This passage in the original being corrupted and mutilated, I can only guess at the meaning.

should

should do the fame, and in every thing obferve the precepts of virtue; like a good archer, who, though he has no adverfary, always exercifes his art againft a proper opportunity.   Our views are not the fame, as we wifh to enjoy your aufpicious letters, and you to receive ours.   But we, though we fhould write a thoufand times, refemble the playful children in Homer, who erect clay-buildings on the fhore, and then foon overwhelm them with fand *: While your letter, however fhort, is preferable to the moft copious ftream.   And in truth, I had rather poffefs one epiftle of Jamblichus than all the gold of Lydia.

If you have any regard for your friends (and fome regard you have, or I am much miftaken), do not neglect us, who, like poultry, are always in want of your fuftenance; but write frequently, and forbear not to nourifh us with your good cheer.   And if we have been deficient, difcharge at once two friendly offices, that of writing to us, and alfo of writing for us.   For fuch a pupil of eloquent Mercury as you are, fhould employ his rod, not in exciting, but in banifhing and difpelling fleep, and in this particular, above all, let him be your model.

* Il. XV. 362, where the poet defcribes the Grecian turrets nodding, and the bulwarks falling, when fhaken by Apollo;

 Eafy, as when afhore, the infant † ftands,
 And draws imagin'd houfes in the fands,
 The fportive wanton, pleas'd with fome new play,
 Sweeps the flight works and fafhion'd domes away.

POPE.

† Julian, quoting by memory, fubftitutes παιδς for παις.

Epiftle

Epiftle XLI. To the fame.

IN obedience to the Delphic oracle, we fhould have known ourfelves, and not prefumed to ftun the ears of a fage like you, whofe very looks it is difficult to encounter, much more to contend with him in genius, as he combines all the powers of philofophic harmony. Every mufician, Ariftæus * not excepted, muft yield to Pan, when he breathes fweet melody; and when Apollo warbles to his lyre, all, though they had the mufical powers of Orpheus, would be filent. Confcious, as we are, of our own inferiority, it is juft that the lefs fhould fubmit to the greater. But he who would put human in competition with divine harmony muft be unacquainted with the cataftrophe of Marfyas † the Phrygian, and with the river named from him, which flows as a punifhment to the mad mufician.

---

* The fon of Apollo by Cyrene, the daughter of Peneus, king of Arcadia. He is faid to have difcovered the ufe of honey, milk, rennet, and other ufeful things. Juft. Hift. xiii. 7. This the poets have turned into a fable. See Virg. Georg. iv. 317, &c. One MS. inftead of Ἀρισαιος, has αριςος, ("the beft" mufician.) The fable of Ariftæus is alfo in the IVth book of the Odyffey.

† A fatyr, who challenged Apollo, and, being overcome by him, was flead alive, and changed into a river. See Ovid. Metam. VI. and Liv. XXVIII. 13.

Nor

Nor can he have heard of the fate of Thamyris *,
who unsuccessfully contended in singing with the
Muses.   Not to mention the Sirens †, of whom
such of the Muses as conquered them still bear a
wing in their foreheads.   All these now suffer, and
will long suffer, for their presumption ‡; we therefore, as I said before, ought to have remained
within our own bounds, and to have been quietly
satisfied with your strains, like those who silently
receive the oracle of Apollo issuing from the sacred

---

* Il. II. 595.

> Superior once of all the tuneful race,
> Till, vain of mortals' empty praise, he strove
> To match the seed of cloud-compelling Jove!
> Too daring bard! whose unsuccessful pride
> Th' immortal Muses in their art defy'd.
> Th' avenging Muses of the light of day
> Depriv'd his eyes, and snatch'd his voice away.
>
> Pope, 732.

As to the wings of the Sirens, see Ælian de natura
anim. *l.* XVII. c. 23.

† This contest of the Sirens with the Muses is thus mentioned by Spenser:

> They were fair ladies, till they fondly striv'd
> With th' Heliconian maids for maisterye,
> Of whom they overcomen were, depriv'd
> Of their proud beauty, and th' one moiety
> Transform'd to fish, for their bold surquedry ‡.
>
> *Fairy Queen*, b. XI. c. 12. st. 31.

which Mr. Spence justly quotes as one instance (among
many) of this great poet's " misrepresenting the stories and
" allegorical personages of the ancients, the Sirens being
" never represented in antiques with a fish-tail, but with
" the upper part human, and the lower like birds." See
Polymetis, p. 302.

Ovid, in his Metamorphoses, v. 553. ascribes their trans-
formation to another cause.

---

‡ Presumption.

shrines.

shrines. But since you lead our song, and by your eloquence, as with the rod of Mercury, rouse us from sleep, we, in the manner of those enthusiasts, who with dances meet Bacchus, when he celebrates his orgies, will join in unison with your harp, as they in tune and measure accompany the leader of the dance. Accept therefore the orations *, which, by the command of the Emperor †, I lately composed on the celebrated junction of the straits ‡; a small work, if compared with yours, and brass for your gold §; but such presents as we have ‖, we offer to our Mercury. Theseus by no means despised the coarse fare of Hecale **; but, urged by necessity, was satisfied with little. And the shepherd Pan disdained not to apply to his lips the pipe of a young herdsman. Such as it is, then, receive it, and scorn not to bestow great attention on a small poem ††. If it have any merit, both the work and its author will be fortunate in receiving such a token of esteem from Minerva.

* These orations are not extant.
† Constantius.
‡ Does he mean the Hellespont joined by Xerxes?
PETAV.
§ II. VI. 236. Julian seems particularly fond of this passage, this being the third time of his quoting or alluding to it in these Select Works.

‖ Οἷς δε εχομεν ξενοις—ιςιωσϊες. Not unlike that expression of St. Peter, Acts III. 6. Ο δε εχω, τϋιο σοι διδωμι. *Such as I have, I give thee.*

** A poor old woman mentioned by Callimachus, as having entertained Theseus with wild lettuce. See Plin. Hist. Nat. XXII. 22. and XXVI. 8.

†† Ολιγω μελει. Could this be one of those which before were styled λογωι (" orations ?")

And

And should a finishing hand be necessary to complete it, disdain not, I intreat you, to supply its defects. Thus of old the God appeared to the archer * who invoked him, and directed his shaft, and thus the harper who was playing the Orthian † tune was answered by Apollo in the form of a grass-hopper ‡.

An Edict relating to Professors §.

27 June,
362.

PROFESSORS and masters should be distinguished first by their manners, and in the next place by their talents. We therefore forbid any,

---

* Paris probably, when Apollo guided his arrow against Achilles. See Ovid. Metam. XII.

† A kind of loud music used by Arion, according to Herodotus. It is introduced by Homer, Il. xi. 11. where
Discord
————— ———Through the Grecian throng,
With horror sounds the loud Orthian song.
POPE, 13.

‡ I am aware that the Greek word τετλιξ, and the Latin *cicada*, mean a different insect from our grass-hopper; for it has a rounder and shorter body, is of a dark green colour, sits upon trees, and makes a noise five times louder than our grass-hopper. It begins its song as soon as the sun grows hot, and continues singing till it sets. Its wings are beautiful, being streaked with silver, and marked with brown spots; the outer wings are twice as long as the inner, and more variegated; yet, after the example of Mr. Pope (see Il. iii. 300.), I retain the usual term.
FAWKES *on Theocritus*.

§ I have taken this Epistle from the Theodosian Code, XIII. t. 3. *De medicis et professoribus.* It is not known from
what

any, whoever they be, to intrude haftily or rafhly
into this important office. He who would keep
a fchool muft be approved by the council of the
town, and alfo have the fanction of the principal
inhabitants; and, as I * cannot be every where
perfonally prefent, let the decree be fent to me for
examination, that the candidate may have the additional honour of feeing the fuffrages of his fellow-citizens † confirmed by our opinion.

Given at * * * * on the fifteenth of the calends
of July. Received at Spoleto on the fourth of the
calends of Auguft, in the confulfhip of Mamertinus
and Nevitta.

what place it was dated, nor to whom Julian addreffed it.
It only appears that he wrote it on the road from Conftantinople to Antioch, as he left Conftantinople in the month
of May, and was at Antioch towards the end of July. It
was made, without doubt, on account of fome profeffor of
Spoleto, a city of Picenum, and confequently was addreffed
either to the Præfect of the Prætorium of Italy, or to the
Præfect of Rome, or perhaps to the Confular of Picenum
(now the march of Ancona), or, laftly, to the inhabitants of Spoleto. The intention of Julian is plain. He
referves to himfelf the right of confirming or annulling
the election of profeffors, in order to exclude the Chriftians
from all literary offices. This law might perhaps be part
of the following edict. I have therefore placed it here.
LA BLETERIE.

* The Emperors generally fpeak in the plural in their
laws; Julian, however, here ufes the fingular. *Sed quia
fingulis civitatibus adeffe ipfe non poffum, jubeo,* &c.   *Ibid.*

† The original is, *Hoc enim decretum ad me tractandum
deferetur ‡, ut altiore quodam honore noftro judicio* (M. de la
Bleterie thinks we fhould read *noftrum judicium*) *ftudiis civi-
tatum accedat.*

‡ In Gothofred's edition, *referetur.*

Epiftle

Epistle XLII.   An Edict, forbidding the Christians to teach polite Literature *.

A. D.
362.

TRUE learning, in my opinion, confists not in words, in elegant and magnificent language, but in the found difpofitions of a well-formed

---

* Two motives induced Julian to reftrain the Chriftian profeffors from teaching: 1. He flattered himfelf, that, in order to keep their chairs, they would change their religion. In this, he did not fucceed, if, as Orofius fays, almoft all rather chofe to quit them. This, in particular, is affirmed of Prohærefius, the fophift, of Athens, and of Marius Victorinus, who profeffed eloquence at Rome. 2. Julian knew, by his own experience, that mafters, when they fhewed their fcholars the ancient authors, never failed to infift on the weaknefs and folly of Paganifm. He was fenfible how much a Chriftian mafter can contribute to the progrefs of religion, when he explains profane authors chriftianly, and equally avails himfelf of the truth and the falfhood which he finds there in order to conduct his pupils to God and Jefus Chrift. This is what he wifhed to prevent. But, inftead of difcovering his true motives, he employs the moft lamentable pretext that can be; fo that this piece of eloquence is a mafter-piece of fophiftry. M. Fleury has inferted moft of it in his Ecclefiaftical Hiftory.

La Bleterie.

His moft illiberal treatment of the Chriftians was, his forbidding the profeffors, who were of that religion, to teach humanity and the fciences in the public fchools. His more immediate defign in this was to hinder the youth from taking impreffions to the difadvantage of Paganifm; his remoter view, to deprive Chriftianity of the fupport of human literature. His own hiftorian, Ammianus Marcellinus, paffes a fevere fentence on this edict, xxi. 10.

Warburton.

His

formed mind, and in juft notions of good and evil, of virtue and vice. Whoever therefore thinks or teaches otherwife feems no lefs deftitute of learning than he is of virtue. Even in trifles, if the mind and tongue be at variance, it is always efteemed a kind of difhonefty. But if in matters of the greateft confequence a man thinks one thing

His driving from their fchools fuch teachers of rhetoric and grammar as profeffed the Chriftian religion, was fevere (*inclemens*), and fhould be buried in eternal oblivion.

AMMIANUS.

He enacted no oppreffive laws . . . . a few excepted; among which was that fevere one, which forbade Chriftian mafters to teach rhetoric and grammar, unlefs they conformed to the worfhip of the Gods. *Ibid.*

Ammianus has twice mentioned this Edict, and always with diflike, as a great hardfhip. Orofius fays, that " when Julian publifhed his edict forbidding the Chrif- " tian profeffors of rhetoric to teach the liberal arts, they " all in general chofe rather to refign their chairs than " deny the faith." And Jerom, in his Chronicle, affures us, that " Prohærefius, the Athenian fophift, in particular, [fee Epiftle II.] " fhut up his fchool, though the Em- " peror had granted him a fpecial licence to teach." Auguftine records the like fteadinefs of Victorinus, who had long taught rhetoric with great applaufe at Rome. But Ecebolus, a Chriftian fophift at Conftantinople [fee Epiftle XIX.], who had been Julian's mafter in rhetoric, was overcome by the temptations of the times, and with great humiliations intreated to be reconciled to the church.

LARDNER.

This Edict may be compared with the grofs invectives of Gregory (*Orat.* III. *p.* 96.). Tillemont (*Mem. Eccl. tom.* VII. *p.* 1201—1204.) has collected the feeming differences of ancients and moderns. They may be eafily reconciled. The Chriftians were *directly* forbid to teach; they were *indirectly* forbid to learn, fince they would not frequent the fchools of the Pagans. GIBBON.

and teaches another *, does he not refemble thofe
mean-fpirited, difhoneft, and abandoned traders,
who generally affirm what they know to be falfe,
in order to deceive and inveigle cuftomers?

All therefore who profefs to teach ought to be
ftrict in their morals, and fhould never entertain
opinions oppofite to thofe of the public; fuch,
efpecially, ought to be thofe who inftruct youth,
and explain to them the works of the ancients,
whether they are orators, or grammarians; but
particularly fophifts, as they affect to be the teachers, not only of words, but of manners, and infift
that civil philofophy is their peculiar province.
Whether this be true or not I fhall not at prefent confider. I commend thofe who make fuch
fpecious promifes, and fhould commend them much
more, if they did not falfify and contradict them-

---

* If the Chriftian profeffors, when they explained in
their fchools Homer, Hefiod, &c. had canonifed the
doctrine of thofe writers, the reproaches of Julian would
have been juft; yet perhaps he would not have made them.
A book may be efteemed in fome refpects, and condemned
in others. No one is deceived by this. To explain the
claffic authors, to commend them as models of language,
of eloquence and tafte, to unveil their beauties, &c. this
is not propofing them as oracles of religion and morality.
Julian is pleafed to confound two things fo different, and
to erect, under favour of this confufion, the puerile fophiftry which prevails through his whole edict.
                                        La Bleterie.

Thus Homer's Achilles, Il. ix. 312.
  Who dares think one thing, and another tell,
  My foul detefts him like the gates of hell.
                                        Pope.

selves by thinking one thing, and teaching their scholars another. What then? Were not Homer, Hesiod, Demosthenes, Herodotus, Thucydides, Isocrates, Lysias, guided in their studies by the Gods, and esteemed themselves consecrated, some to Mercury, and others to the Muses? It is absurd therefore for those who explain their works to despise the Gods whom they honoured.

I do not mean (I am not so absurd *) that they should change their sentiments for the sake of instructing youth; I give them their option, either not to teach what they do not approve, or, if they choose to teach, first to persuade their scholars, that neither Homer, nor Hesiod, nor any of those whom they expound, and charge with impiety, madness, and error, concerning the Gods, are really such as they represent them. For as they receive a stipend, and are maintained by their works, if they can act with such duplicity for a few drachms, they confess themselves guilty of the most sordid avarice.

Hitherto, I allow, many causes have prevented their resorting to the temples; and the dangers that every where impended were a plea for their disguising their real sentiments of the Gods. But now, when the Gods have granted us liberty, it seems to me absurd for any to teach what they do not approve. And if they think that those

* Petau thinks that something is wanting here to perfect the sentence.

I 2

writers

writers whom they expound, and of whom they
fit as interpreters, are truly wife, let them firft
zealoufly imitate their piety towards the Gods. But
if they think their ideas of the moft holy Gods
erroneous, let them go into the churches of the
Galileans, and there expound Matthew and Luke *.
In obedience to your rulers, you forbid facrifices.
I wifh that your ears and your tongues were (as
you exprefs it) regenerated † in thofe things of
which I wifh that myfelf, and all who in thought
and deed are my friends, may always be par-
takers.

* Let all the moral truths which are found, or are fuppofed to be found, difperfed here and there in the Pagan
writers, be collected ; let all profane antiquity, if I may fo
exprefs myfelf, be laid under contribution ; the fyftem
which can be drawn from it will be far lefs valuable
than what we are taught in a few words by the authors of
whom Julian affects to fpeak with contempt, and will fo
far only be rational, as it refembles their doctrine.
                                        LA BLETERIE.

A juft and fevere cenfure has been inflicted on the law
which prohibited the Chriftians from teaching the arts of
grammar and rhetoric. The motives alleged by the
Emperor to juftify this partial and oppreffive meafure might
command, during his life-time, the filence of flaves, and
the applaufe of flatterers.   GIBBON.

† He ridicules the Chriftians by the trite application of an
expreffion ufed by them. Αναγεννησις is commonly underftood
of baptifm, the reformation of the new man, and the
change of ftudies and manners. Therefore forbidding the
Chriftians to read the books of the Heathens, he fays, he
would have their ears and tongues cleanfed from all acquaintance with their writings, that what is depofited
in them may in a manner be born again.   PETAU.

To

To masters and teachers let this be a general law. But let no youths be prevented from resorting to whatever schools they please *. It would be as unreasonable to exclude children, who know not yet what road to take, from the right path, as it would be to lead them by fear, and with reluctance, to the religious rites of their country. And though it might be proper to cure such reluctance, like madness, even by force †, yet let all be indulged with that disease. For the ignorant should, in my opinion, be instructed, not punished.

* This was fair, but would by no means be accepted. Here the bait was half off the hook, and discovered, that to draw them to the schools of the Pagan professors was one end of the edict, which he imagined would necessarily reduce things to this state, either to dispose the Galileans, during their youth, in favour of Paganism, or to disable them, in their adult age, to defend Christianity. So that it appears from hence, his forbidding Christian professors to *explain* Pagan writers to any audience whatsoever, amounted to a prohibition of *learning* them.   WARBURTON.

Mr. Gibbon has adopted the same idea in a former note, p. 113.

† He derides the μωρια Γαλιλαιων (Epist. VII.) and so far loses sight of the principles of toleration as to wish (Epist. XLII.) ακοιλας ιασθαι.   GIBBON.

Epiftle XLIII. To Ecebolus *.

A. D.
362.

SO mild and humane have been my decrees concerning the Galileans, that none of them can fuffer any violence, or be dragged to the temples, or be expofed to any other injury. But they who are of the Arian church, being pampered with riches †, have attacked the Valentinians, and have dared to perpetrate fuch outrages at Edeffa as can never be tolerated in a wellgoverned city. Therefore, as they are taught, in their wonderful law, the moft eafy method of entering into the kingdom of heaven, for this pur-

* This is not the fophift under whom Julian had ftudied, and to whom he addreffed Epiftle XIX. This, no doubt, was the chief magiftrate of Edeffa, the capital of Ofrhoëna, a province beyond the Euphrates and the Tigris.

La Bleterie.

About the fame time that Julian was informed of the tumult of Alexandria, he received intelligence from Edeffa of the diforders which occafioned this mandate. Gibbon

† The Arians were put in poffeffion of the church of Edeffa, under Conftantius. They muft neceffarily therefore be great perfecutors to retain it under Julian. The Valentinians derived their name from the herefiarch Valentinian, who lived in the fecond century after Jefus Chrift, and who, by a mixture of the gofpel, of Platonifm, and the theogony of Hefiod, formed a fyftem fo compounded, fo extravagant, that we do not underftand it, perhaps he did not underftand it himfelf. Some remains of the Valentinians ftill exifted in the Vth century.

La Bleterie.

pofe

pofe co-operating with them *, we have ordered all the wealth of the church of the Edeffenes † to be confifcated and given to our foldiers, and the lands to be annexed to our demefnes. Thus being poor they may become wife, and not fail of that heavenly kingdom to which they afpire ‡.

We alfo command the inhabitants of Edeffa to refrain from all tumults and feditions §, left, if they provoke my humanity, you yourfelf fhould be punifhed for the public diforders by exile, fire, and the fword.

Epiftle

* Julian might boaft as much as he pleafed of not being a perfecutor. Thofe profane and cruel railleries, which fell from the pen of the fovereign, were in themfelves a cruel perfecution, and muft expofe the Chriftians to the fury of the idolaters, wherever they found themfelves the ftrongeft. In order to ill-treat thofe who are not of their religion, the populace only wait for the leaft fignal from the prince, and frequently not even for that.

La Bleterie.

† The effects of the church of Edeffa were probably returned to it by the fucceffors of Julian. At leaft, it was very rich in the vth century. *Ibid.*

‡ Doubtlefs Julian refers to divers texts of the gofpels; perhaps to Matth. v. 3. Luke vi. 20. Matth. xix. 21. or fome other parallel places. But few will allow him to be a good interpreter of fcripture, or that he deduces right conclufions from it. Lardner.

§ Thefe divifions might perhaps be occafioned by the Arians having feized the church and its revenues, though the greater part of the inhabitants was inviolably attached to the Catholic faith. It is notorious, that, nine years after the death of Julian, in the reign of Valens, the bifhop, the clergy, and the laity, ftrictly deferved the glorious title of confeffors. The women, and even the children, fhared the glory of this confeffion. The Edeffenes pretended

Epiſtle XLIV. To LIBANIUS *.

RECOVERING lately from a ſevere and dangerous illneſs, by the providence of the Superviſor of all things, your letter was delivered to me on the day that I firſt bathed. Reading it in the afternoon, I can ſcarce expreſs how much it confirmed me in my opinion of your pure and diſintereſted benevolence, of which I wiſh I were worthy, that I may not diſgrace your friendſhip. I immediately began your Epiſtles †, but could not finiſh them: thoſe from Antony to Alexander I poſtponed to the next day. A week after, my health, by the providence of God, improving to my wiſh, I wrote you this. May you be preſerved, my moſt eſteemed and beloved brother, [by God, who regards all things! may I ſee you, my beſt friend! With my own hand, by your ſafety and my own, by God the ſuperintendant

that their city had the honour of being the firſt that dedicated itſelf to Jeſus Chriſt, and ſhewed in their archives a letter which they believed to have been written to one of their kings by Jeſus Chriſt himſelf in the courſe of his mortal life. We may judge to what degree Julian hated them, and we muſt no longer be ſurpriſed at his writing to Ecebolus, or rather to the whole ſenate of Edeſſa, ſo bitter and ſo threatening a letter.   LA BLETERIE.

* This, in one MS. is addreſſed " to Priſcus."

† What theſe " Epiſtles" were we know not. Poſſibly ſome in aſſumed characters (now loſt), ſuch exerciſes being common with this ſophiſt.

of all things, I have written what I think. Excellent man, when shall I see and embrace you?
For now, like a difappointed lover, I am enamoured even of your name *.]

Epiftle XLV.   To Zeno †.

BESIDES many other proofs of your having
    attained the fummit of the medical art, to
which you have added propriety of behaviour,
good-nature, and regularity of life, this teftimony
now crowns all, your having turned the whole
city of Alexandria towards you in your abfence;
fuch a fting, like a bee, you have left behind you.
And with reafon; for Homer well obferves,

  A wife phyfician, fkill'd our wounds to heal,

Is more than armies to the public weal ‡.
And you are not merely a phyfician, but alfo a
mafter to all who practife phyfic, fo that you are
to phyficians what phyficians are to others. For
this reafon you are re-called from exile, and with
great fplendor. If you were obliged to quit Alex-

A. D.
361.

---

* The words between [ ] are added in one MS.

† Some MSS. give Zeno the title of " Chief Phyfician," (αρχιητρω). He was, it appears, a celebrated profeffor of phyfic, a Pagan without doubt, as Julian expreffes to him fo much efteem and affection.
                            LA BLETERIE.

‡ Il. xi. 514. Pope, 636. The words of Idomeneus on
Machaon. It is needlefs to obferve that the ancient phyficians were furgeons,

andria by the Georgian * faction, as the procefs was unjuft, you may moft juftly return. Return therefore to your former honour, and let acknowledgements be paid to us by both; by the Alexandrians for reftoring Zeno to them, and by Zeno for reftoring to him the Alexandrians.

Epiftle XLVI. To EUAGRIUS †.

I INHERITED from my grandmother ‡ a fmall eftate in Bithynia, confifting of four farms, and with it I reward your affection to me. It is too inconfiderable to elate a man with wealth, or to confer

---

* George had equally perfecuted the Catholics and the Pagans. He muft have procured by furprife fome order of Conftantius to banifh Zeno; for if George had only driven him out by force, this phyfician, fo dear to the city of Alexandria, would not have waited for an order from the fucceffor of Conftantius to return thither. LA BLETERIE.

† It is not known to whom this Epiftle is addreffed. It is very well written; neverthelefs, it is tinctured with pedantry.　　　　　　　　　　　　　　　*Ibid.*

The name of " Euägrius" occurs in the index to Petau's edition. I have therefore added it. He is probably the fame who is mentioned in the conclufion of the xxxviiith Epiftle.

Libanius has two Epiftles to one of this name, and mentions him in feveral others. He held, it appears, fome office under the government, and being accufed of fome mifmanagement in it, was brought to trial, but was acquitted by the intereft of Salluft, whom Libanius thanks for his good offices.

‡ In the Duties of a Prieft, p. 122, Julian mentions his inheriting the whole eftate of his grand-mother, which had been forcibly with-held from him.

felicity,

felicity, but its endowments are by no means unpleasing, as you may judge from the particulars. And there is no reason why I should not be jocular to you who abound with elegance and wit.

It is twenty stadia * distant from the sea, and is therefore undisturbed by trafficking merchants and clamorous or quarrelsome sailors. Yet it is not entirely destitute of the graces of Nereus; for it can always supply a gasping fish fresh-caught, and an eminence near the house commands a view of the Propontic sea, the islands, and the city which bears the name of a great prince †; and instead of being disgusted by sea-weed, and various other kinds of filth that shall be nameless, which are often thrown on the beach and the sands, ground-ivy, thyme, and other aromatic herbs, will afford you a constant regale. When with tranquil attention you have pursued your studies, and wish to relax your eyes, the prospect of the ships and the ocean is delightful. In this retirement I found many charms when I was a boy, for it has fountains also far from despicable, a beautiful bath, a garden, and an orchard; and when I grew up, I was still so fond of it, that I frequently resorted to it, and therefore my obtaining it seemed a fortunate circumstance. It affords too a small memorial of my agriculture, a sweet and fragrant wine, which is

* About two miles and a half.
† Constantinople.

good

good even when it is new *. In short, you will there see Bacchus and the Graces. The grapes, both when they hang on the vines, and are preſſed into the vat, are as odoriferous as roſes. But as ſoon as the wine is in the caſks, to ſpeak in the language of Homer, it is

A rill of nectar, ſtreaming from the Gods †.

Why then, you will ſay, did I not plant many more acres with ſuch vines? Becauſe I was not a very keen huſbandman; and beſides, as mine is a temperate cup, and the neighbourhood abounds with nymphs, I provided enough for myſelf and my few male friends. Such as it is, my dear friend, you will now accept it: however trifling the

* In the original, Ουκ' αναμενοντα τι παρα τυ χρονυ προσλαβειν, literally, "not waiting to receive any thing from time." But the Latin tranſlator has affixed a meaning no leſs oppoſite to the intention of Julian, than to fact and obſervation: *neque temporis diuturnitate vitii quicquam aſſumit.* Though our Imperial author was no votary of Bacchus, his "cup" (as he ſays) being "temperate" (ινφαλιος), he muſt have known, and meant to intimate, that, in general, old wine is proverbially good, and *vice verſâ*. *A new friend,* ſays the wiſe ſon of Sirach, *is like new wine; when it is old, thou ſhalt drink it with pleaſure.* Eccl. ix. 10.

† Τυ νεκλαρος εςιν απορρωξ. *Odyſſ.* ix. 359. POPE, 426. The elogium of Polyphemus on the rich Maronean wine given him by Ulyſſes. This wine alſo, like that of Julian,

Breath'd aromatic fragrances around, ver. (210.) 245.

Julian, it appears, had ſeveral female friends whom he occaſionally mentions, viz. Areta, Theodora, Enodia, &c. but here, to avoid any miſconſtruction, he takes particular care to ſpecify, that though "there were many nymphs "there" (πολυ των νυμφων δε εςιν), thoſe whom he entertained were "a few of the other ſex" (ολιγοι δε εςι το χρημα των ανδρων.)

I

preſent, it is pleaſing to a friend both to give and receive, " from houſe to houſe," according to the wiſe Pindar *.

This is a haſty epiſtle, written by lamp-light. Whatever therefore may be its faults, do not criticiſe them with the ſeverity of one orator towards another †.

Epiſtle XLVII. To the Inhabitants of Thrace ‡.

TO a prince who was avaricious your requeſt would ſeem unreaſonable, nor ſhould the public revenue ever be injured through any favour to individuals. But as it is our view not to collect from our ſubjects as much as poſſible, but rather to do them the utmoſt poſſible good, we remit you what is due. Not indeed the whole, but it ſhall be divided; one moiety you ſhall retain, and the other ſhall be given to the ſoldiers. Of

------

* Οικοθεν οικαδι. I have not found theſe words in Pindar. If I have ſearched well, it muſt be ſuppoſed that Julian took them from one of the works of that poet which has not been tranſmitted to us.　　　　La Bleterie.

M. de la Bleterie has not " ſearched well." They are both in the vith and viith Olympics.

† This concluſion ſavours more of the author than the prince.　　　　　　　　　　　　　　　　*Ibid.*

‡ He remits them the arrears of taxes till a certain time, namely, till the third indiction, or levy, which began in the year of Chriſt, 359. This uſed to be ſtyled " an indulgence." See *Cod. Theod. l. xi. tit. 28. De indulgentiis debitorum.*　　　　　　　　　　　Petau.

this

this no inconfiderable part will alfo be yours, as they preferve you in peace and fafety. We remit you therefore, till the third indiction *, all that is in arrear; after that, you muſt pay it as uſual. For what we have remitted to you is fully fuffi-cient; and the public revenue we muſt not im-pair. I have written on this fubject to the præ-fects, that the favour intended you may have its full effect.

I pray the Gods always to preferve you †.

---

* The name and uſe of the indictions, which ſerve to afcertain the chronology of the middle ages, were derived from the regular practice of the Roman tributes. The Emperor fubfcribed with his own hand, and in purple ink, the folemn edict, or indiction, which was fixed up in the principal city of each diocefe, during two months previous to the firſt day of September. And, by a very eafy con-nection of ideas, the word " indiction" was transferred to the meafure of tribute which it prefcribed, and to the annual term which it allowed for the payment.

The proportion, which every citizen ſhould be obliged to contribute for the public fervice, was afcertained by an accurate *cenfus*, or furvey, and from the well-known period of the indictions there is reafon to believe that this dif-ficult and expenfive operation was repeated at the regular diſtance of fifteen years. The cycle of indictions, which may be traced as high as the reign of Conftantius, or perhaps of his father Conftantine, is ſtill employed by the papal court; but the commencement of their year has been very wifely altered to the firſt of January.   GIBBON.

† This fentence is added in one MS.

Epiftle XLVIII. To * * * *.

MY body is on many accounts in an indifferent
state of health *; my mind, however, is
pretty well.   An epiftle from one friend to another cannot, I think, have a better preface.   Of
what then does this preface confift?   Of a petition, I fuppofe.   For what?   An epiftolary cor-
refpondence; which, I hope, will confirm my
wifhes, and bring me intelligence of your health
and happinefs.

Epiftle XLIX.   To Arsacius, High-prieft
of Galatia †.

THAT Hellenifm ‡ does not yet fucceed as we
wifh is owing to its profeffors.   The gifts
of the Gods are indeed great and fplendid, and far
superior

A. D.
362.
or 363.

* From this and feveral other paffages, which the reader
muft have obferved, it appears, that Julian had frequent
returns of illnefs, owing probably to his great and conftant
fatigue of mind and body, and to his rigid manner of life.

† This pontiff is not known.   I imagine this Epiftle was
written, at the fooneft, towards the end of the year 362, as
it fuppofes that fome time had been employed in endeavouring to re-eftablifh Hellenifm.   Sozomen and M. Fleury have
thought the whole worth being inferted in their Ecclefiaftical
Hiftory.   Indeed it would be impoffible to produce a more
honourable and lefs fufpicious teftimony in favour of our
religion.   But I will not deprive the reader of the pleafure
of

superior to all our hopes, to all our wishes. For (be Nemesis propitious to my words!) not long ago no one dared to hope for such and so great a change in so short a time. But why should we be satisfied with this, and not rather attend to the means by which this impiety § has increased, namely, humanity to strangers, care in burying the dead, and pretended sanctity of life? All these, I think, should be really practised by us.

It is not sufficient for you only to be blameless. Intreat or compell all the priests that are in Galatia to be also virtuous. If they do not, with their wives, children, and servants, attend the worship of the Gods, expell them from the priestly function; and also forbear to converse with the servants,

---

of making himself all the useful reflections which the perusal of this piece supplies.   La Bleterie.

The pastoral letters of Julian, if we may use that name, still represent a very curious sketch of his wishes and intentions.   Gibbon.

‡ This was the style at that time. *Hellenism* is Heathenism, or Gentilism. And Heathens are called *Hellenes*, and Hellenists, by our Ecclesiastical historians, Socrates, Sozomen, and Theodoret, especially in their history of Julian's reign.   Lardner.

§ A singular kind of impiety, which renders man the friend of man, and makes him practise all virtues! To charge good men with hypocrisy is the usual resource of extravagant prejudice and wickedness. Julian, with all his genius, did not and would not see that a society, so numerous as the Christians then were, does not carry on and cannot even conceive such a design. Hypocrisy will never be a popular vice. The multitude, be it what it may, is always honest.   La Bleterie.

children

children, and wives, of the Galileans *, who are
impious towards the Gods, and prefer impiety to
religion. Admonish also every priest not to frequent the theatre, nor to drink in taverns, nor to
exercise any trade or employment that is mean and
disgraceful. Those who obey you, honour; and
those who disobey you, expell. Erect also hospitals in every city, that strangers may partake our
benevolence; and not only those of our own religion, but, if they are indigent, others also.

How these expences are to be defrayed must
now be considered. I have ordered Galatia to supply you with thirty-thousand bushels of wheat †
every year; of which the fifth part is to be given

* Αλλα απεχοιθε τ ι οικθων, η υιιων, η των Γαλιλαιων γαμιθων,
κ. τ. λ. I have attempted a new translation of this passage,
not being satisfied with any other which I have met with.
In Spanheim's edition the Latin version is, *ne patiantur
servos, aut filios, aut conjuges Galilæorum impiè in Deos se
gerere, et impietatem pietati præponere.* And much to the
same purpose is the Latin translation of this Epistle in
Sozomen, made by Valesius, which would be commanding
every Heathen priest and his family to become persecutors;
which cannot be supposed to be probable. Cave, in the
introduction to his History of the Fathers of the ivth century, p. 34. " not suffering their servants, children, or
" wives, to be Galileans, who are despisers of the Gods,
" and prefer impiety before religion," which cannot be
right. For it is a tautology, saying over again the same
thing which had been said just before. And yet Bleterie's
translation is much to the same purpose: *s'ils souffrent dans
leur famille de ces impies de Galiléens.*   LARDNER.
I have adopted this construction.

† The Latin and French translations add here " and
" sixty-thousand *sextarii* (or *septiers*) of wine," words, for
which there is no authority in Petau's or Spanheim's edition.

to the poor who attend on the priefts, and the
remainder to be diftributed among ftrangers and
our own beggars. For when none of the Jews beg,
and the impious Galileans relieve both their own
poor and ours, it is fhameful, that ours fhould be
deftitute of our affiftance *.

Teach therefore the Gentiles to contribute to
fuch minifterial functions, and the Gentile villages
to offer to the Gods their firft-fruits. Accuftom
them to fuch acts of benevolence, and inform them
that this was of old the regal office. For Homer
puts thefe words into the mouth of Eumæus:

————— It never was our guife

To flight the poor, or aught humane defpife;
For Jove unfolds our hofpitable door,
'Tis Jove that fends the ftranger and the poor †.
Let us not fuffer others to emulate our good
actions, while we ourfelves are difgraced by floth ‡,

left

---

* Julian beheld with envy the wife and humane regu-
lations of the church, and he very frankly confeffes his
intention to deprive the Chriftians of the applaufe, as well
as advantage, which they had acquired by the exclufive
practice of charity and benevolence.   GIBBON.
Se: the conclufion of the Duties of a Prieft, Vol. I.
p. 142, &c.

† Odyff. XIV. 56. Pope, 65. This paffage is quoted
by Mr. Harris, on the fubject of the Arabian hofpitality.
See his *Philological Enquiries*, part III. ch. 7.

‡ Who doubts but that, before Chriftianity appeared in
the world, the Pagans performed fome humane actions,
and that fome among them practifed fome moral virtues?
But it was not as Pagans, it was as men that they practifed them: In that they only followed the impreffions of
the law and religion of nature. It was becaufe the corruption

ruption of the heart, the strange idea which the idolaters, at least the people, formed of the divinity, and that monstrous collection of senseless opinions, of scandalous traditions, and of ridiculous superstitions, in which Paganism consisted, had not absolutely extinguished the *light which shineth in darkness.*

The Pagans had a morality, but Paganism had none. It is no less absurd to appropriate virtues to it, as Julian does, than it would be to ascribe to infidelity some virtuous actions, of no consequence, which escape from infidels. Supposing that they have some probity, it is from temper, from interest, from caprice, because they are men, and often because they have preserved some remains of a Christian education. This epistle of Julian shews, how many virtues, even those which by the pleasure that attends their practice carry with them their reward, were rare among the Pagans. Could the finger of God be mistaken in a religion which renders all virtues common; which, founded also on all the proofs of which a fact is susceptible, brings into the world a system of morality the most perfect that can possibly be imagined, supports it by the most powerful motives and examples, regulates even the most secret motions of our souls; in a word, which re-establishes, unfolds, and perfects the principles of the law of nature, almost effaced in the minds of men, and still more in their hearts?

Let us judge of the necessity of Christianity by the horrid crimes which were committed, and are still committed, in the best-governed Pagan nations. To the disgrace of Philosophy, it will, for instance, be always true to say, that mankind are indebted to the gospel of Jesus Christ for the abolition of the barbarous custom of exposing infants. In this respect the most savage animals rise up in judgement, even at the tribunal of reason, against the Greek, the Roman, and the Chinese.

To deprive our religion of a glory which is peculiar to it it would be useless to say, that Mahometanism has been equally serviceable to humanity. Who knows not, that this false religion supposes and acknowledges the mission of Jesus Christ, and is only a corruption of Christianity and Judaism? No one can deny, that the Christian religion has at least sweetened the manners, civilised the barbarous people who have embraced it, enlightened, as to his duties,

the

lest by negligence we lose our reverence for the
Gods. If I hear that you practise this, I shall
overflow with joy.

Visit the dukes * seldom at their houses, but
write to them often. Whenever they enter a city,
let none of the priests go to meet them; but when
they resort to the temples, let them be received
within the vestibule. When they enter, let none of

the rudest Pagan, diffused every where some delicacy of
conscience, and, even among those whom it does not alter,
a tincture of probity. A Christian, moderately instructed,
and of common virtue, knows more in point of morality,
and is more philosophical than a philosopher. Those who,
like Julian, but with less splendor than he, have abandoned the Christian religion, are more indebted to that
religion than they imagine. They, as well as Julian, are
indebted to it for the exactest and purest notions of certain
moral virtues. It is from that that some have retained
those maxims of rigid probity of which they would not
have made parade, if Christianity had not given them reputation. It has already been said, that if, which is impossible, the gospel were false, it would be for the interest of
mankind to believe it true.   LA BLETERIE.

* Or commanders of the troops. See note on Epistle
XXVIII, p. 73. Julian, in what follows, seems very attentive
to the dignity of the priesthood, by endeavouring to prevent
those who were ordained to any holy office from degene-
rating into mere secular politicians, party zealots, and
danglers at the levees (as we now call them) of the great.
What so proper to impress them with a just opinion of their
own rank and importance as to forbid their mixing in
popular assemblies and tumultuous processions, even when
intended to give honour where honour was due, and pay-
ing idle or even ceremonious visits, and rather to confine
them within the precincts of their own temples, where,
without offence, they had an undoubted precedence? In
the Duties of a Priest, in like manner, the priests are allowed to " visit the dukes and præfects." See Vol. I. p. 138.

their

their guards precede them; but let who will follow them. For as soon as they enter the door of the temple, they become private persons. You yourself, you well know, have a right to precede all who are within it, that being agreeable to the divine law. Those who are truly pious will obey you, and none will oppose you but the proud, ostentatious, and vain-glorious.

I am ready to assist the people of Pessinus *, if they can render the Mother of the Gods propitious to them. But if they neglect her, they will not only be culpable, but, which is more harsh to say, will incur my displeasure †.

No law requires that they my care should prove,
Or pity, hated by the powers above ‡.

There-

---

* See Epistle XXI. p. 43.

† An ungenerous distinction was admitted into the mind of Julian, that, according to the difference of their religious sentiments, one part of his subjects deserved his favour and friendship, while the other was entitled only to the common benefits that his justice could not refuse to an obedient people.   GIBBON.

‡ See Odyss. X. 73. What Julian says here does not seem to agree with the order which he has just given to establish some hospitals, where all might be received, Christians as well as Pagans. This contradiction, if such it were, would not have been the only one of which he had been guilty. But it is only apparent. The duties of humanity are strictly just. They are obligatory with regard to all men. But favours are due to none; and it was some favour that the inhabitants of Pessinus had asked of the Emperor.   LA BLETERIE.

These two lines, which Julian has changed and perverted, in the true spirit of a bigot, are taken from the speech of Æolus, when he refuses to grant Ulysses a fresh supply of

 winds.

Therefore assure them, that, if they wish for my protection, all the people must supplicate the Mother of the Gods.

———————

Epistle L.   To Ecdicius, Præfect of Ægypt *.

A. D.
362.

"YOU tell me my dream †," says the proverb. But I am going to tell you what
you have seen waking. The Nile, I am informed,
has

winds. Libanius (*Orat. Parent. c.* 59. *p.* 286.) attempts to justify this partial behaviour by an apology, in which persecution peeps through the mask of candour.   GIBBON.

The lines in Homer are,

Ου γαρ μοι θεμις εςι κομιζεμεν, εδ' αποπεμπειν
Ανδρα, τ' ος κε θεοισιν απεχθηλαι μακαρεσσιν.

His baneful suit pollutes these bless'd abodes,
Whose faith proclaims him hateful to the Gods.

POPE, 85.

Julian has altered them thus, at the expence of a false quantity, and a jingle:

Ου γαρ μοι θεμις εςι κομιζεμεν, η' ελεαιρειν
Ανδρας, οι και θεοισιν απεχθωντ' αθαναλοισιν.

In the last word, probably, his memory might deceive him, as απεχθωλαι μακαρεσσιν would have suited his purpose and metre as well. The other alterations (και perhaps excepted) must have been intentional.

* This Epistle is a good piece of pleasantry on the negligence of Ecdicius. That governor, I fancy, would rather have received a serious reprimand. Nothing was more interesting to the Emperor and the empire than an account of how many cubits the Nile had risen in the autumnal solstice, as on that depended the fertility of Ægypt, and the subsistence of Constantinople. Where the waters rose too much, or too little, the lands could not be sown. "If the increase," says Pliny, (*l.* v. *c.* 9.) "be only
"twelve

has rifen feveral cubits, and overflowed all Ægypt.
If you wifh to know the number, it was fifteen
on the twentieth of September. This intelligence
I received from Theophilus, præfect of the camps.
If you had not heard it before, rejoice at hearing
it now from me.

" twelve cubits, the province is afflicted with famine ; if
" it be only thirteen, it ftill fuffers. Fourteen give joy ;
" fifteen fafety; fixteen abfolute plenty." The Nile fwells
from the middle of July to the folftice. When it is at its
greateft height, the canals are opened, to let it in upon
the lands. It returns to its bed in the month of No-
vember. The feeds are then fown. The corn is reaped in
May.   LA BLETERIE.
    The cubit, by which the rifing of the Nile in Ægypt
was meafured, had been ufually lodged in the temple of
Serapis [at Alexandria]. Conftantine removed it into a
Chriftian church. But Julian ordered it to be replaced in
the temple of Serapis. His ftatue and temple having been
demolifhed, by order of Theodofius I. in the year 391, it
was given out by the Gentiles that the Nile would no
longer overflow. Neverthelefs it rofe the following year
to an uncommon height. The cubit was then again reftored to the Chriftians.   LARDNER.
    Thales, the Milefian, accounted for the inundation of
this river by the Etefian winds blowing againft the mouth
of it at that feafon. But the fame would probably then
happen to other rivers where the like winds are known to
blow. The true caufe is probably the melting of the fnows
on the mountains of Ethiopia, when the fun comes over
them. Yet thefe winds may contribute to make the overflow more regular and lafting, as they are an equal balance
to the waters, and prevent their running into the fea after
thefe have fufficiently fertilifed the land.
    † Το σον οναρ σοι διηγεμαι, " I tell you your dream." That
is, " I tell you what you yourfelf know better than I."
In Suidas this proverb is quoted from fome unknown author, and alfo in Plato *De Republ. l.* VIII. It feems derived
from thofe who confult interpreters of dreams ; whom fome
alfo require to guefs what they have dreamed. ERASMUS.

K 4

Epistle LI.   To the ALEXANDRIANS *.

A. D.
362.

IF your city had had any other founder, any one of thofe who, tranfgreffing their own laws †, had juftly fuffered punifhment for leading a wicked life, and introducing a new doctrine, a new religion, even then it would have been unreafonable for you to wifh for Athanafius. But now, as the founder of your city is Alexander ‡, and your ruler and tutelar deity king Serapis, with the virgin his affociate, and the queen of all Ægypt, Ifis, * * * *, you do not act like a healthy city, but the diftempered part dares to arrogate the

* The Catholics, who were, without doubt, the moft numerous, prefented, in the name of the city, a petition to the Emperor, requefting the repeal of the order which he had iffued againft Athanafius. The Emperor anfwers their petition by this new Edict. M. Fleury quotes the whole of it.   LA BLETERIE.

† Thofe whom Julian here treats as apoftates (a reproach ftrange enough in his mouth), had not abandoned the God of their fathers, to run after ftrange gods. They believed in the fecond revelation, which was only the object, the fequel, and the accomplifhment of the firft. By dying for the doctrine of their mafter, they have proved that they were not deceivers. The proofs of the fact which determined them to embrace it are of fuch a nature, that it is impoffible for them to have been deceived. Could Julian allege any thing fimilar in juftification of his change? He has here given us a very remarkable fketch of his reafons in the pathetic difcourfe which he addreffes to the inhabitants of Alexandria.   Ibid.

‡ See Epiftle X. note †, p. 20.

name

name of the whole. By the Gods, men of Alexandria, I am aſhamed, that any of you ſhould avow himſelf a Galilean.

The anceſtors of the Hebrews were formerly ſlaves to the Ægyptians. But now, men of Alexandria, you, the conquerors of Ægypt (for Ægypt was conquered by your founder), ſuſtain a voluntary ſervitude to the deſpiſers of your national rites, in oppoſition to your ancient laws * ; not recollecting your former happineſs, when all Ægypt had communion with the Gods †, and enjoyed many bleſſings. But tell me, what advantage ‡ has accrued to your city from thoſe who now introduce among you a new religion ? Your founder was that pious man § Alexander of Macedon, who

did

---

* The Hebrews were ſubjected to the ancient kings of Ægypt; the Alexandrians therefore ought to prefer the Greek religion to the doctrine of the Apoſtles : What a ſingular complication of bad arguments ! LA BLETERIE.

† If they recollected it, they recollected but little of it.
Ibid.

Julian makes intercommunity the diſtinguiſhing character of the Pagan religion. For the Imperial ſophiſt, writing to the people of Alexandria, and upbraiding them with having forſaken the religion of their country, in order to aggravate the charge, inſinuates them to be guilty of ingratitude, as having forgotten "thoſe happy times when " all Ægypt worſhipped the Gods *in common*" (ηνικα ην κοινωνια). WARBURTON.

‡ The Chriſtian religion does not promiſe temporal bleſſings; but, if men practiſe it, they will be as happy as they can be on earth. LA BLETERIE.

§ In matters of religion, what authority was that of Alexander ? What conqueſts were his, compared to thoſe

of

did not, by Jove, refemble any one of thefe, or any of the Hebrews, who far excelled them. Even Ptolemy, the fon of Lagus *, was alfo fuperior to them. As to Alexander, if he had encountered, he would have endangered, even the Romans. What then did the Ptolemies, who fucceeded your founder? Educating your city, like their own daughter, from her infancy, they did not bring her to maturity by the difcourfes of Jefus, nor did they conftruct the form of government with which fhe is now bleffed by the doctrine of the odious Galileans.

Thirdly, after the Romans became its mafters, taking it from the bad government of the Ptolemies †, Auguftus vifited your city, and thus addreffed the citizens: " Men of Alexandria, I ac-
" quit your city of all blame, out of regard to
" the great God Serapis, and alfo for the fake of
" the people and the grandeur of the city. A
" third caufe of my kindnefs to you is my friend

of the Apoftles? I beg the reader to recollect that paffage in the epiftle to Themiftius (p. 24.), where Julian raifes Socrates above Alexander; and to determine whether the juft reafons which he has given for preferring the former are not infinitely more ftriking and decifive in favour of the difciples of Jefus Chrift. Here Julian fpeaks like a true fophift. He was well acquainted with Alexander, and would not have wifhed to refemble him in every thing.
LA BLETERIE.

* Ptolemy, the fon of Lagus, was one of the generals of Alexander, who fhared his empire. He founded the kingdom of Ægypt. *Ibid.*

† The family of the Lagides terminated in the perfon of Cleopatra, after having reigned 300 years. *Ibid.*

" Areus."

" Areus *." This Areus, the companion of Augustus Cæsar, and a philosopher, was your fellow-citizen.

The particular favours conferred upon your city by the Olympic Gods were, in short, such as these. Many more, not to be prolix, I omit. Those blessings which the illustrious Gods bestow in common every day, not on one family, nor on a single city, but on the whole world, why do you not acknowledge? Are you alone insensible of the splendor that flows from the sun †? Are you alone ignorant that summer and winter are produced by him, and that to him all things owe their life and origin? Do you not also perceive the great advantages that accrue to your city from the moon, from him and by him the disposer of all things? Yet you dare not worship either of these deities; and this Jesus, whom neither you, nor your fathers have seen, you think must necessarily be God the Word ‡, while him, whom, from eternity, every

* The same who is mentioned in the Cæsars, (Vol. I. p. 193.) and in the Epistle to Themistius, (p. 25.)

LA BLETERIE.

† All nature, and the heavenly bodies, in particular, prove the existence of a Supreme Being, and declare his power, his wisdom, and his goodness. But their splendor, the regularity of their motions, and the uses which they render to mankind do not prove that they are governed by some particular intelligences, and much less that they deserve to be worshipped. *Ibid.*

‡ I have already said that Julian placed the *Logos*, or Demiurgus, in the Sun. *Ibid.*

Θεον λογον. Taken from St. John, i. 1. Θεος ην ὁ λογος, *The Word was G-d.*

generation

generation of mankind has seen, and sees, and worships, and by worshipping lives happily, the great sun, I mean, a living, animated, rational, and beneficent image of the intelligible Father *, you despise. If you listen to my admonitions †, * * * *, you will by degrees return to truth. You will not wander from the right path, if you will be guided by him, who, to the twentieth year of his age, pursued that road, but has now worshipped the Gods for near twelve years.

If you will follow my advice, my joy will be exuberant. But if you will still persevere in that superstitious institution of designing men, agree, however, among yourselves, and do not desire Athanasius. There are many of his disciples who are abundantly able to please your itching ears ‡, desirous as they are of such impious discourses. I wish that this wickedness were confined to Athanasius and his irreligious school. But you have

---

* In another place (*apud Cyril. l.* 11. *p.* 69.) he calls the sun " God, and the throne of God." Julian believed the Platonician Trinity, and only blames the Christians for preferring a mortal to an immortal Logos.   GIBBON.

Though the Alexandrians saw the sun, they by no means saw that he was a divinity; but without having seen the MAN GOD, they had certain proofs of his mission; proofs which, all united, form, in fact, a complete demonstration. It is worth observing, that Julian, in one and the same phrase, speaks the language of Pyrrhonism and that of credulity.   LA BLETERIE.

† Something here is wanting.

‡ Τας ακοας υμων κινησωσας.   Similar to that expression of St. Paul, 2 Tim. iv. 3. κνηθομενοι την ακοην.

among

among you many, not ignoble, of the same sect, and the business is easily done. For any one whom you may select from the people, in what relates to expounding the scriptures will be by no means inferior to him whom you solicit. But if you are pleased with the shrewdness of Athanasius (for, I hear, the man is crafty), and therefore have petitioned, know, that for this very reason he was banished. That such an intriguer should preside over the people is highly dangerous; one, who is not a man, but a puny contemptible mortal, one who prides himself on hazarding his life *, cannot but create disturbances. That nothing of that kind might happen, I ordered him formerly to leave the city, but I now banish him from all Ægypt.

Let this be communicated to our Alexandrians.

* I cannot convey all the energy of the Greek : Μηδὲ ανηρ, αλλ᾽ ανθρωπισκος ευτελης, καθαπερ υιος, ο μεγας (it should be το μεγα) οιομενος περι της κεφαλης κινδυνευειν. *Ne vir quidem, sed homuncio nullius pretii, qualis iste est, qui de capite periclitari magnum aliquid existimat.* La Bleterie.

The present translator may say the same.

M. de Tillemont concludes from this text, that Athanasius was a little man, and that his person had nothing that announced the grandeur and elevation of his mind. The most, I think that we can conclude from this expression of Julian is, that, Athanasius was not of a proper heig t. I say, the most; for it must be observed, that it is an Emperor who speaks of one of his subjects, and who affects to speak of him in a tone of contempt. Gregory Nazianzen (*Orat.* XXI.) says, that Athanasius " had the form of an angel," αγγελικος το ειδος. It even appears, that, when he went to meet the Emperor Constantine the younger, in Gaul, that prince was struck with his advantageous appearance. *Ibid.*

Epistle

Epiſtle LII.   To the BOSTRENIANS *.

Aug.
362.

ITHOUGHT that the prelates of the Galileans had been under greater obligations to me
than to my predeceſſor. For in his reign many
of them were baniſhed, perſecuted, and impriſoned;
and numbers of thoſe, who are ſtyled heretics, were
put to death, particularly at Samoſata and Cyzicus;
and in Paphlagonia, Bithynia, Galatia, and many
other provinces, whole villages were laid waſte
and entirely depopulated †.   In my reign the re-

---

* Boſtra, or Boſra, as it is ſtyled in ſcripture, was a
Roman colony, and the capital of Arabia. It had then
for its biſhop a man equally well verſed in polite literature,
and the doctrine of the church, named Titus.
                                        LA BLETERIE.

In this very remakable Epiſtle to the people of Boſtra,
Julian profeſſes his moderation, and betrays his zeal; which
is acknowledged by Ammianus, and expoſed by Gregory,
(*Orat*, III. *p.* 73.)   GIBBON.

† The ſucceſſor of Conſtantius has expreſſed, in a con-
ciſe, but lively, manner, ſome of the theological calamities which afflicted the empire, and more eſpecially the
Eaſt, in the reign of a prince, who was the ſlave of his
own paſſions, and of thoſe of his eunuchs.   *Ibid.*

Under Conſtantius the Arians, who pretended to be the
Catholic church, had perſecuted not only the orthodox, but
alſo the ſectaries, eſpecially the Novatians, who, without
receiving the council of Nice ſubſequent to their ſchiſm,
were no leſs zealous than the orthodox for conſubſtantiality.
They were the ſubſiſting and unſuſpected proof of the
novelty of Arianiſm; which made them much regarded
by the Catholics, and more odious to the Arians than the
Catholics themſelves.   LA BLETERIE.

verſe

verfe has happened. For they who had been banifhed are allowed to return, and to thofe whofe
goods had been confifcated, all have been reftored. Such, neverthelefs, are their madnefs
and folly, that, becaufe they can no more tyrannife, or perpetrate what they had projected,
firft againft their brethren, and then againft us,
the worfhippers of the Gods, enraged and exafpe-
rated, they move every ftone, and dare to alarm
and inflame the people *; impious towards the
Gods, and difobedient to our edicts, humane as
they are. For we fuffer none of them to be dragged
to the altars againft their will. We alfo publickly
declare, that, if any are defirous to partake of our
luftrations and libations, they muft firft offer facrifices of expiation, and fupplicate the Gods, the
averters of evil. So far are we from wifhing to
admit any of the irreligious to our facred rites
before they have purified their fouls by prayers to
the Gods, and their bodies by legal ablutions +.

The populace therefore, deluded by thofe who
are called the clergy, as the feverity above-mentioned is abolifhed, grow tumultuous. For they
who have been ufed to tyrannife, not fatisfied
with impunity for their paft crimes, but ambitious of their former power, becaufe they are no

* The Arian clergy, who were in poffeffion of a great
number of churches, gave occafion to the invectives of
Julian.   LA BLETERIE.

+ One who fpeaks in this manner was very capable of
having endeavoured to efface his baptifm.   *Ibid.*

7   longer

longer permitted to act as judges *, or make wills †, or embezzle the estates of others, and appropriate every thing to themselves, all, if I may so say, pull the ropes of sedition, and, as the pro_ verb expresses it, heap fuel on the fire, and scruple not to add greater evils to the former by urging the multitude to commotions.

It is my pleasure therefore to declare and publish to all the people, by this edict, that they must not abet the seditions of the clergy, nor suffer themselves to be induced by them to throw stones, and disobey the magistrates. They may assemble together, if they please, and offer up such prayers as they have established for themselves. But if the clergy endeavour to persuade them to foment disturbances on their account, let them by no means concur, on pain of punishment.

* Julian had revoked all the privileges granted to the church, and, among them, the law by which Constantine allowed those who had law-suits to decline the ordinary jurisdiction, and to apply to the bishops, whose sentences were to be executed like those of the Emperor himself.

LA BLETERIE.

† Γραφειν διαθηκας, *scribere testamenta*, may here have three meanings; 1. to make wills; 2. to receive wills in a public capacity; 3. to dictate or suggest wills. Julian had not deprived the clergy of the right of making wills. This is proved by the silence of Christian writers. Among the Romans, to the making of the most solemn will no public person was requisite: there only wanted a certain number of witnesses. The third sense therefore remains. A law of Constantine, which is still in being, allowed wills to be made in favour of the church. Julian having abrogated that law, the ecclesiastics could no longer engage any one to give his

I thought proper to make this declaration to the city of Boſtra in particular, becauſe the biſhop, Titus *, and the clergy †, in a memorial which they have preſented to me, have accuſed the people of being inclined to raiſe diſturbances, if they had not been reſtrained by their admonitions. I will tranſcribe the words which the biſhop has dared to inſert in that memorial: " Though the Chriſtians " are as numerous as the Gentiles, they are re- " ſtrained by our exhortations from being tumul- " tuous." Theſe are the words of the biſhop concerning you. Obſerve, he does not aſcribe your regularity to your own inclination ; unwillingly, he ſays, you refrain, " by his exhortations." As your accuſer, therefore, expell him from the city ‡. And,

for

---

* This Titus, biſhop of Boſtra, taught that we do not die in conſequence of the ſin of Adam, but by the neceſſity of nature ; and that Adam himſelf would have died, if he had not ſinned. In this he was followed by Pelagius.

PRIESTLEY.

† It ſeems as if there was an apprehenſion of ſome commotion in the city of Boſtra. Julian had threatened to make the biſhop, Titus, and his clergy, reſponſible for the whole. The biſhop had preſented, or cauſed a memorial to be preſented, to the Emperor, accounting for his conduct.

LA BLETERIE.

‡ If we did not know how much the mind is narrowed by the ſpirit of party, it would be inconceivable that an Emperor, a man who piqued himſelf on reaſoning, and who publiſhed this himſelf, ſhould be capable of ſuch a trick [*tracaſſerie*.] I uſe this word, becauſe it is a low one, and I know none more proper to characteriſe the artfulneſs of Julian, who was determined, at any rate, to prejudice in the minds of the people an irreproachable

for the future, let the people agree among themselves; let no one be at variance, or do an injury
to another; neither you who are in error, to those
who worship the Gods, rightly and justly, in the
mode transmitted to us from the most ancient
times; nor let the worshippers of the Gods destroy or plunder the houses of those who rather
by ignorance than choice are led astray. Men
should be taught and persuaded by reason, not by
blows, invectives, and corporal punishments. I
therefore again and again admonish those who embrace the true religion in no respect to injure or in-
sult the Galileans *, neither by attacks nor reproaches.

proachable prelate, who employed his authority to main-
tain the public tranquillity. This philosophical Emperor,
in an edict which breathes the principles of mutual support, foments the flame, which he pretends it is his wish
to stifle. If he had banished the bishop, his orders would
have been peaceably obeyed. But does not his advising
the people to drive him out indicate a design to excite a
tumult? Some might consider the advice of the Emperor
as an order, and others only as an advice. History does
not inform us what was the consequence of this affair.
                                        La Bleterie.
    After this, no instance of baseness, or injustice, will be
thought strange. It is remarkable that the author of the
Characteristics has given us a translation of this letter, for
" a pattern," as he tells us, " of the humour and genius,
" of the principles and sentiments, of this virtuous, gallant,
" generous, and mild Emperor." p. 87, &c. 4th edition.
It is true, his translation drops the affair of Titus, their
bishop. So that nothing hinders his reader from concluding
but that the Emperor might be as " gallant and generous"
as he is pleased to represent him.   Warburton.
    * How irreconcileable is this with the above Edict,
[Epistle XLII.] for which he deserved no small reproof from

(i

proaches. We should rather pity than hate those who in the most important concerns act ill. For as piety is the greatest of blessings, impiety, certainly, is the greatest of evils. Such is their fate, who turn from the immortal Gods to dead men *, and their relicks. With those who are thus unhappy we condole, but them who are freed and delivered by the Gods we congratulate †.

Given at Antioch on the calends of August.

Epistle

(in other respects) his chief panegyrist! " It was very un-
" merciful in him (as that excellent writer expresses it) to
" forbid the masters of grammar and rhetoric to teach
" the Christians, unless they embraced the worship of the
" Gods." Amm. Marc. xxv. 4.   SPANHEIM.

* Απο Θεων επι τας νεκρους μεταλλεραμμενες. An expression similar to that of St. Paul, Επεστρεψατε προς τον Θεον απο των ειδωλων: *Ye turned to God from idols, to serve the living God.* 1 Thes. i. 9.

† From this Edict, as well as from other things, it appears that Julian was very fond of Hellenism, or Heathenism. And Sozomen's observations appear to be very pertinent. Julian was very ready to lay hold of every pretence, and to improve every occasion, to rid himself of the Presidents of Christian churches; especially such as had an influence with the people. We see three instances of this, in Athanasius of Alexandria, Eleusius of Cyzicum, and Titus of Bostra, all of them men of great distinction.

Julian here makes repeated professions of moderation and equity toward the Christians. But the letter bears witness against him. Titus was one of the most learned men of the age. His people were peaceable, and he had exhorted them to be so. And yet Julian commands his people to expell him out of their city; under a pretence, that his exhortations to a peaceable behaviour implied an accusation of an unpeaceable temper.

Julian was a man of great ingenuity, sobriety of manners, and good-natured in himself. But his zeal for the religion which he had embraced was excessive, and de-

Epiſtle LIII. To the Philoſopher JAM-
BLICHUS *.

O JUPITER! can it be true that we reſide in
the middle of Thrace, and winter in its ca-
verns, while from the excellent Jamblichus, as
from ſome eaſtern ſpring, letters greet us, inſtead
of ſwallows, though we are not yet allowed to go
to him, nor he to come to us? Who but a Thracian,
or one like Tereus †, can with equanimity ſupport
this?

 O royal Jove! from Thrace the Grecians free ‡,
 Diſpell theſe fogs, and give us but to ſee

generated into bigotry and ſuperſtition; inſomuch that
with all his pretenſions to right reaſon, and all his pro-
feſſions of humanity, moderation, tenderneſs, and equity,
he has not eſcaped the juſt imputation of being a perſe-
cutor.   Lardner.

This learned writer has given an Engliſh tranſlation of
the above Epiſtle in his Jewiſh and Heathen Teſtimonies,
Vol. IV. p. 108.

 * See Ep. XXXIV. note *, p. 80.
 † Tereus was a king of Thrace, but ſeems here introduced for his cruelty and brutality. See Ovid. Metam. vi.

 ‡ Ζευ ανα' αλλα συ ρυσαι απο Θρηκηθεν Αχαιες, altered from Il.
xvii. 645. Ζευ πα[ερ, αλλα συ ρυσαι υπ' ηερος υιας Αχαιων, the
beginning of the celebrated prayer of Ajax, applauded by
Longinus and others. The other line is the ſame as in Ho-
mer. Pope has thus tranſlated them:
 ——————————— Lord of earth and air!
 O King! O Father! hear my humble prayer!
 Diſpell this cloud, the light of heaven reſtore,
 Give me to ſee, and Ajax aſks no more.   727.

sometimes our Mercury, and to salute his shrine, and embrace his images, as Ulysses is said to have done, when, after his wanderings, he at last saw Ithaca *; though the Phæacians departed, after laying him out of the ship, like a bale of goods, in his sleep †. But sleep does not seize us till we are allowed to see the great blessing of the world. You too are jocose in saying that I and my companion Sopater ‡ have transported all the East into Thrace. For if the truth must be spoken, while Jamblichus is absent, I seem involved in Cimmerian § darkness. Besides, you desire one of these alternatives,

* Ulysses, at his return to Ithaca, Odyss. xiii.

——————With joy confess'd his place of birth,
And on his knees salutes his mother earth ; POPE, 403.
but where Julian found the two other circumstances mentioned above, I cannot say.

† Odyss. xiii. 116.
Ulysses sleeping on his couch they bore,
And gently plac'd him on the rocky shore, &c.
POPE, 138.

‡ Could this be the Sopater, who afterwards entertained him at Hierapolis, (see p. 70.) whom he " had (then) " scarce ever seen before ?"

§ The Cimmerians were a people of Italy who dwelt in a valley, between Baiæ and Cumæ, so surrounded with hills, that it is said they never saw the sun. There was the Sibyl's grot, and there was supposed to be the descent to hell.

Great obscurity, or darkness, of the mind, is called " Cimmerian darkness." This adage arose from the prodigious darkness of the Cimmerian region, which Strabo describes in his first book of his Geography, and quotes

alternatives, either that I would go to you, or that you may come to me; one of which, namely, that I would return to you, and enjoy your advantages, is very defirable to me. The other exceeds all my wifhes. But as this is not only inconvenient to you, but alfo impracticable, remain at home, fare you well, and continue to enjoy your prefent tranquillity. As to me, whatever the Gods fhall allot, I will bear with fortitude: for it is the character of the virtuous to cherifh good hopes, and to perform their duty; but always to fubmit to fatal neceffity.

> There, in a lonely land, and gloomy cells,
> The dufky nation of Cimmeria dwells;
> The fun ne'er views th' uncomfortable feats,
> When radiant he advances, or retreats:
> Unhappy race, whom endlefs night invades,
> Clouds the dull air, and wraps them round in fhades,
>   BROOME, 15.

Tully alfo mentions the Cimmerians in the ivth book of his Academic Queftions. And in this country Ovid, in the xith book of his Metamorphofes, has built a temple to the God of Sleep.   ERASMUS.

Epiſtle LIV. To George, the Catholic *.

LET Echo be, as you ſay, a Goddeſs, and talkative, and alſo, if you pleaſe, the wife of Pan †. I ſay nothing to the contrary. Though Nature would teach me, that Echo is the ſound of the voice reverberated by the percuſſion of the air, and reflected back to the ear, yet, by the opinion both of ancients and moderns, as well as by yours, I am induced to think that Echo is a Goddeſs. But what is this to me, who in love to you far exceed Echo? For ſhe does not reply to every thing ſhe hears, but only to the laſt words of the voice, like a coy miſtreſs, who receives the ſalute of her lover on the extremity of her lips. In this as I gladly lead the way, ſo again challenged by you, like a tennis-player, I return the ſtroke. You ſhall not eſcape, but ſhall be convicted by your own letter; and in that image you may diſcover a reſemblance of yourſelf, as you re-

* Epiſtle VIII. is addreſſed to the ſame.
† The Mythologiſts fable, that Echo was deſperately beloved by Pan. See, among others, Hephæſtion in the Writers of poetic hiſtory, publiſhed by Thomas Gale, p. 333.
WOLFIUS.
And thus Libanius ſays to his friend Demetrius, “ You “ have tranſmitted me ſo ſweet a voice by your epiſtle, “ that I was quite captivated by it, and enamoured of its “ charms, admiring the beauty of the words no leſs than “ Pan admired the Goddeſs!” Ep. ccccxLII.

          ceive

ceive much and return little, not of me, who endeavour to excell in both. But whether you return with the same measure that you receive, or not, whatever I receive from you is agreeable to me, and shall be deemed a full and satisfactory answer.

Epistle LV. To Eumenius and Pharianus*.

A. D.
359.

WHOEVER has persuaded you that any thing is more pleasing and beneficial to mankind than philosophising in ease and security, is deceived himself, and deceives you. If you retain your former spirit, and, like a sparkling flame, it be not suddenly extinguished, I deem you happy. Four years have now elapsed, and almost three months more, since we parted. I would gladly therefore learn what progress you have made in that time. As to me, it is a wonder that I can even speak Greek, such barbarism I have contracted in this country†. Despise not oratory,

* These were probably two of Julian's fellow-students, whom he left with regret at Athens, in 355, when he was summoned to court by Constantius, and created Cæsar. I have therefore dated this Epistle as above. I know not that their names occur any where else.

Among the Epistles of Libanius, preserved (in Latin) by Zambicari, are two to Eumenius, (III. 237, 8.) which probably means this Eumenius, especially as in one of them

nor neglect rhetorick, nor be inattentive to poetry. But let your principal study be philosophy; and in this bestow all your labour on the maxims of Aristotle and Plato. Be this your chief work; be this the base, the foundation, the walls, the roof. Let the rest be no more than offices; which, however, you may finish with more skill than some can build a mansion.

This advice is given you by one, who, by divine Nemesis, loves you both with a brotherly affection, as having been his school-fellows and intimate friends. If you retain a regard for me, my affection will increase. If not, I shall grieve. And what at length may be the consequence of continual grief, for the sake of a better omen, I suppress.

Epistle LVI. To Ecdicius, Præfect of Ægypt.

IF any thing particularly deserves our serious attention, it is sacred music. Selecting therefore from among the Alexandrians some youths of good families, order two *artabæ* * to be distributed every month to each; and some oil, wheat, and wine. The præfects of the treasury shall supply them with cloaths. They shall be chosen by

---

* Among the Ægyptians, that an *artaba* made twenty *modii* we are told by Jerom on Isaiah, ch. v.

Among the Persians it was different, as we learn from Herodotus, *l.* 1.   ROBERTSON.

their

their voices. Mean time, let those who are proficients in that art be informed, that we have allotted rewards for their labours. And, besides these encouragements from us, they may also be assured by those who have a right judgement in these things, that they will profit their souls by purifying them with divine music. So much for these youths. As to what relates to the scholars of the musician Dioscorus, let them cultivate that art with more attention, and they shall receive from us all possible assistance *.

Epistle LVII. To the Philosopher ELPIDIUS †.

THE pleasure even of a short letter is great, when the friendship of the writer is measured, not by the conciseness of his epistle, but by the greatness of his mind. Therefore if my present mental salutation be rather short, do not from thence form a judgement of my regard. But as you well know the extent of my love for you, excuse the brevity of this address, and answer it with-

* This Epistle is a proof of the Emperor's great esteem for music. And indeed it is impossible to read his works without being convinced, that he was ignorant of nothing which was then necessary to be known to render a man an universal scholar.   LA BLETERIE.

It is omitted, however, by this translator.

† This philosopher, and the Emperor's kindness to him, are mentioned by Libanius in one of his Epistles to Julian. See Vol. I. p. 305.

out delay. For whatever you send me, though it be small, I esteem as a specimen of every thing that is good.

———————

Epistle LVIII.   To the ALEXANDRIANS.

YOU have a stone obelisk *, I am informed, of a proper height, but that, as if it were worthless, it lies on the shore. Constantius, of blessed memory, had constructed a vessel on purpose to convey it to my country, Constantinople †. But as he, by the will of the Gods, has taken a fatal departure from hence, that city now requests this present from me, being my country, and consequently more nearly connected to me than to him. His was a brotherly, but mine is a filial, love ‡;

for

* In a remote but polished age, which seems to have preceded the invention of alphabetical writing, a great number of these obelisks had been erected in the cities of Thebes and Heliopolis, by the ancient sovereigns of Ægypt, in a just confidence that the simplicity of their form and the hardness of their substance would resist the injuries of time and violence.   GIBBON.

† Constantius caused one of the obelisks that are still seen at Rome to be transported thither from Ægypt. It is that which was erected by Sixtus V. Constantius was desirous of procuring a like decoration for New Rome.
                    LA BLETERIE.

A vessel of uncommon strength and capaciousness was provided to convey this uncommon weight of granite from the banks of the Nile to those of the Tyber.   GIBBON.

‡ Julian, I think, might have said that *Constantine* loved the city as his " daughter ;" and then he would have had

no

for I was born there, I was educated there, and therefore I cannot be ungrateful to her *.

As your city is no less dear to me than my own country, instead of a triangular stone engraved with Ægyptian characters, I allow you to erect the colossal statue †, which has lately been made, of a man whose resemblance you desire. And as it is generally reported that some persons repose on the top of that obelisk, and pay it adoration ‡, it

no occasion to magnify his affection for that place above *Constantine's.* However, the more to satisfy the Alexandrians, he promises them a column of brass, of a large size, in the room of the Ægyptian obelisk of stone. And thus Julian does what had been blamed in *Constantine.* He robs and strips Alexandria to enrich and adorn Constantinople.

LARDNER.

. This learned writer, it is observable, has here mistaken " Constantine" for " Constantius." Yet he refers to Spanheim's edition, where we read ὁ μακαρίτης Κωνσάντιος.

* In the editions of Julian the Epistle ends here. M. Muratori found the conclusion in a MS. of the Ambrosian library, and has published it in his *Anecdota Græca,* from whence M. Fabricius has inserted it in his *Bibliotheca Græca.*

LA BLETERIE.

† I imagine this was a statue of Julian himself.   *Ibid.*

‡ Τινὲς εἰσιν οἱ θεραπευόντες καὶ προσκαθευδόντες αὐτὰ τη κορυφη. M. Muratori translates it, *quosdam esse therapeutas qui obelisci hujus vertici indormiunt.* He thinks that these *therapeutæ* were some monks, who, no doubt in the spirit of mortification, slept on that obelisk. M. Fabricius adds, that these were certainly some Stylites. But, 1. in order to find therapeuts here, a force must be put upon the text, and no regard paid to the conjunction copulative which connects the two verbs: *cultum adhibentes et indormientes ejus vertici.* 2. The Stylites were entirely unknown before the illustrious St. Simeon, who did not ascend his pillar till about the year 423 ; and it is remarkable that the anchorets

it fhould, I am convinced, on account of that fuperftition, be removed. For thofe who fee them
fleeping there, amidft the filth which muft fur-

chorets of Ægypt fent and declared to him, that they
feparated themfelves from his communion, becaufe they
could not approve fo new a kind of life. Nor did they
again unite with this faint till they had had proofs of his
obedience and humility. It is better therefore to tranflate
it as I have done, and to fay that fome Heathens paid adoration to this obelifk. It is well known, that all the obelifks
were dedicated to the fun, a reafon fufficient to miflead
fome Chriftian anchorets ; and the hieroglyphics which were
feen on this might render it ftill more refpectable to idolaters. Some, hoping no doubt to have divine dreams,
went to fleep on the point, or rather near the point, of
this obelifk, which lay on the fea-fhore. The heat of the
climate will not admit a doubt that this was in the night ;
and this nocturnal fuperftition ferved as an occafion and a
pretext for fome diforders which completed the difcredit
of Paganifm. Julian, if I may be allowed the expreffion,
was defirous of removing that *ftone of offence*, and of preferving from this ridicule his unhappy religion, which had
already too much of it. *Ibid.*

· This obelifk might be that which Spon faw at Conftantinople in the fquare of the Armeydan, where was formerly the Hippodrome. It is of Ægyptian granite, fifty
feet high, and covered with hieroglyphics. The infcription
on the bafe relates that " Theodofius undertook to erect
" this monument, which lay on the ground, and that Pro-
" clus accomplifhed the work in thirty-two days." Julian, no
doubt, was dead before his obelifk was erected, and Valens
had neglected it. In the reign of Theodofius they were
far from giving the honour of it to Julian, or from faying
that it had been tranfported from Ægypt by the orders of
that apoftate. It may be objected that the obelifk of Spon is
fquare, but that this which Julian mentions was triangular,
τριγωνα. But this word is a correction of M. Muratori, as
the MS. gives τριτωνα, which has no meaning. Probably we
fhould read τετραγωνα, efpecially as, according to M. Muratori himfelf, all the other obelifks are fquare. *Ibid.*

round

round the place, and the shameful actions there committed, can by no means regard this stone as sacred, and the superstition of those who dwell on it confirms unbelievers in their infidelity. You should therefore second me in my undertaking, by sending this obelisk to my country, which, when you navigate our seas, receives you with such hospitality, and thus contributing your assistance to the outward embellishment of that city. Nor can it be disagreeable to yourselves to have something of your own extant among us, which, as you sail towards the city, you may hereafter view with pleasure.

Epistle LIX *. To Dionysius †.

[M]ORE prudent was your former silence than your present defence;] for then, though perhaps you devised scandal, you did not utter it. [But now, teeming, as it were, with slander against us, you pour it forth most abundantly; unless I ought not to deem slander] and abuse your thinking

---

* For an account of this Epistle and the former, see p. 2. In the editions of Rigalt, Petau, and Spanheim, it is imperfect. The above is translated from a copy in the *Lux Evangelii* of Fabricius, p. 326. collected by Rostgaard. The additions are inserted within [].

† The Medicean MS. has this inscription: Ἰουλιανὸς κατα Νειλε. The beginning of the Epistle is wanting in the editions.　　　FABRICIUS.

me like your friends; to each of whom you offered
your services unasked *, but particularly unasked by
the first, and the second only hinting that he should
be glad of your assistance, you immediately com-
plied. Whether I resemble Constns and Magnentius †, facts, as the saying is, will shew. But
you, like Astydamas in the comedy, are your own
panegyrist ‡; and this is evident from what you
have written. For those expressions, " intrepidity,"
and " great boldness," and, " I wish you knew who
" and what I am," and the like, for shame! what
boasting and ostentation do they exhibit! But, by
Venus and the Graces, if you are so bold and noble-
minded, [why were you so fearful of being under the
necessity of offending a third time? For those who
have incurred the displeasure of princes, if they
are wise, find an ease, and perhaps a pleasure, in

* Suidas : ακληῖος, ανωνυμος, δεδωκας σεαυῖον ακληῖον τω δευῖερω.
He alludes to the words of Julian. By πρoῖερον (" the
" former,") understand Constans (" the second,") ο δευῖερος,
is Magnentius.   FABRICIUS.

† Constans, the youngest son of the great Constantine,
was engaged in a civil war with his eldest brother Constantine, who was killed in the course of it. Magnentius revolted against Constantius, and usurped the West.
By comparing Julian to them, Dionysius perhaps meant
to stigmatise him with the murder of Constantius and usurpation of the empire.

‡ In the MS. σεαυῖον επαινεις, not σαυῖης επαινεις, γυναι, as
even Rigalt to Onosander, in his edition, p. 90. It refers
to Philemon, the comic poet, as appears from the Proverbs
of Apostolius, Centur. XVII. 30. and Suidas on σαυῖης επαινεις.
See also Zenobius, v. 100. Julian quotes the same proverb
in his XIIth Epistle,   FABRICIUS.

being

being difcharged from bufinefs; or if they muft be-
fined, they fuffer in their fortunes; or the utmoft
effect of refentment is that incurable evil, as it has
been called, the lofs of life. All thefe things are
fcorned and defpifed by you, who have renounced
your friend, a man, from common and general report, well known to us, dull as we are. Inftead
of this, you fay, you invoke the Gods that you
may not offend a third time. My anger therefore
will not from being good make you wicked. He
that could do this would be a prodigy indeed. According to Plato, it might indeed have the contrary
effect *. But virtue being perfectly free, you ought
to have no fuch ideas. You, however, think it a
great matter to flander all men, to utter the bittereft farcafms, and to convert the temple of peace
into a brothel.]

Do you think that your paft faults are in general
excufed, and that your late courage has atoned for
your former cowardice? You know the fable of
Chabrias †. A cat was once in love with a handfome
youth ‡. Learn the reft from the book. What-

* De Legibus, vi.

† The words τον Χαβριυ are in the Medicean and Barro.
MSS. and this is in the xvith fable of Chabrias, or Ba-
brias, a Greek poet, who has put the fables of Æfop into
Iambic verfe.

‡ Rather, according to our fables, a young man was
in love with a cat. Dionyfius could no more diveft himfelf
of his natural pufillanimity, &c. than the cat (tranf-
formed to a woman) could forego her purfuit of mice.
The Latin tranflator renders it *muftela* ("a weafel"); but
γαλη fignifies alfo "a cat."

ever you may fay, you will perfuade no one that
you were not what you were, and what many have
long known you to be. But your unfkilfulnefs and
temerity are owing, not to philofophy, the Gods
forbid! but rather to what Plato calls "a double
ignorance *." For though experience might have
taught you, as it has me, that you know nothing,
yet you think yourfelf the wifeft of all men, paft,
prefent, or to come ; fo great is your ignorance, fo
abundant your felf-conceit.

But enough concerning you. Some apology
perhaps is neceffary to others for fo readily giving
you a fhare in the conduct of my affairs. I am
not the firft, nor the only one, Dionyfius, who has
been miftaken. Your name-fake alfo deceived
Plato †. [And fo did Callippus the Athenian ‡,
whom, he faid, he knew to be wicked, but that he
was profligate to fuch a degree he never could have
fufpected.] And need I add, that the greateft of
phyficians, Hippocrates, faid, " in my opinion of
" the futures of the head I was miftaken § ? Thus
they were deceived in what they ought to have
known,

* The one is when men acknowledge their ignorance,
the other when they think they know that of which they
are ignorant. *In Alcib.* I.

† Dionyfius the younger fent for Plato into Sicily, to inftruct him in philofophy. See the Life of Dion in Plutarch.

‡ A hearer of Plato, who murdered Dion.

§ The following is doubtlefs the paffage to which Julian
alludes : " Autonomus of Omilus died of a wound on his
" head, on the fixteenth day, having received a hurt by a

known, and even a phyſician was ignorant of a theorem of his own art. Is it ſtrange then that Julian, hearing that Nilöus *, or Dionyſius, had on a ſudden behaved bravely, ſhould be miſtaken?

You have heard of Phædon † of Elis, and you know his hiſtory. If not, read it with attention. He thought that no one is ſo depraved that philoſophy cannot cure him, and that it purifies human life from the paſſions, deſires, and all ſuch diſorders. For that it ſhould be ſerviceable to thoſe who are well born, and well educated, is not at all extraordinary. But if it brings back into the light thoſe whoſe minds are ever ſo much darkened by depravity, this ſeems to me truly admirable. And on that account, as all the Gods know, I began by degrees to form a more advantageous opinion of you.

"ſtone on the ſutures. I did not think it neceſſary to "open it; for that the ſutures themſelves were injured by "the blow eſcaped me." (εκλειψαν δε μυ την γνωμην αι ραφαι, κ. τ. λ.) *Hipp. de morb.* V. 7. 27. The words above quoted, as from Hippocrates, are, ισφηλαν δε μυ την γνωμην αι περι την κεφαλην ραφαι. But though in a particular caſe (as above) this great phyſician had the candour to own himſelf miſtaken, it does not follow, nor does it appear, that he was ignorant of the nature of the ſutures in general. Julian truſted to his memory, which, though good, was not infallible.

This candid confeſſion of Hippocrates is mentioned alſo with applauſe by Celſus, VIII. 4. and Plutarch *de profectu in virtutem*, p. 82.

* Τον Νειλων. MS. Τον Ναιλον.   FABRICIUS.

† A ſcholar of Socrates, ſo much beloved by Plato, that he inſcribed his divine book, on the immortality of the ſoul, *Phædon.*

Not that I placed you in the firſt, or even in the ſecond, rank of worthies, as you yourſelf perhaps may know. If not, aſk the excellent Symmachus *,] for he, I am perſuaded, being naturally diſpoſed to ſpeak truth, will never utter a wilful falſhood.

[But if you reſent my not raiſing you to the higheſt, I reproach myſelf for not degrading you to the loweſt, rank. And I thank all the Gods and Goddeſſes for preventing me from forming an intimacy with you, and making you privy to my counſels, as a boſom friend. Though the poets have ſaid many things of Fame, as a Goddeſs; ſhe is rather, if you pleaſe, a Dæmon. For Fame is not always to be credited; and therefore her nature is dæmoniacal, being not abſolutely pure or perfectly good, like that of the Gods, but allayed with ſome degree of evil †. And though it may not be proper to ſay this of the other Dæmons, I know I may ſafely affirm of Fame, that ſhe utters many falſhoods, as well as many truths ‡. For I

---

* A Roman orator and præfect, well known by his epiſtles ſtill extant, and by his writings againſt Chriſtianity, refuted by Prudentius and St. Ambroſe. Three epiſtles to him are extant from Libanius, to whom, it appears, he wrote in Latin, as his letters required an interpreter. He was conſul in 391.

† And had not the Gods, as well as Fame and the Dæmons, of Julian and the Heathens, much evil in their nature? Not to mention the notorious vices of Mars, Bacchus, Apollo, and the reſt of them, in what was their Jupiter, their Supreme, ſo pre-eminent as in his debaucheries?

‡ *Tam falſi pravique tenax quam conſcia veri.* Virg.

would by no means be accused of bearing false
witness.]

You value your freedom of speech at four
oboli *, as the saying is. [But know you not, that
Thersites, among the Greeks, was also a free-speaker,
and in return was chastised by the wise Ulysses with
his sceptre † ? and that the drunkenness of Thersites was less regarded by Agamemnon than the flies
in the proverb were by the tortoise ‡ ?]

What avails our reproaching others? We should
rather be irreproachable ourselves. If you are so,
convince me of it. [When you were young, you
told fine stories of yourself to your elders. These
adventures, with the Electra of Euripides §, I pass

---

* That is, at ever so high a rate. Suidas on Τετλαρων
οβολων, quoting this passage of Julian.   FABRICIUS.

He quotes it, as usual, without naming his author. An
obolus was a small Athenian coin of silver, weighing about
twelve grains; in our money five farthings.

† Il. II. 199.

———— Cowering as the dastard bends,
The weighty sceptre on his back descends. POPE, 336.

‡ Suidas quotes these words from an author to me unknown, τω δε Αγαμεμνον. κ. τ. λ. Flies cannot hurt a tortoise,
on account of the shell with which it is furnished. Similar
to this is, " an elephant does not regard a fly." It would
be more pleasant if applied to the mind. A mind fortified
by virtue and philosophy no more fears the attacks of fortune than " a tortoise flies."   ERASMUS.

The passage above quoted by Suidas is this of Julian,
which has been brought to light long since the time of
Erasmus. It is also quoted anonymously by Apostolius, in
his Centur. XX. proverb. 66.

§ Eurip. Electr. ver. 946. 1122.

I never with the opening morn forbore
To breathe my silent plaints, &c.   POTTER.

in filence. But when you became a man, and joined the army, you did, by Jove, juft what you fay of truth; it gave you offence, and you deferted it. By how many witneffes can I prove this, and thofe not of the vulgar and abandoned, but fome by whom you yourfelf, were repulfed, who came to us from that neighbourhood?] To depart from princes in enmity, moft fagacious Dionyfius, is no proof either of courage or wifdom. Much more would it become you to conciliate, by your intercourfe with mankind, their affections to us. But fuch, by the Gods, will never be your conduct; nor that of thoufands more who are like-minded. ..

If rocks dafh againft rocks, and ftones againft ftones, inftead of being ferviceable to each other, the ftrongeft eafily breaks the weakeft. I fay not this with Laconic brevity; for I think on your fubject I feem more loquacious than the Attic grafs-hoppers *. For your drunken abufe † of me, with the leave of the Gods, and powerful Nemefis, I will inflict upon you a deferved punifhment. " To what purpofe?" you fay. [To reftrain as much as poffible your mind and tongue, and] to

---

* This is faid of a man immoderately talkative, or very mufical; becaufe this infect, living only on dew, chiefly delights in finging. And Socrates, in the Phædron of Plato, relates that fome who were fo abforbed by mufic that, neglecting their food, they were famifhed, were changed by the Gods into grafshoppers.   ERASMUS.

† See the Fragment (from Suidas) on Mufonius.

preven

prevent your offending [in the leaſt] either by words or deeds; in ſhort, to diveſt your ſcurrilous tongue of ſo much ſlander. I well know that the ſandal even of Venus is ſaid to have been ridiculed by Momus *. But you ſee that Momus, though envious of all her beauties, could find nothing but her ſandal to depreciate. May you grow old, fretted, in like manner, with envy, more decrepid than Tithonus, more wealthy than Cinyras, and more effeminate than Sardanapalus, ſo as to verify the proverb, " Old men are twice children ! † "

[But why does the divine Alexander ſeem to you ſo renowned? Why do you profeſs yourſelf his imitator and rival? Is it for that with which the youth Hermolaus ‡ reproached him? Of that no one is ſo ſilly as to ſuſpect you; but of the contrary, for which Hermolaus, grievouſly complaining, ſuffered ſtripes, and, it is ſaid, would have killed Alexander, there is no one who is not per-

---

* Viz. The creaking of it. See Philoſtrati Epiſt. XXI.

† On the word Καλαγηρασαι, Suidas has the above paragraph (not mentioned as a quotation from Julian) with this addition, " which is ſaid of thoſe who live long. For " Tithonus, being ſuperannuated, was, at his own deſire, " changed into a graſshopper. Cinyras, a deſcendant of " Pharnaces, king of Cyprus, was famous for his riches. " And Sardanapalus, the laſt king of Aſſyria, fell a victim " to intemperance and luxurious delights."

‡ " We conſpired to kill you," ſaid Hermolaus, " be- " cauſe you have begun not to govern us as free-men, but " to tyranniſe over us as ſlaves."   Q. Curtius.

ſuaded

fuaded that you are guilty *. From many, by the
Gods, who faid they had a great regard for you,
I have heard feveral things advanced by way of
extenuating this offence; and one there was who
difbelieved it. But he was a fingle fwallow, who
does not make a fpring †. Perhaps Alexander
appears great to you, becaufe he cruelly flew
Callifthenes ‡; or becaufe Clitus ‡ fell a facrifice
to his intemperance; and alfo Philotas ‡, and
Parmenio ‡; whofe fon Hector was afterwards
fmothered in the whirlpools of the Ægyptian Nile,
or of the Euphrates, for both have been mentioned §. I omit his other follies, that I may not
feem to revile a man, who, though by no means
diftinguifhed for virtue, was a moft valiant and excellent commander. Of both which, virtue and

---

* Hermolaus, a noble youth, of the royal guards, for
killing a boar, which the king had deftined for his own
fpear, was by his command fcourged; a difgrace which
he fo bitterly refented that he wept, and formed the above-
mentioned confpiracy. Q. Curtius.

† See Erafmi Chiliad. xciv.

‡ The cruel deaths of this philofopher and thefe generals
are well known, and are related at large by Quintus
Curtius. "One," faid Hermolaus, [Clitus] "fprinkled
" your table with his blood; another [Philotas] fuffered
" more than one kind of death. Parmenio was maffacred
" unheard, &c."

§ According to Curtius, as this youth, one of the few dear
to Alexander, was attempting to follow him down the Nile,
the fmall veffel in which he had embarked, being over-
loaded, funk. Hector, after long ftruggling with the ftream,
at length reached the bank, but there, for want of affiftance,
perifhed. Of this, however, Alexander feems to have been
innocent. Philotas was alfo a fon of Parmenio.

M 4

valour,

valour, you have a lefs portion than fifh have of
hair.   Now hear with calmnefs what I advife:
     Not thefe, O daughter, are thy proper cares!
     Thee milder arts befit, and fofter wars *.

What follows, by the Gods, I am afhamed to
tranfcribe.   I would have you, however, attend to
it, fince it is highly reafonable that deeds fhould
follow words, and that one who has been remifs
in his deeds fhould never ftart at words.   But you,
who revere the fhades of Magnentius and Conftans,
wage war with the living, and, in fome way or
other, afperfe the beft characters.   Are the living
lefs able to revenge affronts? This you will by no
means think proper to affirm, be the confidence
which you mention, whatever it may.   Rejecting
that plea, will you admit this, that you deride
them becaufe they are infenfible? Nor is this, I
prefume, the true reafon.   For who among the
living is fo ftupid, or pufillanimous, as to think
your good opinion of the leaft importance, and
would not prefer being totally unknown to you, or,
if that were impoffible, would not rather choofe to
be reviled by you, as I am now, than honoured?
I would by no means err fo egregioufly in my
judgement as not to think your praifes better than
your reproaches.   But even this, perhaps, that I
am now writing to you, proves that I am hurt.
By no means, I call the preferving Gods to witnefs; I only wifh to check the intolerable arrogance

* Il. V. 428. Pope, 519.

of

of this reviler, the petulance and prurience of his
tongue, the frenzy of his mind, and his fury on
all occasions. If I were injured by you, I might
by deeds, not words, have a legal remedy, as
you, being a citizen, and of the senatorial rank,
have disobeyed the command of the Emperor.
But for this there was no occasion, nothing
but the last extremity requiring it. I did not think
proper therefore to subject you to any punishment,
but rather chose first at least to write to you, hoping
that a short epistle might effect your cure. But
as you persevere in these crimes, or rather exhibit
to the public the frenzy which was before concealed, let no one, for the future, think you a
man, who are not a man, or mistake the fury,
which transports you, for courage, or suppose you
to be learned who are an utter stranger to literature, as may easily be proved from your epistles.]

None of the ancients, for instance, ever used το
φρυδον, to signify " manifest,"* as you have, besides
many other blunders, in your letter. No one, in
the longest discourse, could express your loose
and indecent behaviour, your self-prostitution. For
you

----

* Φρουδος is rather αφανες, ικπεδων, αφανλον. ("Far distant, obscure.)" See Hesychius and Harpocratio.   FABRICIUS.

† Among the flagrant crimes of which he accuses Dionysius, Julian here condescends to arraign his phraseology,
and, like a former Dionysius, exchanges his sceptre for a
rod. Thus a mistake in the meaning of a word, or in the
graces of style, is put on a level with treachery and treason,
and seems as unpardonable to this Imperial critic, as an
offence against the graces of behaviour was to a late British
peer.

you feduce, not only fuch as are willing and forward, * * * * nor thofe who hunt after public
employments, but thofe who, in confequence of a
found judgement, act right, [and therefore have
been felected by us for their prompt obedience.

You make fair promifes, though not by way of
intreaty, or fubmiffion, if we will again employ
you in fome place of truft. But fo far is that
from my intention, that when others have been
admitted, I never fent for you, as I have for many,
known and unknown to me, of the inhabitants
of that heaven-beloved city, Rome. Such value
I fet on your friendfhip; of fuch attention I
thought you worthy! I fhall therefore act in the
fame manner probably for the future. And this
epiftle, which I am now writing, I intend, not only
for your perufal, but think it neceffary to be communicated to many more. I will give it indeed
to all, for all, I am perfuaded, will readily receive
it; fuch a general indignation your infolence and
arrogance have excited.

You have here a complete reply, fo that you
can defire from us nothing farther. Nor do we
wifh any return from you. Make what ufe you
pleafe of our letters; for you have fold our friendfhip. Farewell; amidft your banquets abufing me!]

peer. The above criticifm is perfectly in the fpirit of
Bentley *verfus* Barnes. But Julian fhould have recollected
that this Roman wrote Greek in compliment to him.

Epiftle

Epiftle LX. To Jamblichus.

YOU came, and acted. For you came, though absent, by your letter. But, by the ardour of the friendship which I feel for you, I do not decline your love †, * * * nor in any respect desert you, but, as if you were present, I view you with my mind, and am with you, though absent, nor can any thing else give me complete satisfaction. You are never weary of obliging the present, and not only delighting, but preserving the absent by your writings. For being told that a friend was arrived with a letter from you, though I had been three days ill of a pain in my stomach, and was much indisposed with a fever, yet hearing, as I said, that a letter from you was at the gate, like one not master of himself and divinely inspired, I sprung up and rushed out to him before he could enter. But as soon as I had taken the letter into my hands, I swear by the Gods themselves and that regard for you which inflames me, my pain at once abated, and the fever instantly fled, abashed, as it were, at the evident presence of some tutelar deity. And when I had opened and read it, what, think you, were my sensations, or how great was my satisfaction, praising immoderately, and loving

† Imperfect.

the

the moſt friendly, as you ſtyle him, * * * * †, who
is really deſerving of love, and the miniſter of
good, for being inſtrumental in forwarding to me
your letter, and conſigning it to me, like a bird,
by a favourable and proſperous gale, which not
only gave me the delight of hearing that your
affairs were in a proper ſtate, but alſo recovered
me from illneſs! As to other things, how ſhall I
expreſs what I felt when I firſt read that epiſtle,
or how can I ſufficiently demonſtrate my affection?
How often did I turn back from the middle to the
beginning! How much did I fear, leſt, when I
had finiſhed it, I ſhould forget it! How often, as
in the circuit and compaſs of a ſtanza, did I carry
back the concluſion to the beginning, repeating at
the cloſe, as in a muſical compoſition, that meaſure
with which the ſong began! And what followed?
How often did I apply the letter to my lips, as
mothers kiſs their infants! How cloſely did I preſs
it to my mouth, as if I had been embracing my
deareſt miſtreſs! How frequently did I accoſt and
kiſs even the ſuperſcription, which, as a well-
known ſignature, you had written with your
own hand; and then fixed my eyes upon it, rivetted,
as it were, by the fingers of that ſacred hand on
the traces of the letters?

  † Imperfect. The name of the friend who forwarded
the letter ſeems all that is wanting.

" Much

" Much falutation from us attend you !" as fays the
fair Sappho * ; and, not only during our feparation,
but fare you well always, not failing to write, and,
as is fitting, to remember us ! As to ourfelves,
there will never be a time, there can never be an
occafion, there will never be a difcourfe, in which
we fhall not remember you * * * *. And if Jupiter fhall ever allow me to revifit my native country, and again to enter your facred manfion, fpare
not the fugitive; but, as a deferter from the Mufes,
brought back from flight, bind him, if you pleafe,
to your delightful benches, and, when properly
chaftifed, reprimand him. I will by no means decline the punifhment, but will fubmit to it volun-
tarily and chearfully ; as to the provident and falu-
tary correction of an indulgent father. But if you
will permit me to pronounce my own fentence, I will
with pleafure acquiefce in this ; the being faftened,
my noble friend, to your veft, fo as never to be
feparated from you, but clofely to adhere to you,
and every where to be carried about with you, as
fables feign of double men : unlefs they ludi-
croufly mean it as an allufon to the excellence of
friendfhip, expreffing the congenial agreement of
each foul in the bond of communion.

* Χαιρε δε και αυτος ημιν πολλα. This muft be in fome
poem that is loft.

Epiftle

Epistle LXI. To the same.

I HAVE suffered, I confess, sufficient punishment for my absence from you, partly in the
fatigues which I endured in my journey, but
chiefly on account of my long separation from you.
Though I have every where met with a variety of
accidents, so as to have left none unexperienced;
though I have sustained the tumults of battles, the
distress of sieges, the wanderings of flight, with ter-
rors of every kind, and also the severities of winter,
the dangers of diseases, and many and various other
calamities from Upper Pannonia to the passage of
the Chalcedonian strait, I can truly say, that nothing has happened to me so grievous and perplex-
ing, since my leaving the East, as my not having
seen, for such a length of time, you, the general
blessing of the Greeks.   Wonder not therefore, if
I say, a kind of darkness and thick clouds hang
over my eyes.   For, in truth, the sky will be
serene, the light of the sun more splendid, and a
most beautiful spring of life will, as it were, be
renewed to me, when I can embrace you, the great
ornament of the world.   Then, like a darling son,
escaped from war, or returned from a long voyage,
and restored unexpectedly to an excellent father,
relating to you all my sufferings, and the dangers
that I have surmounted, and resting, as on a sacred
anchor,

anchor, I shall find a sufficient solace for my sorrows. For calamities are consoled, and sufferings alleviated, by communication, and by the knowledge of our friends participated. Mean while I tender you my best services, nor will I ever fail to write to you, and during the whole time of my absence to send you such epistolary tokens. If I can obtain the same from you, the perusal of your letters, like an auspicious omen, will abate my grief. Receive mine with complacence, and be more favourably disposed to make a return. For whatever good you shall express or communicate, I shall prefer to the eloquent voice of Mercury, and the skilful hand of Æsculapius.

Epistle LXII. †. To **** (Imperfect.)

* * * * * * * *
SHOULD not the same indulgence, which is given to wooden blocks, be allowed to men ‡ ? For suppose that one invested with the priesthood be unworthy, should he not be spared, till, having

ascer-

----

† The Gentiles, who peaceably followed the customs of their ancestors, were rather surprised than pleased with the introduction of foreign manners; and in the short period of his reign, Julian had frequent occasions to complain of the want of fervour of his own party. See Epistles LXII. and LXIII.   GIBBON.
Many of the Epistles of Julian are the effusions of pri-

afcertained the enormity of his offence, he can be removed from the minifterial function, and deprived of the name of prieft, injudicioufly perhaps conferred upon him, and may be fubjected alfo to cenfure, fine, and other punifhments? If you underftand not this, you cannot have even a fuperficial knowledge of any thing; for how ignorant muft you be of what is juft and right, not to know the difference between a prieft and a private man! And what muft have been your temper, if you have beaten one to whom you ought to have rifen from your feat! Nothing can be more fhameful, in you it is particularly unbecoming, in the fight both of Gods and men. The bifhops and prefbyters of the Galileans perhaps affociate with you; and if not publickly, through fear of me, yet by ftealth and

---

juftly ftyled by Mr. Gibbon " paftoral letters," and are dictated by the Emperor as Sovereign Pontiff. In this pontifical character he addreffes the Epiftle, of which this fragment only is preferved, to a Gentile prieft, who, forgetting the nature of his fpiritual warfare, had violently affaulted and beaten one of his brethren. As a Chriftian Pontiff would have quoted St. Paul to Titus, *A bifhop muft be no ftriker*, this Gentile apoftle appeals to the Didymæan oracle, and then pronounces a fentence of fufpenfion.

‡ This paragraph is unintelligible, for want of that which precedes it. Julian perhaps had been fpeaking of fuch images of the Gods as were worn out and decayed, which he has mentioned alfo in his long Fragment. " If " any one," fays he, " thinks, that, becaufe they have " been once called the images of the Gods, they can " never decay, he feems to me to have loft his fenfes. " For then they could not have been the workmanfhip of " men," &c.

at home with your concurrence. But the priest
has been beaten. Otherwife your pontiff would
not have preferred fuch a complaint againft you.
Paffages from Homer you think fabulous; hear
therefore the oracle of the Didymæan lord, and
confider whether he rightly admonifhed the Greeks
of old, and afterwards, in his difcourfes, taught
men to be wife and virtuous:

They, whom depravity and folly lead
To fcorn the priefts of heaven's immortal powers,
And to the wife intentions of the Gods
Their own vain thoughts contemptuoufly oppofe,
In fafety live not half their days, condemn'd
To perifh by th' eternal Gods, who deem
Their fervants honour facred as their own *.

Not only thofe, you fee, who beat or infult priefts,
but fuch as deny them honour are [declared †] to
be enemies to the Gods; fo that he who beats them
is guilty of facrilege. I therefore, as the Sovereign Pontiff of the religion of my country, having
now obtained the præfecture of the Didymæan
oracle, forbid you to interfere in any thing that
relates to the priefthood for three whole months.
If, within that time, you fhould appear deferving,
on my hearing from the chief-prieft of your city,
I will confult the Gods whether you fhall be re-
inftated. To this punifhment, which I inflict upon

---

* This paffage has been quoted before, in the Duties of
a Prieft, p. 127.

† Some fuch word is wanting in the original.

you for your rashness, the ancients used formerly
to add, by words and in writing, the curses of the
Gods. But of this I do not approve, as it never
seems practised by the Gods. And in other respects, knowing that the priests are the ministers
of our prayers, I join my hopes and prayers to
yours, that by many and earnest intreaties you may
obtain the pardon of the Gods.

———

Epistle LXIII. To the High-Priest Theo-dore *.

A. D.
361.

THE Epistle that I have addressed to you differs
from that which I have transmitted to others †,
as I think your friendship for me superior to theirs.
It is no inconsiderable circumstance, that we have

* This High-Priest Theodore was, as may be inferred
from this Epistle, a zealous Pagan, the disciple of Maximus, who, like Julian, had been initiated by Maximus,
and instructed, like that prince, in the principles of theurgy.
This letter is inserted in the edition of F. Petau, but only
in Greek. It had been copied from a MS. so defective,
that it was not possible to translate it. M. Spanheim, from
a MS. less imperfect, has given it, with a Latin version,
which is not answerable to the reputation of that learned
writer.   La Bleterie.

† Julian had sent, without doubt, a circular letter to
the Pagan pontiffs as soon as he was in peaceable possession
of the empire. As this seems to have been written at the
same time, I assign it to the year 361.   *Ibid.*
Julian must then have been at Constantinople.

one

one common master, and you well remember *.... In a conversation that passed between us, a few evenings ago, it gave me great pleasure to hear him express the highest regard for you. In my friendships I am usually very cautious. As for you, I had never seen you. Before we can love, we must know; and before we can know, we should try. But a certain reason determined me †. I have therefore thought proper to rank you among my friends. And now I entrust to you an affair very interesting to me, and highly advantageous to all men. You will transact it, I doubt not, with propriety, which will afford me much joy here, and better hopes hereafter ‡. For I differ in opinion from those who

---

* He intimates by half a word, and a mysterious air, what they saw, or thought they saw, when they were initiated by Maximus. LA BLETERIE.

† It is impossible to guess this reason; but we may partly discover, that, in the initiation of Theodore, something happened which induced Julian to conclude that a man so agreeable to the Gods deserved to be the minister and the assistant of the apostle of Paganism. *Ibid.*

‡ As this Epistle was not written to be shewn, it proves to what a degree Julian was fanatical and convinced of his false religion. It shews, at the same time, that he believed a providence, another life, and the immortality of the soul. He detested the materialists. In one of his works he speaks with horror of Pyrrhonism, and of the doctrine of Epicurus. He thanks the Gods for having extinguished those sects, and caused most of the books which contained their pernicious tenets to be destroyed. [See the Duties of a Priest, p. 134.] Probably the free-thinkers would not have triumphed in his reign. Why

who think that the foul perifhes before or with the
body *. We rely, however, on no man, but only on
the Gods, as they only can be well acquainted
with thefe things, or rather they alone neceffarily
know them. Men may form conjectures, but
knowledge belongs to the Gods. The commiffion
that I now give you is the fuperintendence of all
the priefts in Afia, both in the cities and in the
country, with full powers to treat every one according to his deferts.

In a high-prieft the principal requifite is moderation, together with kindnefs and benevolence to
the deferving. As to thofe who are unjuft or in-
folent to men, and irreligious to the Gods, let
them be rebuked with boldnefs, or punifhed with
feverity. Whatever is neceffary to be regulated
in common, in order to render divine worfhip as
perfect as poffible, I will foon direct, with many
other particulars. Some of them, in the mean time,
I will here mention, in which it is right for you to

then fhould they defend him ? But fome common interefts
often ferve to unite in appearance irreconcileable enemies. *And the fame day they were made friends together;
for before they were at enmity between themfelves.* Of this the
affection which Julian teftified for the Jews is a remarkable
inftance.   *Ibid.*

* Thofe who believed the foul to be immortal, and even
the materialifts, diftinguifhed in the foul the intellectual
part, νεϛ, and the fenfitive part, ψυχη. There were fome who
imagined, no doubt, that the intellectual part was withdrawn, and others that it was deftroyed, when they faw the
body reduced to a mere animal life.   *Ibid.*

be

be advifed by me. For on many of thefe fubjects I fpeak, as all the Gods know, with much premeditation. In circumfpection no one exceeds me, and I am an enemy, and have been fo ftyled, to all innovation, efpecially in matters of religion, thinking it highly proper to adhere to our ancient paternal laws *, which were certainly given us by the Gods. They could not be fo excellent, if they proceeded from men. But by the prevalence of riches and pleafures they have been fo neglected and corrupted, that they require, I think, a new foundation. Seeing therefore fo great an indifference among us towards the Gods, and all fenfe of religion banifhed by debauched and luxurious manners, I have continually lamented in private.

* Paganifm, in general, had no religious code, unlefs it were fome pretended oracles, apparently very modern, as to the ceremonies which ought to be obferved in facrifices, and the victims which were fuitable to every kind of Gods. Eufebius quotes fome paffages of thefe oracles in the fourth book of his Evangelical Preparation. I imagine that the laws which Julian here mentions are principally the ancient rites of every nation, city, and temple. Thefe rites had in time fuffered various alterations, and in the decline of Paganifm fome were abolifhed.

Julian, deeply verfed in antiquity, was defirous of reftoring things to their former ftate. As to the wifdom quite divine which he admires in thefe rites, that is the work of his imagination. He confiders them as fymbolical. Being an ingenious and fruitful allegorift, by the force of arbitrary explanations he difcovered fome wonderful things in the worfhip, as well as in the hiftory, of his Gods. To be convinced that he every where found all that he chofe, we need only read his difcourfe " on the Mother of the Gods."

LA BLETERIE.

For

For those who are distinguished in the school of
impiety * are so zealous as to suffer want and
famine rather than taste swine's flesh ✝, or that of
any thing strangled, or even killed by accident;
while we are so regardless of the Gods as to forget the laws of our ancestors, and not even to
know whether any such exist. But these men are
in part only religious, as the God whom they worship is really most powerful, and most benevolent,
and governs the visible world ‡.

They therefore who do not transgress the laws
seem to me to act right. I blame them only for

* Δυσσιβειας σχολη προσχονlας, " Those who are attached
" to the school of impiety." I think that we should read
προιχονlας, " the chiefs, the principal teachers." The sequel
shews that this refers to the Jews.   La Bleterie.

✝ This would only prove that Julian speaks of the Jews.
Indeed the Christians, through respect for the Council of
Jerusalem, abstained from blood and things strangled longer
than the reasons subsisted on which the prohibition was
founded; and the Oriental Christians continue to abstain
from them still. But after God had revealed to St. Peter
(Acts xv.) that the distinction of meats was abrogated,
no Christian scrupled eating swine's flesh, except the Ju-
daising Christians, who were not tolerated till the second
destruction of the Jews, which happened under the Emperor Hadrian.   Ibid.

‡ In the books of Julian against the Christian religion,
of which St. Cyril, in refuting them, has preserved a considerable part, this prince says, in direct terms, that " he
" worships the God of Abraham, of Isaac, and of Jacob :"
Αη προσκυνων τον Θεον Αβρααμ, και Ισαακ, και Ιακωβ. But it
appears, in the same books, that he means, by this God,
the *Demiurgus*; in which he is mistaken if he makes
the *Demiurgus*, or *Logos*, of a different nature from the
Being, το ον, τ'αγαθον.   *Ibid.*

worship-

worshipping God alone, and despising the worship of other Gods. Hurried into this frenzy by the pride of Barbarians *, they think that he is hidden from us Gentiles only. But from the Galilean impiety, like a pestilential distemper † * * * *.

[The remainder is wanting in the original.]

* Whatever incense Julian gave the Jews in the Epistle which he wrote to them, this text, and many others, shew that he despised them. In general, what most prejudiced the Pagans against both the Christian and Jewish religions, was their being exclusive and admitting no community with any other. But they endured the Jews with less impatience, and contented themselves with despising them, because the latter gained few proselytes. The barrenness, with which the synagogue was struck, made it find grace in the sight of our common enemies; but the fertility of the church alarmed and enraged them. They foresaw that she would at length destroy their altars. Julian, in particular, kept good terms with the Jews, because they entered into his plan, 1. By their implacable hatred to the Christians; 2. from the design which he had formed to restore the nation and the temple, in order to falsify the scriptures. Besides, the religion of the Jews ordained sacrifices, and in this point of view was agreeable to Julian, who, as may be seen in his life and his works, had a taste for bloody sacrifices more worthy of a butcher than a philosopher. La Bleterie.

† It is evident that Julian here launched forth against Christianity and the Christians; perhaps in a manner so atrocious as to shock the transcribers. *Ibid.*

Epistle

Epiſtle LXIV. *. To the People †, cla-
morouſly applauding in the Tychæum, or
Temple of Fortune.

A. D.
361.

WHEN I enter the theatre, even privately,
you may applaud; but in the temples be
ſilent, and transfer your applauſes to the Gods.
Praiſes are much more properly due to them.

---

* This Epiſtle was firſt publiſhed by Muratori, in his
Anecdota Græca, from a MS. 700 years old, in the Ambroſian library, and is copied by Fabricius, in his *Bibliotheca Græca*.

In the edition of Wolfius, it is the mccxxth Epiſtle of
Libanius. And the editor ſubjoins in a note, " I neither
" underſtand what Libanius here means, nor the occaſion
" on which he wrote this Epiſtle." Yet as Muratori and
Fabricius had previouſly given it to Julian, I cannot account
for its being there aſcribed to Libanius. Surely it ſeems
much more characteriſtic of a prince than of a ſophiſt;
and is beſides a ſubject, which Julian has diſcuſſed in the
Miſopogon, Vol. I. p. 241, &c.

† Probably " of Conſtantinople." Fabricius inſcribes it
Byzantiis, like Epiſtle XI. But ſee a note on that Epiſtle,
p. –†.

Epistle LXV. To a Painter *.

* Not being able to satisfy myself as to the meaning of the first part of this short Epistle, I will add the original, with the Latin translation of Muratori, by whom this also is preserved:

Προς ζωγραφον.

Ει μεν μη ειχον, και εχαριζω μοι, γνγνωμης κουα αξιος. Ει δε ειχον μεν, κα' εχρισαμην τε, τες Θεος εφερον, μαλλον δε υπο Θεων εξεφομην. Συ μοι αλλοτιον σχημα πως εδ.δυς, εφαιρε; Οιον με ειδες, τοιουτον και γραψον.

Ad Pictorem.

Siquidem non haberem, et mihi fuisses gratificatus, venia dignus esses. Sin autem haberem, neque uterer, Deos ferrem: imo potius, Dii me ferrent. Tu vero quare alienum mihi habitum dedisti, O amice? Qualem me vidisti, talem etiam pingito.

The meaning of the two last paragraphs is sufficiently clear. " But why, my friend, have you given me a foreign "dress? Paint me as you see me." The painter perhaps had drawn him, like a Roman Emperor, with a small beard, and not like a Grecian Philosopher, with a large one;

Epiſtle LXVI. To Arsaces, Satrap of Armenia *.

A. D. 363.

ARM, arm, Arſaces, againſt the furious Perſians, and haſten to join my forces, ſwift as thought. My martial preparations and determined reſolution have one of theſe ends in view; either

---

* The feeble Arſaces Tiranus, king of Armenia, had degenerated, ſtill more ſhamefully than his father Choſroes, from the many virtues of the great Tiridates ; and as the puſillanimous monarch was averſe to any enterpriſe of danger and glory, he could diſguiſe his timid indolence by the more decent excuſes of religion and gratitude. He expreſſed a pious attachment to the memory of Conſtantius, from whoſe hands he had received in marriage Olympias, the daughter of the præfect Ablavius ; and the alliance of a female, who had been educated as the deſtined wife of the emperor Conſtans, exalted the dignity of a Barbarian king. Tiranus profeſſed the Chriſtian religion ; he reigned over a nation of Chriſtians ; and he was reſtrained by every principle of conſcience and intereſt from contributing to the victory which would conſummate the ruin of the church. The alienated mind of Tiranus was exaſperated by the indiſcretion of Julian, who treated the king of Armenia as his ſlave, and as the enemy of the Gods. The haughty and threatening ſtyle of the Imperial mandates awakened the ſecret indignation of a prince, who, in the humiliating ſtate of dependence, was ſtill conſcious of his royal deſcent from the Arſacides, the lords of the Eaſt, and the rivals of the Roman power. GIBBON.
This Epiſtle, printed, for the firſt time, in the *Anecdota Græca* of M. Muratori, is inſerted in the *Bibliotheca Græca*, [*tom.* VII. *p.* 86.] of Fabricius. It is in very bad Greek, vulgar, brutal, meanly vain-glorious, without genius, con-

trary

either to pay the debt of nature, bravely fighting, and exerting my utmost efforts, if fuccefs fhould attend the Parthians; or, if the Gods fhould affift me, to return triumphant, and to erect trophies

trary to policy; and, what is ftill more remarkable, it contains expreffions that could not proceed from the pen of a fuperftitious Pagan, at the eve of a great enterprife, and in circumftances where the leaft word of bad omen was fcrupuloufly avoided, as capable of being fatal. Can it be fuppofed that Julian would have ventured to fay, even by way of circumlocution, that " he was refolved to perifh ?" Would he have communicated the prediction that we find at the end of the Epiftle? Whatever the illuftrious M. Muratori may fay of it, I can fcarce believe that it is the fame which Sozomen has mentioned; efpecially as this does not contain all that the Ecclefiaftical hiftorian relates. I do not infift on this laft reafon, becaufe it may be anfwered, that we have not the whole Epiftle. But, after all, it is fo ftrange a piece, that, inftead of afcribing it to Julian, I would rather fay, which is not neceffary, that Sozomen was deceived by a fpurious piece.

LA BLETERIE.

Muratori has publifhed an Epiftle from Julian to the Satrap Arfaces, fierce, vulgar, and (though it might deceive Sozomen) moft probably fpurious. La Bleterie tranflates and rejects it.

GIBBON.

And fo does the prefent tranflator.

The paffage of Sozomen, to which M. de la Bleterie refers, is as follows: " He wrote alfo to Arfaces, king of
" the Armenians, an ally of the Romans, to join him in
" the field. In this Epiftle, after boafting immoderately,
" and extolling himfelf as fit to reign, and dear to the Gods
" whom he worfhipped, and ftigmatifing Conftantius as
" pufillanimous and impious, he threatened Arfaces moft
" contumelioufly. And as he had heard that he was a
" Chriftian, in order to aggravate his reproaches, he ut-
" tered fome wicked blafphemies againft Chrift, with great
" pride and oftentation, fignifying, that the God whom
" he worfhipped would by no means defend him, if he
" neglected his commands." *Hift. Eccl. l.* VI. *c.* I.

taken

taken from the enemy. Shake off therefore your inactivity, forego all evasions, and thinking no longer of that Constantine of happy memory *, or of the wealth of the nobles, which was lavished on you and other Barbarians, by the effeminate and too aged † Constantius, now cultivate the friendship of Julian, Sovereign Pontiff, Cæsar, Augustus, the servant of Mars and the Gods, the destroyer of the Franks and Barbarians, but the deliverer of the Gauls and Italians. If you have any other design, for I hear that you are very crafty, a bad soldier, a boaster, I shall not be surprised, as you now secrete a public enemy, trusting to the chance of war. To destroy the enemy, we need only the assistance of the Gods; but if Fate, whose decree is their will, should determine otherwise, I shall submit with fortitude and complacence. Know, however, that you, in consequence, will be subjected to the Persian power, your house and your whole family will be destroyed by fire, and the kingdom of

* Μακαρίτην εκεῖνον Κωνςαντῖνον, "That blessed Constantine." Julian would hardly have spoken so favourably of his uncle, the constant object of his hatred and ridicule. It appears by the conclusion of the Cæsars, p. 220, that he rather thought him cursed than " blessed."

† Πολυέτης Κωνςαντίω, annosi Constantii. Constantius lived only 44 or 45 years.   LA BLETERIE.

In like manner, Julian, in his 1st oration, styles Licinius " an old man," (γεροντος), at the Battle of Cibalis in 314, though he was then not 50. M. de la Bleterie translates πολυέτης "qui n'a vécu que trop long tems (" who had lived too " long.")

Armenia

Armenia subverted. The city of * Nisibis will also share your misfortunes. This the Gods revealed to us long ago.

Epistle LXVII.   To the People [of Antioch †.]

SOME are so audacious as to prophane the sepulchres and consecrated graves of the dead, though to remove from them even a stone, or to dig the earth, and pull the turf, was always deemed by

12 Feb. 363.

* The bulwark of the East, given up to the Persians by Jovian, now reduced to 150 houses. See *Voyages de Niebuhr*, tome ii. *p.* 300—309.

Be this letter genuine, or not, "Arsaces," as M. de la Bleterie expresses it, " attentive only to his own interest, " and dissatisfied with Julian, would not leave his own " frontiers." This prince, in the reign of Valens, was treacherously seized, imprisoned, and put to death, by Sapor, king of Persia, as Ammianus relates, xxvii. 12.

† I take this law from the Theodosian Code, ix. xvii. 3. *tit. De sepulchris violatis.* It is the only piece of any length that is left of the Latinity of Julian. It is forcible and elaborate, but much less pure than his Greek. The reader perhaps will not dislike being enabled to judge for himself. The following is the whole Epistle.

IMP. JULIANUS A. AD POPULUM.

Pergit audacia ad busta diem functorum et aggeres consecratos; cùm et lapidem hinc movere, terram solicitare, et cespitem vellere, proximum sacrilegio majores semper habuerint. Sed ornamenta quidam tricliniis, aut porticibus, auferunt de sepulchris. Quibus primis consulentes, ne in piaculum incidant contaminatâ religione bustorum, hoc fieri prohibemus penâ Majori vindice adhibenda.

Secundum

by our ancestors next to sacrilege. Some take away the ornaments of tombs to adorn their porticoes or parlours. To prevent, in the first place, the criminal impiety of polluting sepulchres, we prohibit it under pain of the punishment that is due to those who offend the Manes *.

Secundum illud est, quod efferri cognovimus cadavera mortuorum per confertam populi frequentiam et per maximam insistentium densitatem, quod quidem oculos hominum infaustis incestat aspectibus. Qui enim dies est benè auspicatus à funere? Aut quomodo ad Deos et templa venietur? Ideóque, quoniam et dolor in exequiis secretum amat, et diem functis nihil interest, utrùm per noctes, an per dies, efferantur, liberari convenit populi totius aspectus; ut dolor esse in funeribus, non pompa exequiarum, nec ostentatio, videatur.

Datum prid. id. Feb. Antiochiæ, Juliano Aug. IV. et Sallustio, Coss.   LA BLETERIE.

* The profanation of sepulchres was considered in all times among the Romans as a kind of sacrilege. Those who dug up the body, or the bones, of a dead person were punished with death, if they were of mean condition. They were confined in an island, if they were of genteel rank. Those who destroyed a sepulchre, or took any thing away from it, were condemned to the mines, or banished. Constantine, in a law, whose object was to render divorces less frequent, and to make the Roman jurisprudence as to marriage again somewhat like the gospel, by restraining divorce to certain cases, specifies, among the crimes which gave a woman a right to repudiate her husband, murder, poisoning, and the violation of tombs. *Si homicidam, vel medicamentarium vel sepulchrorum dissolutorem maritum suum esse probaverit.* III *Cod. Theod. tit.* XVI. *De repudiis.* But the respect for the dead, and their tombs, which nature herself seems to inspire, was carried to an excess among the Pagans. They honoured the souls of the dead as divinities, and sepulchres as temples.

The Christian religion, which enlightened the world as to the fate of those wretched divinities, and the impiety of the worship that was paid them, no sooner became the

religion of the empire, than many individuals fell into an
excefs oppofite to that of Paganifm.   A zeal ill underftood,
and, under the mafk of zeal, avarice, always ready to draw
from the trueft principles falfe conclufions which favour
it, deftroyed tombs, applied the ftones and ornaments to
other ufes, and difperfed the afhes of the dead, in order
to find fome valuable ftuffs, or trinkets, which fuperftition
might have interred with them.

M. Muratori, in his *Anecdota Græca*, has inferted near
eighty fhort copies of verfes compofed by St. Gregory
Nazianzen, againft the violators of fepulchres.   As feveral of
them feem made in order to be engraved on the tombs of
his friends, of whom the majority at leaft profeffed Chriftianity, we may infer that the tombs of the Chriftians were
not fpared, were it only by the Pagans, who, without
doubt, ufed reprifals.   The law, above quoted, fhews what
the Emperor Conftantine, long after his converfion,
thought of thefe diforders, which not only outraged
nature, but alfo might render Chriftianity odious, on whofe
account they had become more common, though it had
always condemned them.   However, in the reign of
Conftantine, the laws were not executed with rigour.   It
appears by a law of Conftans, that fome individuals, and
even fome of the magiftrates, had violated them with impunity.   He caufed a fearch to be made for the guilty:
but he moderated the feverity of the ancient laws, and reduced it to pecuniary penalties.   Conftantius renewed and
even augmented it, as he fuffered the pecuniary penalties
to remain, when he re-eftablifhed the punifhment of death.
Other chriftian princes, particularly Valentinian III. ex-
erted themfelves, in like manner, againft this crime.

Julian, who confidered the worfhip of the Manes as an
effential part of Hellenifm, here condemns from fuperftition what thofe princes condemned from a principle of
humanity and Chriftianity, though fome Pagan expreffions
have crept into their ordinances, which, without doubt,
muft be afcribed to their fecretaries.   The firft part of the
law of Julian is in the Code of Juftinian, with fome alteration.   That which favoured too much of Paganifm has
been reformed.   LA BLETERIE.

If an ancient were to revifit the world, with what af-
tonifhment would he be ftruck in the amphitheatre of the

Secondly, we have heard that dead corpses are carried to interment through large crowds of people and numerous spectators, a sight, that defiles the eyes of men by its inauspicious appearance. For what day is well-omened by a funeral? And how can we afterwards approach the Gods and the temples?

For these reasons, and because funereal grief loves privacy, and as it is of no consequence to the deceased, whether they are interred by day or by night, it is proper that funerals should be secreted from the public view, so as to be expressive of sorrow, rather than of pomp and ostentation *.

bodies! A corpse was esteemed by the ancients a sacred object, which was respectfully placed under a funeral pile; and he who dared to lay hands on it was declared impure. What would he say on seeing that corpse horribly cut and mangled; and all the young surgeons, with their arms stripped and bloody, joking and laughing amidst those dreadful operations!   *Tableau de Paris.*

* Whatever respect the Pagans had for the dead, by a contradiction, of which I will not here trace the origin, they considered a human corpse as the impurest thing in the world. They thought they ought not to enter into a temple on a day when they had attended a funeral. But, delivered from a vain superstition, the Christians, and perhaps some Pagans, after their example, paid the last duties to the dead in open day. Julian was desirous of reviving the ancient practice, and even endeavoured to support, by philosophical ideas, the Pagan notions on which that practice was founded. This second part of his law is in the Theodosian Code, though it does not appear to have been observed after his death.   La Bletérie.

Of the laws which Julian enacted in a short reign of sixteen months [Dec. 361—June 363.] fifty-four have been admitted into the Codes of Theodosius and Justinian. (Godefred. Chron. Legum. pp. 64—67.)   Gibbon.

Given

Given at Antioch, on the day preceding the ides of February, Julian Aug. (for the ivth time), and Sallust being Consuls.

Epiftle LXVIII.   To LIBANIUS *.

YOU have made a proper return to Arifto-phanes † for his piety to the Gods, and his affection for you, by making what was formerly a difgrace to him redound to his glory, not only

A. D.
362.

---

* This Epiftle was copied by the illuftrious Roftgaard from the Modenefe MS. D. collated with the two Medicean E. and F. and is not to be found among thofe which have been publifhed, except, with many more, in the *Salutaris Lux Evangelii* of our Fabricius, p. 323. But it is here more en-larged.   It is thus infcribed : Ιυλιανος Αυτοκρατωρ Λιβανιω τω Σοφιςη χαιρειν.   WOLFIUS.

Libanius anfwers this Epiftle (occafioned by his oration in defence of Ariftophanes) in his DCLXXth, which fee Vol I. p. 317. The original of it is inferted by Wolfius, in his notes on that Epiftle.

Muratori obferves that in one of the Ambrofian MSS. [at Milan] there was a fhort Epiftle of Julian, not yet publifhed; " but," he adds, " the evanefcent letters made me totally de-" fpair of reading it. I hope, however, that it will fome time " or other be publifhed, together with fome other remains " of the Apoftate, by Frederick Roftgaard, a noble Dane. " For when he was travelling through Italy, and collecting " the Epiftles of Libanius from various MSS. in order to " give them to the public, he thought he had fagacity " enough to decypher alfo this Ambrofian MS."

See the firft note on the next Epiftle.

† Meaning Ariftophanes, a Corinthian, the fon of Me-nander, for whom there is an oration of Libanius, in Vol. II. of Morell's edition, p. 210.   FABRICIUS.

at prefent, but in future times; as the calumny of
Paul *, and the fentence of that judge †, can by
no means be compared with your orations. For
fuch fiery proceedings were inftantly detefted, and,
together with their authors, are now extinct; while
your orations delight the true Greeks of the prefent
age, and, unlefs I am much miftaken, will alfo delight their pofterity.

Be affured, in fhort, that you have convinced
me, [or rather that you have induced me to retract
my opinion of Ariftophanes, and that I think him
fuperior to all the allurements both of profit and
pleafure. Can I refufe to concur with the moft
philofophical of orators, the greateft partifan of
truth? After this, perhaps you may afk, why
we have not placed his affairs in a more profperous

---

* This Paul, who pleaded for the informers againft Ariftophanes, before the Emperor Conftantius, is mentioned
in the fame oration of Libanius, p. 222.   FABRICIUS.

Julian has ftigmatifed Paul as a " notorious flanderer,"
in his Epiftle to the Athenians, Vol. I. p. 92. See alfo Ammianus, xix. and xxii.   He was burnt alive, by the order
of that prince, foon after his acceffion to the empire; a
fate to which he feems to allude above by αἰθυλα, (" fiery")
and σνναπισθη, (" extinguifhed together.")   In Fabricius it
is αιθυλα, (" at their firft appearance.")

Libanius, in the oration above mentioned, fays, in one
place, " Ariftophanes received many fevere ftripes from
" balls of lead" [tied, probably, to ftrings], " which
" Paul thought fit inftruments of death;" and in another,
that " he had irritated Paul by fome expreffions fuitable
" indeed to him, but which it would have been better to
" have fuppreffed."

† The Emperor Conftantius.   FABRICIUS.

                                   ftate,

state, and removed every inconvenience attending his disgrace.

When two their efforts join, &c. *.
You and I will confer together. For you are worthy to be consulted, not only as to the propriety of assisting a man who devoutly honours the Gods, but also in what manner, of which indeed you have given some hints. But of these matters it will be better perhaps to discourse than to write. Farewell, my most dear and beloved brother †.]

* Συν τι δυ' ερχομινω, κ. τ. λ. Iliad X. 224.
An expression of Diomed, enforcing the propriety of an assistant in his nightly expedition. The same meaning is conveyed by our English proverb, " Two heads are better " than one."

† This was immediately followed by Ανιγνων δε χθες τον λογον, κ. τ. λ. (" Reading yesterday your oration, &c.") which is the XIVth Epistle of Julian [see p. 28.] published by Ezech. Spanheim, among his works, as a single Epistle, and (as is very probable) totally unconnected with the former.   WOLFIUS.
The concluding farewell is exactly the same with that of Epistle III. to Libanius also.

All that is between [ ] is only in the copy published by Wolfius.

Epistle

Epiſtle LXIX *.   To Sosipater †.

WHEN an opportunity offers of writing to our friends by a domeſtic, the pleaſure it affords is much augmented. For thus your letters convey to them ſomething more than a mere image of your mind. So fortunate am I at preſent. And therefore, as I was ſending to you Antiochus, the tutor of my ſons ‡, I could not omit this opportunity of informing you, that if you wiſh to have any intelligence concerning us, you may learn it particularly from him. And if you have a regard for your friends, and that you have ſome I am certain, when you have a ſimilar opportunity of writing, you will by no means neglect it.

* This, and the ſeven following Epiſtles (and alſo great part of the LIXth and LXVIIIth, as has been obſerved in the notes on each) were firſt publiſhed by Fabricius, in his *Lux Evangelii*, 1731, with a Latin tranſlation. He was indebted for them, he ſays, to Count Chriſtian Danneſhiold de Samſoa (then lately deceaſed), who purchaſed them in 1726, together with many hundreds of unpubliſhed epiſtles of Libanius, at the public auction of the library of the " moſt " noble and learned Frederick Roſtgaard," having been tranſcribed by him in Italy, from the Vatican, Medicean, and Ambroſian libraries. See p. 193, note *.

† Or was it " to Sopater," the ſon-in-law of Jamblichus, who is frequently mentioned in the XXVIIth, XLth, and LIIId Epiſtles of Julian?   FABRICIUS. See p. 70, note †.

‡ This probably muſt be the perſon mentioned by the ſame appellation (Τροφευς των υιεων παιδιων) in Epiſtle XL. See p. 102, note †.

                                    Epiſtle

Epiftle LXX. To Philip *.

WHILE I was Cæfar, the Gods can witnefs, I wrote to you, and, I think, more than once. Great certainly was the impulfe I felt, but many and various were my avocations; and, befides, as the friendfhip between me and the bleffed † Conftantius, in confequence of my advancement, was that of wolves, I was extremely cautious of writing to any one beyond the Alps, left I fhould involve him in the greateft difficulties. Confider my writing to you now as a proof of my friendfhip, for frequently the tongue refufes to correfpond with the heart. And fubjects perhaps have reafon to exult and glory in being able to fhew the letters of princes, difplaying them to the unexperienced, like rings to perfons unacquainted with

---

* This feems to be the fame to whom there are feveral Epiftles of Libanius, in [one of] which he fays, that the letters which he received from Philip were written " not " with ink, but with a Pegafean liquor." Fabricius.

Libanius had two correfpondents of this name, one a præfect, whom he mentions in his Life, p. 25, and the other a poet.

It muft have been written in the fpring of 362, probably at Conftantinople, when Julian was preparing to remove to Antioch.

† So Julian ufed to ftyle Conftantius, now dead, as he calls him μακαρίης in his XXXIft and LVIIIth Epiftles, and in his XXIIId, εκεινω μεν ων, επειδη μακαριης εγενετο, καφη γη.

Ibid.

fuch

such trinkets.   True friendship is generally found between equals; but there is a second kind, when one has a real, not a pretended, esteem for the other, and though superior in rank and genius, is loved for his good-nature, affability, and discretion. But such epistles are apt to be filled with vanity and trifles.   And I often reproach myself for making them too prolix, and being too loquacious, when I should teach my tongue a Pythagorean silence.

I have received your presents, a silver cup, a pound in weight, and a piece of gold coin.   I am indeed desirous, as you say in your letter, of having your company here.   But now the spring approaches, the trees begin to blossom, and the swallows, though not yet expected, when they arrive, will expell us, engaged on a like expedition, from our houses, and bid us remove to a distant country.   Therefore, as we shall pass near you, it will be better for you, if the Gods permit, to meet us in your own neighbourhood.   This, I hope, will soon happen, unless something providential prevents; which may the Gods avert!

Epistle

Epiftle LXXI. To Eutherius.*

WE live, preferved by the Gods †. Offer facrifices therefore to them in acknowledgement of my fafety; but not for the fafety of one individual only, but of all the Greeks ‡ in general. If you have leifure to pafs over § to Conftantinople, I fhall think myfelf not a little honoured by your company.

A. D.
361.

* To this Eutherius I have three Epiftles of Libanius in MS. **Fabricius.**
There are fix in the edition of Wolfius. Julian muft have written this foon after his arrival at Conftantinople in the winter of 361.

† Ζωμεν υπο των Θεων σωθεντες. On the fame occafion Julian ufes an expreffion very fimilar to this in his XIIIth Epiftle, to his uncle: Ζωμεν δια τας Θεας. In the Latin of Fabricius it is mifprinted *Vicimus*.

‡ Meaning the Gentile worfhippers of idols.
Fabricius.

§ This expreffion (διαβηναι) fhews, that Eutherius was then on the oppofite fide of the Bofphorus.

                    Epiftle

Epiſtle LXXII. To the Patriarch *.

THIS is the ſecond letter that I have ſent in favour of Amogila †, my former having been rendered ineffectual by the powerful influence of her oppreſſors. Lamenting therefore the fate of my former Epiſtle, pay due regard to this, and make it not neceſſary for us to write a third.

* Mention is made of Julus, the Patriarch of the Jews, whom he calls " moſt venerable," in the XXVth Epiſtle of Julian. FABRICIUS.

See p. 50.

This, as has been obſerved of the LXIVth Epiſtle, p. 184. has alſo, by miſtake, been aſcribed to Libanius, being printed in the edition of Wolfius, as the DCCCXXXVth of his Epiſtles. There are ſix more ſo inſcribed. But a MS. of one of them in the Vatican library has the addition of Ἀντιοχίας. This therefore, and all of them, were probably addreſſed, not to the Jewiſh Patriarch, as Fabricius ſuppoſes, but to the Chriſtian Patriarch of Antioch, who in the year 361 was Meletius.

† Αμωγιλης. In the copy (above mentioned) aſcribed to Libanius, the name is Αμμωνιλλης, (" Ammonilla.")

This is followed in Fabricius, by

" To ÆTIUS. (See p. 78.)

" Κοινως μεν απασι, &c. This, in the editions of Petau and " Ez. Spanheim, is the XXXIſt Epiſtle, p. 405, but inſtead " of Κοινως, (" in general,") we there read Λοιποις, (" the " reſt,") and then inſtead of the words μιχρι τε ſραλοπεδε " τε εμε, (" as far as [my] camp,") there is only in the " Medicean MS. μιχρι τε ſραλοπεδε. This Epiſtle, by which " we find the biſhops, whom Conſtantius had baniſhed, " recalled by Julian, is mentioned by Sozomen, l. v. c. 5."

Epiſtle LXXIII. To Diogenes *.

AFTER your departure, Diogenes, your ſon came to me, and ſaid, you were angry with him, and as much enraged as a father could be with a ſon : he begged me therefore to intercede for him, and to reconcile you to him. If his offence be ſlight, and ſuch as may eaſily be forgiven, yield to nature, and, recollecting that you are a parent, reſtore your ſon to favour. But if it be ſuch as cannot be pardoned, you yourſelf are the beſt judge which is moſt expedient, to act generouſly on this occaſion, and to conquer the diſpoſition of your ſon by the beſt advice, or to truſt his amendment, and the reparation of his fault, to length of time.

* An Athenian philoſopher, to whom there are ſome Epiſtles of Libanius. FABRICIUS.

In one of them he acquaints Diogenes with the death and burial of his wife. He is alſo mentioned by Julian in his XXXVth Epiſtle. See p. 90. He was the uncle of Ariſtophanes, the Corinthian, mentioned p. 193.

Epiſtle LXXIV. To Priscus *.

_{A. D.}
_{362.}

ON receiving your letter, I immediately diſpatched Archelaus †, and gave him ſome
epiſtles for you, with a paſſport, as you deſired,
for a longer time. If you are inclined to ſpeculate
the ocean, every thing, under God, will proſper
to your wiſh, unleſs you dread the inelegance of
the Galatians, or a ſtorm. But this will be as God
ſhall think fit. I ſwear to you by him, who is to
me the giver and preſerver of all good, that I wiſh
to live only for the ſake of being uſeful to you.
By you, I mean the true philoſophers; of whom
convinced that you are one, you well know how
much I have loved, and love you, and wiſh to ſee
you. May divine Providence preſerve you in
health many years, my moſt eſteemed and friendly
brother! The excellent Hippia, and your children,
I ſalute.

* The father of the præfect Anatolius. Fabricius.
Anatolius was maſter of the offices, and was killed in
the ſame ſkirmiſh in which Julian himſelf was mortally
wounded. He would otherwiſe perhaps have ſucceeded
that prince, as he himſelf is ſaid to have wiſhed. For an
account of Priſcus, ſee p. 6. note †.

† To this Archelaus, as I ſuppoſe, Libanius has four
Epiſtles, in one of which he expoſtulates with him for
enviouſly burning ſome of his declamations.

Epiftle LXXV. To Libanius, Sophift and Quæftor *.

HOW fortunate was our difappointment of a public carriage! For inftead of the terror and apprehenfion attendant on fuch a vehicle, where we meet with drunken muleteers, and mules, like thofe in Homer, "pampered with barley †," fuch are their idlenefs and repletion, and are annoyed with clouds of duft and the intolerable diffonance of clamorous drivers and fmacking whips ‡, I now travel at my leifure on a pleafant fhady road, abounding with fountains, and having many commodious inns, and when the hour of refrefhment arrives, I reft wherever I pleafe, beneath the fpacious, fragrant boughs of the plane or cyprefs, with the Myrrhinufian § Phædrus ‖, or fome other work of Plato, in my hands. As I thus enjoy an unembarraffed journey, did I not communicate this pleafure to you, my deareft friend, I fhould think myfelf inexcufable.

---

* So ftyled alfo in Epiftle XXVIIth. But here, for a reafon given below, I fufpect it to be an anachronifm.

† Ακερσαοι. Iliad. VI. 506. xv. 263.

‡ The inconveniences of the public vehicles in thofe days feem by this account very fimilar to thofe experienced in our times. Had Julian then been Emperor, or even Cæfar, all the public carriages, with their motions, would have been at his command.

§ Of Myrrhinus in Attica.   FABRICIUS.

‖ The book of Plato fo infcribed, from his fcholar of that name.

Epiftle

Epiſtle LXXVI. To the Philoſopher Euclid *.

WHEN did you leave us, that we muſt write to you? or when do we not view you, as if you were ſtill preſent, with the eyes of our mind, ſeeming not only to be conſtantly enjoying your company and converſation, but alſo taking the ſame care of your affairs as when you were here? If, however, you would have me write to you as to one who is abſent, conſider whether this requeſt does not prove that you are really abſent. Be that as it may, if it gratifies you, even in this we readily obey you. Indeed, according to the proverb, you will ſpur to the field a free horſe. See then that you make a ſimilar return, and fail not to be punctual in your replies. Though I am unwilling to interrupt your labours for the pnblic good, yet, as I obſerve that you purſue what is excellent, far from offending I ſhall ſeem to render an eſſential ſervice to all Greece by diſmiſſing you unmoleſted, like a generous hound, to track learning through all her paths, through every footſtep †. If you have ſuch alacrity as neither to neglect your friends, nor to diſcontinue theſe purſuits, haſte, and exert yourſelf in both thoſe courſes.

---

* I do not recollect that this philoſopher is elſewhere mentioned, either by Julian or Libanius. An Eucladius occurs in the DCLXXIIId Epiſtle of the latter.

† Βηματα, otherwiſe Αιμματα, ("argument.") FABRICIUS.

Epiſtola

Epiſtola LXXVII *. Ad Photinum †.

TU quidem, O Photine, veriſimilis videris et proximus ſalvare, benefaciens nequaquam in utero inducere quem credidiſti Deum. Diodorus ‡ autem Nazaræi magus ejus pigmentalibus mangoneis acuens irrationabilitatem acutus apparuit ſophiſta religionis agreſtis. * * * * Quod ſi nobis opitulati fuerint dii, et deæ, et muſæ omnes, et fortuna, oſtendemus infirmum et corruptorem le-

---

* This Epiſtle, mentioned by Fabricius, in his *Lux Evangelii*, p. 310. is preſerved by Facundus, biſhop of Hermania in Africa, in his book dedicated to the Emperor Juſtinian, in defence of the " three chapters," as they were called, which were the writings of Theodore of Mopſueſtia, Theodoret of Cyprus, and Ibas of Edeſſa, againſt all which Juſtinian had publiſhed an edict, A. D. 544. See Moſheim, I. 299. It was printed by Sirmond, at Paris, 1629, 8vo; and from that edition, p. 163, this letter is extracted.

This letter of Julian, if not written originally in Latin, ſeems to have been tranſlated in a very bombaſt ſtyle. He here threatens his work againſt the Chriſtians. I will not give it in Engliſh.

† Photinus, biſhop of Sirmium, publiſhed, in the year 343, his opinions concerning the deity, which were equally repugnant to the orthodox and Arian ſyſtems. His temerity was chaſtiſed, not only by the orthodox in the councils of Antioch and Milan, held in the years 345 and 347, and in that of Sirmium, whoſe date is uncertain, but alſo by the Arians, in one of their aſſemblies held at Sirmium, in the year 351. In conſequence of all this, Photinus was degraded from the epiſcopal dignity, and died in exile in the year 372. MOSHEIM.

For his extravagant notions ſee vol. I. of this hiſtorian, 223.

‡ Of Antioch, biſhop of Tarſus, an orthodox prelate. See Moſheim, I 188, and Moreri, article *Diodore d' Antioche.*

{ m,

gum, et rationum, et mysteriorum paganorum, et
deorum infernorum, et illum novum ejus deum
Galilæum quem æternum fabulosè prædicat indignâ
morte et sepulturâ denudatum confictæ a Diodoro
deitatis! Iste enim malo communis utilitatis Athenas
navigans, et philosophans, imprudenter musicorum
participatus est rationem, et rhetoricis confecti-
onibus odibilem adarmavit linguam adversus cæ-
lestes deos usque adeo ignorans paganorum mys-
teria omnemque miserabiliter imbibens, ut aiunt,
degenerum et imperitorum ejus theologorum pisca-
torum errorem.   Propter quod jam diu est quod ab
ipsis punitur diis.   Jam enim per multos annos in
periculum conversus, et in corruptionem thoracis
incidens, ad summum pervenit supplicium.   Omne
ejus corpus consumptum est : nam malæ ejus conci-
derunt, rugæ vero in altitudinem corporis descen-
derunt, quod non est philosophicæ conversationis
indicio, sicut videri vult a se deceptis, sed justitiæ
pro certo deorumque pœnæ quâ percutitur com-
petenti ratione usque ad novissimum vitæ suæ finem
asperam et amaram vitam vivens et faciem pallore
confectum.

FRAGMENTS

OF

EPISTLES OF JULIAN,

Translated from SUIDAS.

Article AMPHION.

.... FOR you have leisure, you have excellent natural endowments, and, if any one ever had, a love for philosophy. These three united were sufficient to render Amphion the inventor of ancient music *; namely, time, divine inspiration, and the love of harmony. The want of instruments cannot be any impediment to these; and he who is possessed of these three will easily find those. Have we not heard that Amphion not only invented music, but also the harp, either by the wonderful powers of his genius, or some divine assistance, or some unusual co-operation? And most of the ancients, by principally attending to these three, seem to have philosophised without disguise, and to have required nothing else.

* The lute, on which Amphion played so harmoniously as to bring together the stones with which the tower of Thebes was built, is said by others to have been presented to him by Mercury. Some suppose that there were two Amphions, and that the younger, called the Dircæan, from the river Dirce, in Bœotia, was the musician and the inventor of music.

Article

Article HERODOTUS.

WHO is ignorant of what the Æthiopians said of the moſt nouriſhing food we have? On taſting ſome of our bread, " they wondered", they ſaid, " how we could live upon dung," if we may credit the Thurian hiſtorian *. Thoſe who have treated on the various climates of the earth alſo relate that there are nations of men who feed on fiſh and fleſh, and never, even in a dream, ſaw ſuch diet as ours. If any one of them ſhould attempt to adopt our mode of living, he would fare no better than thoſe who ſwallow hellebore or hemlock.

---

* Herodotus, ſo called from Thurium in Magna Græcia, where he lived and died. Julian gives him the ſame appellation in Epiſtle XXII. The paſſage to which he here alludes is in the iiid book of that hiſtorian, and is part of the enquiry which the Æthiopians made of the *Ichthyophagi*, or " fiſh-eaters," whom Cambyſes ſent to explore that country. Their king, they ſaid, lived upon bread, explaining the nature of wheat, and that eighty years was the longeſt period propoſed by a Perſian. The Æthiopian anſwered, " I do not wonder, as you live upon dung, that " you are ſo ſhort-lived; and, were it not for this " beverage (wine), you would not live ſo long."

This extraordinary perſon was born at Halicarnaſſus, a Grecian colony in the leſſer Aſia, not long before the invaſion of Greece by the armies of Xerxes. In his youth he retired from his native city to Samos, in order to avoid the arbitrary proceedings of Lygdamis, the grandſon of the famous Artemiſia, who acquitted herſelf with much honour in the naval engagement of Salamis. There he formed himſelf upon the dialect of Ionia, and compiled his

hiſtory

hiſtory, which begins with Candaules and Cyrus, and comes down to the battle of Mycale, towards the latter end of the reign of Xerxes, a period of 120 years. In the mean time he ſpared no pains to inform himſelf of all that was neceſſary, in the beſt manner which he could. To this end he travelled into Ægypt, ſurveyed its chief towns, conversed with the prieſts of Thebes and Memphis, and penetrated into the principles of their religion and learning, as far as his own ſagacity could carry him, and their recluſeneſs would permit him. He travelled through the ſeveral diſtricts and republics of Greece, ſaw the principal cities of Aſia, and viſited the borders of Thrace, Scythia, and Arabia. Returning, however, after a long voluntary exile, into his own country, he bore a conſiderable ſhare in the expulſion of the tyrant; but meeting with envy from his fellow-citizens, inſtead of that gratitude which he expected, as the juſt reward of his ſervices, he went to Athens, and after about a twelvemonth's ſtay there, departed into Italy with a colony of Athenians, to build a city called Thurium (hence the above appellation) near the ruins of the ancient Sybaris. As ſoon as he had drawn up his hiſtory from the materials he had collected with ſuch infinite diligence and induſtry, he determined to expoſe it to the judgement of all Greece. It happened, that during his reſidence at Athens, beſides the feaſt of Panathenæa where he read his work aloud, the Olympian exerciſes were performed, to which the Grecians reſorted in general from each ſtate, and thus he had a very favourable opportunity of putting his deſign into execution. Many of his auditors had, no doubt, been perſonally engaged in ſome of the battles againſt Xerxes and Mardonius, and not one of them could be unacquainted with the principal facts of a war, ſo honourable to Greece, and ſo inglorious to Perſia. In the midſt of this aſſembly he declared, that " he appeared be-
" fore them not ſo much a ſpectator of their games, as a
" competitor for the prize of reputation;" and recited his work publickly a ſecond time with univerſal applauſe. Of this nothing can be a greater teſtimony than that the names of the nine Muſes have been given to the nine books of his hiſtory, as if the compoſition were above the ſtandard of humanity, and the joint labour of thoſe celebrated divinities.

Article MUSONIUS *.

THE drunken abuse, with which the commander in Greece † has loaded me, you have borne with serenity, thinking that it did not in the least concern you. As to your earnest defire to be ferviceable to the city in which you refide, that is a certain proof of a philofophical mind. The firft feems to me fuitable to Socrates, the fecond to Mufonius. He faid that it was wrong for a good man to fuffer himfelf to be injured by the wicked ‡. For he had the fuperintendence of the towers when he was banifhed by Nero.

* For an account of Mufonius, fee the Epiftle to Themiftius, Vol. I. p. 25. note ‖.

† This poffibly might be Dionyfius, whofe " drunken " abufe" Julian mentions in Epiftle LIX. p. 165. The words in the original are fimilar, παροινιαν and πεπαρωηκας.

‡ Though I have literally tranflated this paffage, I do not clearly apprehend its meaning, or its connection with what follows.

Article ΧΡΗΜΑ.

OUR journey lay through the Hercynian forest *. There I saw a most wonderful sight (χρημα, εξαισιον). I can confidently assure you, that you have never seen the like, though I know that there are many of the kind in the Roman dominions. But let any one think of the inaccessible Thessalian Tempe, or of Thermopylæ †, or of steep and extensive Taurus ‡; and all these will seem insignificant when compared in ruggedness with the Hercynian forest.

* This seems also to be styled the Hercynian forest by Zosimus, *l.* III. It is at present called *der Spessard*, formerly a part of the Hercynian forest, and is on the left bank of the Mayne, not far from the confluence of the Rhine and Moselle, as Cluverius says, *l.* III. *c.* 7.

VALOIS.

In Cæsar's time this forest extended from the country of the Rauraci (Basil) into the boundless regions of the North. Julian mentions his being " sent into the Hercynian forest when he had scarce arrived at manhood," in the Misopogon, p. 275; and Ammianus, XVII. I. where it is styled *sylvam squalore tenebrarum horrendam.*

† Straits between the mountains of Thessaly and Phocis, which divide Greece, famous for the defence of Leonidas against the Persians.

‡ The highest and most extensive mountains in Asia.

 INDEX

INDEX TO THE EPISTLES.

N. B. Those translated by M. de la Bleterie are marked with Arabic figures, which shew the chronological order in which he has endeavoured (as far as he could) to arrange them. Gallus to Julian, and Julian to Themistius, are his two first. And those to the Athenians and Constantius he has omitted.

THE

THE
LIFE
OF
LIBANIUS, the SOPHIST.

From the Latin

Of JOHN ALBERT FABRICIUS, D. D. *

LIBANIUS was born of an ancient and noble family at Antioch, on the Orontes, in the year of our Lord 314. Suidas calls his father " Phafganius;" but this was the name of one of his uncles †; the other, who was the elder, was named Panolbius. His great grandfather, who excelled in the art of divination, had publifhed fome pieces in Latin, which occafioned his being fuppofed by fome, but falfly, to be an Italian. His maternal and paternal grandfathers were eminent in rank and in eloquence; the latter, with his brother Brafidas, was put to death, by the order of

---

* In his Bibliotheca Græca, vol. VII. p. 378.
† Libanius, in his Life (which he fays, p. 19, he wrote when he was fixty), vol. II. p. 6. and 40, and *Orat.* XXIV. p. 534. He mentions, p. 46. that he attained his fiftieth year under Jovian; and, p. 48, his fifty-feventh under Valens.   FABRICIUS.

Diocletian,

Diocletian, in the year 303, after the tumult of
the tyrant Eugenius. Libanius, of his father's
three sons the second, in the fifteenth year of his
age, wishing to devote himself entirely to literature, complains that he met with some " shadows
" of sophists." Then, assisted by a proper master *,
he began to read the ancient writers at Antioch,
and from thence, with Jasion, a Cappadocian, went
to Athens, and residing there for more than four
years became intimately acquainted with Crispinus
of Heraclea, who, he says, enriched him afterwards
with books at Nicomedia, and went, but seldom, to
the schools of Diophantus.   At Constantinople he
ingratiated himself with Nicocles of Lacedæmon (a
grammarian, who was master to the Emperor Julian),
and the sophist Bemarchius. Returning to Athens,
and soliciting the office of a professor, which the pro-
consul had before intended for him when he was
twenty-five years of age, a certain Cappadocian happened to be preferred to him. But being encouraged
by Dionysius, a Sicilian, who had been præfect of
Syria, some specimens of his eloquence, that were
published at Constantinople, made him so generally
known and applauded, that he collected more than
eighty disciples, the two sophists, who then filled
the chair there, raging in vain, and Bemarchius
ineffectually opposing him in rival orations, and
when he could not excell him, having recourse to

* This was probably the same whom Libanius freed
from the resentment of the Emperor Constantius, as he
relates, p. 34.   FABRICIUS.

5   the

the frigid calumny of magic. At length, about
the year 346, being expelled the city by his com-
petitors *, the præfect Limenius concurring, he
repaired to Nice, and soon after to Nicomedia, the
Athens of Bithynia, where his excellence in fpeaking began to be more and more approved by all, and
Julian, if not a hearer, was a reader and admirer
of his orations. In the fame city, he fays, he
was particularly delighted with the friendſhip of
Ariftænetus †, and the five years, which he paſſed
there, he ftyles " the fpring, or any thing elſe that
" can be conceived pleafanter than fpring, of his
" whole life." Being invited again to Conftantinople, and afterwards returning to Nicomedia, being
alſo tired of Conftantinople, where he found Phœnix
and Zenobius, rival fophifts, though he was pa-
tronifed by Strategius, who fucceeded Domitian as
præfect of the Eaft, not daring, on account of his
rivals, to occupy the Athenian chair, he obtained
permiſſion from Gallus Cæfar to vifit, for four
months, his native city Antioch, where, after
Gallus was killed in 354, he fixed his refidence
for the remainder of his life, and initiated many

---

* The jealoufy of his rivals, who perfecuted him from
one city to another, confirmed the favourable opinion which
Libanius oftentatiouſly difplayed of his fuperior merit.

GIBBON.

† The death of this Ariftænetus, præfect of Bithynia,
who was overwhelmed at Nicomedia by an earthquake in
358, he laments, p. 40, and in his XXIXth and XXXIft
Epiftles. See alſo the following Monody.

in the facred rites of eloquence. He was alfo much
beloved by the Emperor Julian, who heard his difcourfes with pleafure *, received him with kindnefs,
and imitated him in his writings. Honoured by
that prince with the rank of quæftor †, and with
feveral Epiftles [of which fix only are extant ‡],
the laft § written by the Emperor during his fatal
expedition againft the Perfians, he the more lamented his death in the flower of his age, as from
him he had promifed himfelf a certain and lafting
fupport both in the worfhip of idols and in his
own ftudies. There was afterwards a report that
Libanius, with the younger Jamblichus, the mafter
of Proclus, enquired by divination who would be
the fucceffor of Valens ‖, and in confequence with

difficulty

---

* Fabricius corrects this miftake in his *Lux Evangelii.*

† See p. 65.

‡ Viz. the iiid, xivth, xxviith, xlivth, lxviiith, and
lxxvth.

§ The xxviith.

‖ In the year 373, or 374, whilft Valens was at Antioch,
a difcovery was made of a confultation which fome Gentiles
had together for finding out the name of the perfon who
fhould fucceed the Emperor. There are accounts of it
in feveral of our Ecclefiaftical hiftorians, and in divers
Heathen authors, particularly Ammianus Marcellinus, who
is the fulleft of all, and was then in the Eaft, and poffibly
at Antioch. The confeffions made by Patritius and Hilary,
both fkilful diviners, he thus particularly relates:

“ A tripod made of laurel was artificially prepared, and
“ confecrated with certain prefcribed fecret charms and
“ invocations. It was then placed in the middle of a
“ room, perfumed with Arabian fpices. The charger, on
“ which it was fet, had on its utmoft brim the four and
“ twenty letters of the alphabet, neatly engraved, and fet
“ at due diftances from each other. Then a perfon, clad

“ in

"in linen veſtments, with linen ſocks upon his feet, and
"a ſuitable covering upon his head, came in with laurel
"branches in his hands, and, after ſome myſtic charms
"performed, ſhook a ring, hanging at a curtain, about
"the edge of the charger; which jumping up and down,
"fell upon ſome letters of the alphabet, where it ſeemed
"to ſtay; the prieſt alſo then compoſing certain heroic
"verſes in anſwer to the queſtions that had been propoſed.
"The letters, which the ring pointed out in this caſe, were
"four, Θ, E, O, Δ, which being put together, one that
"was preſent immediately exclaimed, that the oracle
"plainly intended Theodorus" [then ſecond in the ſecre-
taries office], "nor did we make any farther enquiries,
"being all well ſatisfied that he was the perſon intended,
"though himſelf was totally ignorant of this proceeding."

Cave's Tranſlation.

Zonaras gives a different account of the method of divination then made uſe of. He ſays, "that the four and
"twenty letters of the alphabet were written upon the
"ground, and at each one was placed a grain of wheat or
"barley. Then, after ſome myſtic forms, a cock * was let
"out, which picked up ſuch grains as lay at thoſe four
"letters." But it is much more reaſonable to rely upon
Ammianus, who was contemporary, and likely to be well
informed. His account alſo is agreeable to that in Sozomen and Zoſimus, who have both mentioned the tripod.

When Libanius ſays, that "Valens hoped to have had
"him alſo accuſed as one of the conſpirators," I take it to
be a mere flouriſh. He was willing to make a merit of
ſome danger with the reſt of his friends, though really he
was ſafe enough.   LARDNER.

For this conſultation and divination many were put to
death, viz. Simonides and Maximus, philoſophers, the
latter the friend and perverter of Julian, Diogenes, who
had been præfect of Bithynia, and Theodorus, the perſon
named, perhaps with many more who owned the fatal
ſyllables. Theodoſius ſucceeded. Alypius too (ſee p. 73.)
who had been vice-prefect of Britain, was condemned, but
only baniſhed; and his ſon Hierocles, when he was leading
to execution, was happily ſaved, it is ſuppoſed, by a tumult
of the people.

* To this method Fabricius plainly alludes by the word *alectryomania.*

The

difficulty escaped his cruelty *, Irenæus attesting the innocence of Libanius. In like manner he happily escaped another calumny, by the favour of Duke Lupicinus, when he was accused by his enemy Fidelis, or Fidustius, of having written an elogium on the tyrant Procopius †. He was not, however, totally neglected by Valens, whom he not only celebrated in an oration, but ob-

---

The inquisition into the crime of magic, which, under the reign of the two brothers, was so rigorously prosecuted both at Rome and Antioch, was interpreted as the fatal symptom, either of the displeasure of heaven, or of the depravity of mankind. Lardner has copiously and fairly examined this dark transaction. GIBBON.

* That future events may be conjectured by the motions of the stars Libanius does not deny, in an Epistle [the xivth of Zambicari, *l.* I.] to Eustolius. That he also studied the interpretation of dreams may be deduced from Vol. II. of his works, p. 74. FABRICIUS.

† Procopius, a relation of the Emperor Julian, who had hastily promoted him, from the obscure station of a tribune and a notary, to the joint command of the army of Mesopotamia, retired, after the death of that prince, to his ample patrimony in Cappadocia. But being suspected and ordered to be apprehended by the new sovereigns Valentinian and Valens, A. D. 365, he escaped from his guards, passed over to the country of Bosphorus, and, after remaining many months in that sequestered region, embarked for Constantinople, and assumed the sovereignty. Being joined by some Gallic soldiers, whose numbers rapidly increased, he subdued the unarmed provinces of Bithynia and Asia, the city and island of Cyzicus, &c. but being at last deserted by his troops, in two engagements, after wandering some time among the woods and mountains of Phrygia, he was betrayed by his desponding followers, conducted to the imperial camp, and immediately beheaded.

Abridged from GIBBON.

tained

tained from him a confirmation of the law againſt
entirely excluding illegimitate children from the
inheritance of their paternal eſtates, which he ſo-
licited from the Emperor, no doubt, for a private
reaſon, ſince, as Eunapius informs us, he kept a
miſtreſs *, and was never married. The remainder
of his life he paſſed, as before-mentioned, at Antioch, to an advanced age, amidſt various wrongs
and oppreſſions from his rivals and the times, which
he copiouſly relates in his Life, though, tired of
the manners of that city, he had thoughts, in his
old age, of changing his abode, as he tells Euſebius
in his DLIVth Epiſtle [edit. Wolf.] He continued
there, however, and on various occaſions was very
ſerviceable to the city, either by appeaſing ſe-
ditions, and calming the diſturbed minds of the
citizens, or by reconciling to them the Emperors
Julian and Theodoſius. That Libanius lived even
to the reign of Arcadius, that is, beyond the
ſeventieth year of his age, the learned collect from
his oration on Lucian and the teſtimony of Cedrenus;
and of the ſame opinion is Godfrey Olearius, a
man not more reſpectable for his exquiſite knowledge of ſacred and polite literature, than for his
judgement and probity, in his MS. prælections, in

* He laments her death, and mentions a ſon, whom he
had by her, in his Life, p. 82. and in ſeveral of his Epiſtles.
In others it appears that his name was Cimon; that his
father ſent him to ſtudy at Athens, and that he died before
him.

which,

which, when he was profeſſor of both languages in the univerſity of his own country, he has given an account of the life of this ſophiſt.

The writings of Libanius * are numerous, and he compoſed and delivered various orations, as well demonſtrative as deliberative, and alſo many fictitious declamations and diſputations. Of theſe Frederick Morell † publiſhed as many as he could collect in two volumes, folio, in Greek and Latin. In the 1ſt vol. Paris, 1606, are XIII. Exerciſes (*Pro-*

---

* The voluminous writings of Libanius ſtill exiſt; for the moſt part they are the vain and idle compoſitions of an orator, who cultivated the ſcience of words; the productions of a recluſe ſtudent, whoſe mind, regardleſs of his contemporaries, was inceſſantly fixed on the Trojan war, and the Athenian commonwealth.   GIBBON.

† The Latin tranſlation of Morell has been obſerved by many of the learned to be often obſcure, and in numberleſs places to have miſtaken the ſenſe of Libanius. Whoever therefore ſhall undertake another edition of this author, muſt new tranſlate many paſſages, eſpecially in the IId volume. It is ſaid, neverthleſs, that Morell applied to his verſion with ſuch intenſe application, as not to ſuffe himſelf to be interrupted by an account that his wife was at the point of death, if we credit Iſaac Voſſius, in Colomeſius, p. 99. of his works: " I have heard from M. " Voſſius, that while Frederick Morell was employed on " Libanius, ſome one came to inform him that his wife " was very ill:" to which he replied, " I have only three " or four ſentences more to tranſlate, and then I will go " and ſee her." Another coming to tell him that ſhe was dying; " I have only two words," ſaid he, " I will be " there as ſoon as you." At laſt, being informed that his wife was dead, " I was very happy," he anſwered coldly, " ſhe was an excellent woman."   FABRICIUS.

gymnaſmata)

gymnafmata) XLIV Declamations *, and 111 moral differtations, and in the 11d vol. Paris, 1627, are the Life † of Libanius, and XXXVI other orations, moft of them long and on ferious fubjects.

Befides what are contained in thofe volumes, and his Epiftles, ten other works of this fophift have been feparately publifhed, moft of them orations ‡, and in the *Excerpta Rbetorum* of Leo Allatius,

---

* That his Declamations were " poffeffed, read, and " thought worthy of being imitated by many," appears from an Epiftle of Libanius to Archelaus [XLIVth of Zambicari, *l.* 1.], who, from envy, had committed fome of them to the flames. Eràfmus (I. 550.) has tranflated the 1ft of them, the " oration of Menelaus," which Morell has adopted *verbatim*, without acknowledgment, (I. 189.) his name being prefixed as the tranflator of them all.

† Libanius has compofed the vain, prolix, but curious narrative of his own life, of which Eunapius (p. 130—135.) has left a concife and unfavourable account. Among the moderns, Tillemont, Fabricius, and Lardner have illuftrated the character and writings of this famous fophift.

GIBBON.

‡ Of thefe, as of all the others, Fabricius has given the titles and fubjects. The Vth of them, " an oration " for the Temples," that they may not be deftroyed, to Theodofius the Great, 390, firft publifhed by Godefroi, Geneva, 1634, 4to. is tranflated into Englifh by Dr. Lardner, in his Jewifh and Heathen Teftimonies, Vol. IV. p. 137—158, with Obfervations. The VIth, " On reveng- " ing the death of the Emperor Julian," addreffed to the fame Theodofius, 379, was firft publifhed, from the Bodleian MS. by Olearius above-mentioned, Leipfic, 1701, 8vo. to which he afterwards added a Latin tranflation, and learned notes, at the defire of Fabricius, which he publifhed, in Bibliotheca Græca, Vol. VII. p. 145—179, with the original, and alfo with the VIIth, " To thofe who " called him troublefome," 373 ; and the VIIIth, " To " the Antiochians, on appeafing the refentment of the " Emperor"

Allatius, Greek and Latin, Rom. 1641, 8vo. are
xxxix Narrations, vii Defcriptions, and vii more
Exercifes of Libanius, with tranflations by Allatius.   His unpublifhed works are,

1. Many hundred Epiftles * yet concealed in various libraries, a mode of writing in which it appears he excelled by the teftimony even of the
ancients, particularly Eunapius and Photius ; and
of that the perufal of them will eafily convince
the intelligent reader ; for they abound with Attic
wit and humour, and every where recommend
themfelves by their pointed concifenefs no lefs than
by their elegance and learning †.

2. Several

"Emperor" [Julian], 363, both for the firft time, and a
correct copy of the " funeral oration on Julian," with
tranflations of them all by the fame Olearius.

* Eleven years after Fabricius printed the above, John
Chriftopher Wolfius, his pupil, friend, and collegue, affifted
by the collections of Frederick Roftgaard, a noble Dane,
(fee p. 196.) publifhed at Hamburgh, in one volume, folio,
1738, with learned notes, MDCV Epiftles of Libanius, in
Greek and Latin, two-thirds of them collected from various
MSS. to which he added DXXII Epiftles of the fame author,
in Latin only (xc of them duplicates, being alfo in the
Greek), tranflated from the originals, collected in Greece,
and publifhed at Cracow, about the middle of the XVth
century, by Francis Zambicari of Bologna, and republifhed
there by John Sommerfeld, M. A. 1504. See Vol. I. p.
330, note *.

† The critics may praife their fubtle and elegant brevity ;
yet Dr. Bentley (Differtation upon Phalaris, p. 487,)
might juftly, though quaintly, obferve, that " you feel by
" the emptinefs and deadnefs of them, that you converfe
" with fome dreaming pedant, with his elbow upon his
" defk."   GIBBON.

2. Several Orations, as in a MS. of the Barberini library, of excellent character, moſt correctly written on vellum, from which Allatius aſſerts *, that all the publiſhed works of Libanius might alſo be given much more correct and perfect.

3. Various Declamations, in the above MS. and one in the Vatican library.

And that there are many MS Epiſtles, Orations, and Declamations of Libanius in the Imperial library [at Vienna], Neſſelius has obſerved, affirming alſo that ſeveral Greek ſcholia are frequently inſerted in the margin.

Though ſo many of the writings of this ſophiſt are preſerved, there is no doubt that many both of his Epiſtles and Orations have been loſt †.

The MDLXXIVth Epiſtle of Libanius occurs among thoſe of Phalaris, and is inſcribed to Antimathius, n. XXVII.

It is thought at preſent by almoſt all the learned, Bentley, the prince of critics (*viro κριτικωτατω*) at their head, that theſe Epiſtles of Phalaris may juſtly be aſcribed to ſome ſophiſt. It may be worth while to conſider whether all of them perhaps were not fabricated by Libanius. I recollect, at leaſt, that in my notes I have frequently compared the phraſes and expreſſions of Phalaris with thoſe of Libanius. See, for inſtance, the notes on Ep. MCXLI.   WOLFIUS.

* *Præf. ad Excerpta Rhetorum Græcorum.*

† Of XI of theſe, mentioned by Libanius himſelf in different parts of his works, Fabricius recapitulates the titles, beſides various Counſels (συμβϗλαι ‡) to the Emperor Theodoſius, mentioned in the beginning of his oration for the temples of the Heathens. And many more, which Fabricius has omitted, might be ſpecified from ſeveral of his epiſtles.

‡ Tranſlated by Dr. Lardner, " Orations, and the counſel delivered in them."

A MONODY

A MONODY* by LIBANIUS,

On NICOMEDIA,

Deſtroyed by an Earthquake †.

HOMER never ſuffers even a tree to periſh without commiſeration; but, as if he himſelf had been the planter or gardener, when he ſees it ſtretched on the ground, he ſings a lamentation

A. D. 358.

---

* A mournful ſong, recited by one only on the ſtage, without a chorus, was called Μονωδια. And mention is made of a *Monodiaria*, or of a woman who ſung a monody.
WOLFIUS.

Libanius, in his XXXIſt Epiſtle, mentions two Monodies which he compoſed on this occaſion; one (which is now before us) relating to the city, the other, no doubt, to Ariſtænetus, Præfect of Bithynia, who periſhed in it (ſee the next note); but the latter is loſt. "I alſo," ſays he, (Ep. xxv.) "am one of thoſe who are overwhelmed by "that great calamity. For Ariſtænetus, O Jupiter, has "periſhed; and, beſides this, we have ſuffered another "ſtroke, as fate has not ſpared the head of Hierocles."

All the ancients ſpeak of Nicomedia as a place of great note: Pliny calls it "a famous and beautiful city;" Ammianus, "the mother of all the cities of Bithynia." In this city the Roman emperors reſided, when the affairs of the empire called them into the eaſt. Conſtantine the Great choſe Nicomedia for the place of his abode after he retired from Rome, and there remained till the buildings that he had begun at Byzantium were finiſhed. This city, once ſo famous, is now but a ſmall village, known to the Turks by the name of Schemith ‡. UNIVERSAL HISTORY.

‡ According to Pococke, Iſmit.

Q 2

At

† At break of day, on the 9th of the calends of September, the sky, which before was clear, was obscured by thick dark clouds; and the light of the sun being veiled, neither near nor contiguous objects were discernible. Then the Supreme Deity throwing, as it were, fatal thunder-bolts, and removing the winds from their very hinges ‡, the fury of the storm abated; and to these hurricanes and whirlwinds succeeded an horrible earthquake, which totally overthrew the city and suburbs. And on account of the declivity of the hills, some houses fell upon others, all resounding with the dreadful crash of the ruins. Mean time the lofty roofs re-echoed with various cries of those who were seeking their wives and children, or dearest friends. After the second hour, but long before the third, the sky, now fair and clear, discovered the funereal carnage. For some, crushed by the overwhelming force of falling rafters, perished under the weight of them : some, buried up to the neck, though they might have survived if they had had timely assistance, died for want of help; others hung fixed to the tops of standing beams; many men were killed a little before by one blow; then were seen promiscuous slaughtered bodies; some, the roofs of their houses falling in, were confined unhurt, victims to anguish and famine. Among whom Aristænetus, who governed the diocese lately desired with vicarial power, to which Constantius, in honour of his wife, had given the name of the Eusebian Piety ‖, by this calamity, long tortured, expired. Others, crushed by sudden bulky ruins, are still covered by the same heaps. Some, who had their sculls fractured, or had lost their arms or legs, between life and death, imploring with earnest intreaties those who were assisting others, were deserted. And the greater part of the inhabitants might have survived the sacred and private buildings, had not flames, widely dispersed, for fifty days and nights, consumed whatever was combustible.

AMMIANUS.

See also an Epistle on this subject from Libanius to Julian, Vol. I. p. 303.

---

‡ *Ventosque ab ipsis excitante cardinibus.*
Not unlike to this are Milton's " winds," that
—————— rush'd abroad
From the four hinges of the world.   *Par. Reg.* IV. 409.

‖ After the example of the Julian Piety, a name given to Pola in Istria (of which see Plin. l. III. c. 19.)   LINDENBROG.

3

over

over it *. And can I permit Nicomedia, where I increafed my knowledge of the liberal arts, efpecially eloquence, and acquired, befides, a degree of reputation which I had not before, to be deftroyed, can I fee fuch a city, a city no longer, reduced to afhes, unmourned, unwept? This concern I fhare in common with the vulgar; let her alfo participate of the oratory which fhe cherifhed. As, if I had been a mufician, and had gained many victories there in mufical contefts, fhould I have fuffered others to lament without joining in the lamentation?

Let me now addrefs the Gods, fuppofing them prefent, and thus endeavour to eftimate our calamity.

When, fitting in the palace of Jupiter, with the other Gods, you, O Neptune, were enraged on account of the wall which the Grecians had built

---

* Homer deplores the deftruction of plants in Iliad ix and xviii.   MORELL.

    —————— a monftrous boar,
That levell'd harvefts, and whole forefts tore.
                  POPE, ix. 659.
Much more expreffive in the original.

In the xviiith I find a plant, or a tree, mentioned only thus,
    Like fome fair olive, by my careful hand
    He grew, he flourifh'd, and adorn'd the land.
              POPE, 175 and 512.

If Libanius had been acquainted with the Pfalmift, and unprejudiced by Paganifm, he could not have overlooked that beautiful allufion of the " vine brought out of " Ægypt," and the complaint of its being " rooted up, " burnt, and cut down." Pf. lxxx. 8—16.

at Troy to cover their ſhips, was not their neglect
of the Gods, when they laid the foundation, the
principal ſubject of your complaint *? And therefore, when Troy was taken, you judged right in
thinking it neceſſary to deſtroy that wall; which
you eaſily accompliſhed by turning againſt it the
rivers that ruſhed from Ida †. But in the foundation of this city what was the offence that induced you to treat it in the ſame manner? Did not
its firſt founder ‡, deſigning to build a city on the
ſhore

---

* Hom. Il. VII. 450.
See the long walls extending to the main,
No God conſulted, and no victim ſlain, &c.   POPE, 535.

† Ibid. XII. 17.
Then Neptune and Apollo ſhook the ſhore,
Then Ida's ſummits pour'd their watery ſtore;
Rheſus and Rhodius then unite their rills, &c.

.   .   .   .

Theſe, turn'd by Phœbus from their wonted ways,
Delug'd the rampire nine continual days;
The weight of waters ſaps the yielding wall,
And to the ſea the floating bulwarks fall.
Inceſſant cataracts the Thunderer pours,
And half the ſkies deſcend in ſluicy ſhowers, &c.
POPE, 15.
This is a noble paſſage in the old bard; ſtorm, inunda-
tion, and earthquake magnificently combined.   B.
Milton alludes to it in his viſion of the Deluge, b. xi.
———————————— Then ſhall this mount
Of Paradiſe, by might of waves, be mov'd
Out of his place, puſh'd by the horned flood,
With all his verdure ſpoil'd, and trees adrift,
Down the great river to the opening gulf,
And there take root, an iſland ſalt and bare,
The haunt of ſeals, and orcs, and ſea-mews' clang. 829.

‡ Nicomedia is ſaid to have been firſt built by Olbia,
and had its firſt name from him. It was afterwards re-built

fhore oppofite to that where it now ftands, or rather
where it once ftood, begin his work from you?
Were not the altars covered with victims, and furrounded by a crowd of worfhippers? But by an
eagle and a prodigious fnake you diverted their attention to the hill; of thefe, the former with her
talons fnatched the head of the victim from the fire;
and the latter, large and refembling thofe which
are bred in India, iffued from the earth. The one
cleaving the fea, and the other the air, repaired to
the brow of the hill. The people followed, led,
as they thought, by the guidance of the Gods.
Thefe omens were all deceitful. The city was at
firft overwhelmed by the torrent of war *. Be it
fo. Your own Corinth † alfo, and the land of

by Nicomedes I. king of Bithynia, though Olbia feems
rather to have been near it, and that the inhabitants of it
were tranfplanted to this place.   Pococke.

  Nicomedia, Aftacus, and Olbia are fpoken of by
Ptolemy as three neighbouring but diftinct cities. Strabo
writes that Nicomedes, the fon and fucceffor of Zipœtes, deftroyed Aftacus, and transferred its inhabitants to Nicomedia.
          Universal History.

  * This muft probably have been in the reign of Nicomedes III. who was twice driven from his throne by Mithridates the Great, king of Pontus.

  † Among other names which Corinth anciently had we
find that of Heliopolis, or city of the fun, for which this
reafon is commonly given; that the poets feign Apollo and
Neptune to have contended for it, and that Jupiter having
appointed Briareus, the Cyclop, their umpire, he adjudged
the Ifthmus to the latter, and the Promontory, which commands the city, to the former.   Universal History.

Q 4

Cecrops,

Cecrops *, your beft beloved, have experienced the fame fate †. Another founder came, who, making the Gods his principal leaders, and, by the fuperior magnitude of his offering, rendering your minds more propitious, reftored the city. How then, like the land of Ætolia, for the offence of Œneus ‡, did fhe deferve to be punifhed with contempt? Is it right, has it been ufual, for the Gods to deftroy with their own hands works like thefe, in which they have co-operated with mortals, and to imitate the paftime of children, who are accuftomed to pull down what they have erected §? Or did it become you, O Neptune, to enter into a conteft with your niece for an Attic city not then in being, and to overflow a citadel fo diftant from

* An Ægyptian fugitive, who introduced religion into Greece, and founded the Athenian monarchy. See note * p 233.

† Corinth was furprifed by Antigonus and Aratus, taken and burnt by the Romans, &c. Athens was deftroyed by Mardonius, taken by the Lacedæmonians and Sylla, &c.

‡ Oeneus, king of Ætolia, or Calydon (its chief city) facrificing to the reft of the deities, neglected his duty to Diana, who in confequence fent a wild boar to ravage and deftroy the country, which was killed by his fon Meleager, and his company. See Hom. Il. IX. 530.

§ Thus Tibullus, ———— *puer è virgis extruet arte cafas.*
           l. II. el. 1.
 And Horace of a boy, ———— *amata relinquere pernix.*
           Morell.

Libanius had here, no doubt, in his view that paffage in the Iliad to which Julian alfo refers in his XLth Epiftle. See p. 106.

the

the fea *, yet to difplay no regard for fuch a great
and important city as this, but even to fubvert it
from the foundations? What city was more beautiful? I will not fay larger, for in fize it was exceeded by four †, but contemned all that increafe
of extent, which would have wearied the feet of
its citizens ‡. In beauty alfo it yielded to thefe,
and was equalled, not excelled, by fome others:
for, ftretching forth its promontories, with its arms

---

* Cecrops not knowing what name to give to his new-
built city, an olive-tree, and a fountain of water (or, as
others fay, a horfe) appeared. The oracle, being confulted,
anfwered, that "Neptune and Minerva were contending
" for the honour of naming it, that the olive was the gift
" of Minerva, and the fountain (or horfe) that of Nep-
" tune; and that that which they efteemed moft benefi-
" cial to mankind fhould adjudge the prize to the giver."
The men and women being affembled to give their judgement, the former gave it for the God; but the women,
who were more numerous, gave it for the Goddefs; and
the city was named from her *Athena*. Neptune, in revenge
of the affront, overflowed their territories. Apollodorus.

Here we have an account of the ῥόθιον mentioned by Libanius, which Morell has rendered *Procella*, though it
fignifies properly " the violence and force of water, a billow
" of the fea:" as, in the poem on Hero and Leander, the
poet fays, he ftood on the fhore,

Μαινομενων ροθιων πολυηχεα βομβον ακουων·

where βομβον excellently expreffes the heavy found occafioned
by the fall of the waves. B.

† Rome, Byzantium, Antioch, and Alexandria.

‡ Τοσετον αιμασασα τα μεγεθες, οσοι εμελλε λυπησειν των οικη-
τορων τας ποδας. This is an odd paffage, and feems to me a
puerile conceit. Morell's marginal reading, ισ. παιδας (for
ποδας) is pleafant enough. I wonder he fhould think any
alteration neceffary, as he underftood the true fenfe of the
place; for men may be fatigued as well as children. I have
no doubt that he was a great walker. B.

it embraced the fea. It then afcended the hill
by four colonnades extending the whole length.
Its public buildings were fp'endid, its private
contiguous, rifing from the loweft parts to the
citadel, like the branches of a cyprefs, one houfe
above another, watered by rivulets, and furrounded
with gardens *. Its council-chambers, its fchools
of oratory, the multitude of its temples, the
magnificence of its baths, and the commodi-
oufnefs of its harbour I have feen, but cannot
defcribe. This only I can fay, that, frequently
travelling thither from Nice †, we ufed on the
road to difcourfe on the trees, and the foil, abundant in all productions, and alfo of our families,
our friends, and ancient wifdom. But after we had
paffed through the intricate windings of the hills,
when the city appeared, at the diftance of a hundred and fifty ftadia ‡, on all other fubjects a profound filence inftantly enfued, and, no longer engaged either by the towering branches of the
gardens, or by the fruitfulnefs of the foil, or by

---

* In like manner, Dr. Pococke defcribes the prefent town
as " fituated at the foot of two hills, and all up the fouth
" fide of the weftern one, which is very high, and on part
" of the other: it is near the N. E. corner of the bay. All
" the houfes have fmall gardens, or courts, to them, efpe-
" cially thofe on the hills. The gardens are planted with
" trees §, and the vines, being carried along on frames built
" like roofs, make the city appear exceedingly beautiful.
" There are very few remains of the ancient Nicomedia."
  † Thirty-two miles.   Pococke.
  ‡ About nineteen miles.

  § Κηποι ανεζευμενοι τοις κλαδοις are the words of Libanius.

the

the traffic of the fea, our whole converfation turned on Nicomedia. And yet mariners, or thofe who labour at the oar, and enfnare the fifh with nets, or hooks, naturally attract the obfervation of travellers. But the form of the city, much more fafcinating, by its beauty tyrannifed over our eyes, and fixed their whole attention on itfelf. Similar were the fenfations of him who had never feen it before, and of him who had grown old within its walls. One fhewed to his companion the palace, glittering over the bay; another the theatre embellifhing the whole city; others various other rays darted from various objects: which furpaffed it was difficult to determine. Revering it as a facred image, we proceeded; in our way to Chalcedon, it was neceffary to turn, till the nature of the road deprived us of the fight *. This feemed like the ceffation of a feaft.

A city fo great, fo renowned, ought not the whole choir of the Gods to have furrounded and protected, exhorting each other to decree that it fhould never be fubjected to any calamity? But now fome of you have deceived, others have deferted, and none affifted her. And all thefe particulars, which I have mentioned, once were, but remain no longer. What a beautiful lock has For-

* He firft mentions the pleafure arifing from the profpect of the city, as they approached; and then their concern at lofing fight of it, as they proceeded from it to Chalcedon.   B.

tune now fevered from the world *! How has fhe blinded the other continent by thus bereaving it of its illuftrious eye! What a deplorable deformity has fhe diffufed over Afia; as if her moft fpacious grove had been felled, as if her moft confpicuous feature † had been lopped off! O moft injurious earthquake, why didft thou perpetrate this? O departed city! O name of it in vain remaining! O grief difperfed over land and fea! O dire intelligence, diftrefsful to the hearts of all ranks, of all ages! for what heart is fo ftony, what heart is fo adamantine, as not to be wounded by this relation? who is fo deftitute of tears as now to with-hold them? O dreadful misfortune, which has reduced the innumerable ornaments of the city to one ruinous heap! O unpropitious ray ‡, what a city

didft

---

* Thus Pindar ftyles Ætna " the front," or forehead, " of the fruitful earth," ευκαρποιο γαιας μίτωπον, Pyth. I. and Nicomedia was a beautiful city " high-mounted on a " hill," as Sandys fays of fome other. I am afraid the hill of Nicomedia hardly deferved the name μίτωπον γαιας; but a panegyrift may make mountains of molehills.   B.

† Βοςρυχος, οφθαλμος, what next? αλσος, ριν (" The lock, " the eye, the grove, the nofe.") In the name of propriety, what has αλσος to do here? Are we to underftand it of the hair of the head?   B.

This idea feems anticipated by βοςρυχος. The metaphor indeed feems here loft, " a grove," or " wood," being no feature, like the others. Pιν. feemed in Englifh to require a circumlocution.

‡ Ω δυςυχες αχτινος, οιαν μεν προσεβαλλε την πολιν ανασχεσα· οιαν δε αφεισα καταδυ. Morell tranflates αχτινος tridentis radius. But why fhould it not mean (as ufual) the " fun's ray?" Ανεχω and καταδυνω are ufed for the " rifing and fetting of the

fun."

didſt thou ſmite at thy riſing, what a city ſunk with thee! The day had almoſt advanced to noon *; the tutelar deities of the city abandoned the temples, and ſhe was left like a ſhip deſerted by its crew. The lord of the trident ſhook the earth, and convulſed the ocean; the foundations of the city were diſunited; walls were thrown on walls, pillars on pillars, and roofs fell headlong. What was hidden was revealed, and what had appeared was hidden. Statues, perfect in beauty, and complete in every part, were blended by the concuſſion in one confuſed maſs. Artificers, working at their trades, were daſhed out of their ſhops and houſes. In the harbour was much deſtruction, and alſo of many worthy choſen men collected about the Præfect †. The theatre involved in its ruins all who

ſun." I do not recollect that αχων is uſed abſolutely, as here, for the " prong of the trident." The trident too is thruſt under the foundation. See the beginning of the Phœniſſæ of Euripides, where Jocaſta, addreſſing the Sun, complains of his darting an " unpropitious ray" on Thebes. Ηλιε, θοαις ιπποισιν, κ. τ. λ.

  O thou, that glorying in thy fiery ſteeds,
  Rolleſt the orient light, reſplendent Sun,
  How inauſpicious didſt thou dart thy beams
  That day on Thebes, &c. POTTER. Poſſibly Libanius may allude to it.   B.

 * Μικρον μεν απειχεν ημερα περι πληθυσαν αγοραν ειναι.
Literally, " it was near high market." But Ammianus ſays, that it happened at break of day; and George Cedrenus, in the night.

 † Ariſtænetus, the great friend and patron of Libanius, who, in ſeveral of his epiſtles to him, celebrates his eloquence and ſweetneſs of manners. See p. 227. note *. He was afterwards buried at Nice, of which he was a native.

            were

were in it. Some buildings, which had long stood tottering, and others which had yet escaped, with all who were in them, shared at last the general fate. The sea, violently agitated, deluged the land. Fire, which abounded every where, seizing the rafters, added to the concussion a conflagration * ; and some wind, it is said, fanned the flames. Much of the city, much of the ramparts, still remains. Of those who have escaped, a few still wander about wounded.

O all-seeing Sun, what were thy sensations on seeing this? Why didst not thou prevent such a city from leaving the earth? For the oxen profaned by the famished mariners † such was thy resentment as to threaten the celestial powers that thou wouldst give thyself up to Pluto ‡ ; but for the glory of the earth, for the labour of many kings, for the fruit of prodigious cost, destroyed in the day-time, thou hast no compassion.

O fairest of cities, on what a faithless and froward hill didst thou fix thy seat ; which, like a vicious horse, has dismounted its excellent rider? Where are now thy winding walks ? where are thy

---

* Thus at Lisbon, Messina, and in all great earthquakes, fire has been their constant attendant.

† Hom. Odyff. xii. Libanius has before taken Neptune to task ; he here reprimands Apollo.

‡ Alluding to what Apollo says on that occasion in the same book of the Odyssey.
" Vengeance, ye Gods, or I the skies forego,
" And bear the lamp of heaven to shades below."
Pope, 450.

por-

porticoes? where are thy courses, thy fountains, thy courts of judicature, thy libraries, thy temples? Where is all that profusion of wealth? Where are the young, the old? Where are the baths of the Graces and of the Nymphs? of which the largest, named after the prince, at whose expence it was built, was equal in value to the whole city *. Where is now the senate? Where are the people? where the women? the children? where is the palace? where is the circus +, stronger than the walls of Babylon ‡? Nothing is left standing; nothing has escaped; all are involved in one common ruin.

O numerous streams, where now do you flow? what mansions do you lave? from what springs do you issue? The various aqueducts and reservoirs are broken. The plentiful supply of the fountains runs to waste, either forming whirlpools, or stagnating in morasses; but drawn or quaffed by no one, neither by men nor birds. These are terrified

---

* As Diocletian, according to Lactantius, embellished Nicomedia with a great number of stately buildings, with a design of equalling it to Rome, possibly these baths might be part of them, and named after him, as we know his baths, now magnificent in ruins, were at Rome; which, says Ammianus, with no small exaggeration, "seemed rather a "province than a building."

+ He [Diocletian] built there several basilics, a circus, a mint, an arsenal, a palace for his wife, and another for his son. LACTANTIUS.

‡ The walls of Babylon were so celebrated among the ancients as to grow proverbial. Libanius mentions them in like manner in his cxcvith Epistle.

by

by the fire which rages every where below, and,
where it has a vent, flames into the air. This city,
once fo populous, now in the day time is deferted
and defolate, but at night is poffeffed by fuch a
multitude of fpectres, as I think muft crowd the
inhabitants of the infernal regions after they have
paffed Acheron.

Celebrated of old were the difafters of Lemnos *,
and the Iliad fings the woes of Troy. Their remembrance will be flighted, but the excefs of our
calamities any one may hence determine. Former
earthquakes, though they deftroyed fome parts of the
city, fpared others; but this has overwhelmed the
whole. Other cities have alfo perifhed, but never one
of fuch a magnitude. If it had been deprived only
of bodies infected with the plague, or of thofe
perfons who, contrary to the laws †, were celebrating

---

* Great misfortunes were proverbially ftyled " Lem-
" nian;" fome fay, from the flaughter of the Attic
women, and the children which they had by them, by the
Pelagians, who inhabited Lemnos ; others, from the murder of their hufbands, on account of their offenfive breath,
by the Lemnian women. See Ludolph Kufter on Suidas,
tom. II. p. 441. Bayle's Dictionary, vol. II. p. 1780. and
Erafmus, in his Chilcades.   WOLFIUS.

Libanius, in his xxivth Epiftle, thus alludes to this
paffage; " I faid little when I expreffed the ruin of Ni-
" comedia by the misfortunes of Lemnos."

† Κατα νομον. It feems a little hard that people fhould be
deftroyed for facrificing " according to law ;" yet κατα νομον
is certainly " according to law." Let us fuppofe an error of
the prefs, and make it νομω. He alludes to fome event, which
I do not recollect. I fufpect that he has taken a line from
fome Greek poet, and accommodated it to his purpofe.   B.

Though

brating a general sacrifice without the city, and had not itself fallen, the stroke might have been supportable. The whole would not have been defolated; now both lie proftrate, and the form of the city is confufed with the flaughter of the citizens.

Lament therefore, every ifland and every continent, peafants and mariners, cities, villages, cottages, every thing that is connected with human nature; and let tears prevail over all the world, as in Ægypt whenever Apis dies *. Even rocks fhould now be indulged with tears, and birds with reafon, to join in an elegiac fong. O harbour, which fhips now carefully avoiding, rather fteer into the ocean, their cables flipped, which formerly were filled with loaded veffels, but now cannot boaft even a pleafure-boat, and art more dreaded by mariners than even the manfion of Scylla! O difappointment to travellers, who no longer frequent the road, which, gloomy and in the form of a crefcent, beautifully winded round the dykes of the haven, but embarking fail to-

---

Though Libanius, like Julian, was probably acquainted with the Mofaic hiftory, I will not affirm that he here alludes to it; but certain it is, that this paffage has no diftant affinity to the earthquake that fwallowed up Korah and his company, for offering unhallowed incenfe, and to the plague that deftroyed their abettors. *Numbers* xvi.

* When Apis dies, they behave as if they had loft their deareft children, and bury him in the moft fumptuous manner. Nor do the people ceafe from lamenting till the priefts have found a calf with the fame marks. DIODORUS SICULUS.

wards the hill, to which they formerly haftened
[by land], trembling as at Charybdis, and unable to
conjecture in what part of the fea they ufed to
ftand on the fhore! O deareft of cities! in your
ruin you have involved your inhabitants; you have
deftroyed them by your fall; fo that all mankind
apply themfelves to fupplications, thinking the extinction of their whole race determined. After the
lofs of this moft valuable poffeffion, nothing hereafter, they apprehend, will be fpared. Who will
fupply me with wings to waft me thither? Who will
place me on an eminence to view the diftrefsful
fight? For a lover has fome confolation in being
furrounded by the objects of his affection, though
in ruins *.

    * For the notes on this and the following Monody,
marked B, I am obliged to a learned and amiable friend.

A MONODY by LIBANIUS,

ON THE

Daphnæan Temple of Apollo, deſtroyed by Fire, or, as it is ſaid, by Lightning *.

FELLOW-citizens, whoſe eyes, like mine, are now involved in darkneſs †, this city we ſhall no longer ſtyle beautiful or great ‡.

A. D. 362.

---

* The Greek title of this Monody is more perfect in the Royal MS. which I have followed, than in the Bavarian; in which it is only ſtyled, "'A Monody on the Daphnæan " Temple of Apollo." But the corollary, which is added to the inſcription here adopted, does not give the ſentiments of Libanius, who had conceived an idea, that ſome incendiary by a ſmall ſpark had kindled this great conflagration, as he ſays, in the beginning; and ſoon after, that he may obviate the opinion of thunder from heaven, he adds, that " it happened in a clear and cloudleſs ſky ;" which to the orthodox increaſes the miracle, of which St. John Chryſoſtom, the contemporary of our Libanius, in his 1ſt Diſcourſe on the Martyr St. Babylas, p. 725. " As " ſoon as the bier was brought to the city, lightning " fell from heaven on the head of the image, and con- " ſumed every thing." And the Emperor Julian too was well aware of this; " he knew that the blow came from " heaven ;" though he aſſerts, in the Miſopogon, that " the " temple was deſtroyed by the negligence of the keepers, " and the preſumption of the impious." MORELL. After the interment of St. Babylas, Apollo gave oracles as before; and Julian cauſed a ſuperb colonnade to be built round his temple. But in the night of the 22d of October, 362, a fire conſumed the wood work of that ancient edifice, and the ſtatue itſelf; nor could Julian, who haſtened

to

to the place, fupply any remedy. That fire was afcribed by the Chriftians to the divine vengeance, and by Julian to the refentment and jealoufy of the Chriftians. He fufpected the facrift, and the minifters who kept the temple, of being in a confederacy with them. But thofe idolaters, being put to the torture, accufed no one. On the contrary, they conftantly affirmed, that the fire began from above; and fome peafants, who were that night on the road in their way to the city, faid, they faw fire from heaven fall on the temple, though the weather was very calm, and there was no appearance of a ftorm. Julian, however, either by way of reprifal, or to prevent the Chriftians from triumphing, ordered the great church of. Antioch to be fhut, and its riches to be carried to the imperial treafury.

LA BLETERIE.

See alfo Vol. I. p. 247, 248.

† What darknefs hangs over the eyes of the Antiochians ? Is it the darknefs of a cloud, which

With mifts and films involves their mortal fight ? Such as the Pallas of Homer boafts to have removed from Diomed, and the Venus of Virgil from Æneas ? Or is it the gloom of forrow, which, hanging over the eyes of the mind, obfcures the ufe of reafon and thought ? MORELL.

‡ On the beauty and extent of Antioch, fee Philoftratus on the Life of Apollonius, *l.* I. *c.* xii. *p.* 21. " Apollonius " came to Antioch the Great," &c. and our Libanius, in his oration to Theodofius the Great, on the fedition, in behalf of the Antiochians, where, in the conclufion on the misfortunes of that city, he adds, as here, " our city is be- " come different, or, to fpeak more truly, it is no longer " a city." Aufonius celebrates it among the famous cities,

Tertia Phœbeæ lauri domus Antiochia.

With the Phœbean laurel grac'd, the third Is Antioch.

After the firft fentence, Chryfoftom in the fame place declares, that Libanius added fomething of the fable of Daphne, and perhaps it was the fable which Philoftratus, in the above mentioned paffage, calls " Arcadian," and explains as follows: " He entered the fane of Daph- " næan Apollo, to which the Affyrians afcribe the Ar- " cadian fable. For the[illegible] Daphne, the daugh- " ter [illegible] turned; and the river

. . . [A king of Persia, one of the ancestors of him who is now at war with us, having by treachery taken and burnt the city, as he was preparing the same fate for Daphne, was so thoroughly di. verted from his purpose by the Deity, that, throwing away the torch which he brandished, he prostrated himself, and adored Apollo : so appeased was his resentment, so checked was his fury *.] He, though he led an army against us, thought proper to preserve this temple, and the beauty of the image restrained his barbaric fury. But now, O heaven and earth, who and whence is that traitor, who wanting neither light † nor heavy-armed foot ‡, nor

---

* This I have not published in the Greek, because it was not in our Royal and Bavarian MS. And John Chrysostom himself, though he did not insert it in its proper place, hurried away by the eddy of his discourse, yet afterwards pays it as a debt, or brings it back as a fugitive, with this introduction, " You read this in the beginning of the " Monody, " A king of Persia," &c. [as above]. But who was this king of Persia, unless it were Sapor, the second king, who, according to Zosimus, succeeded Artaxerxes the first king ?] The same took Antioch, and held it till the Emperor Gordian, having defeated the Persians in several battles, dispossessed king Sapor, and recovered Antioch, with Carrhæ and Nisibis, all which were under the Persian dominion, as Julius Capitolinus relates in his Gordian.

MORELL.

† The light-armed foot of the Greeks fought with arrows, darts, and slings ; and were placed either in the van to begin an engagement, or on the flank of the wings to gall the enemies cavalry, and prevent their breaking in.

‡ The heavy-armed soldiers engaged with long spears, broad shields, and cutting swords. The Grecian cavalry was not very numerous.

R 3

horse,

horfe, has confumed the whole with a fmall fpark? Nor was our temple deftroyed by a violent ftorm, but in a ferene and cloudlefs fky. Hitherto, Apollo, your altars thirfting for blood, you have remained the conftant and careful guardian of Daphne; and though neglected, and fo far contemned as to be ftripped of your outward ornaments, you acquiefced. But now, when many fheep, many oxen, have been offered to you; when the facred lips of an Emperor * have impreffed your feet; feen by him whom you have exalted, feeing him whom you have proclaimed, and delivered from the hateful neighbourhood of a certain dead body †, which difturbed you, you have withdrawn from the midft of your worfhip.

How can we now expect to be honoured, in future, by thofe who have a veneration for temples and images! When fatigued in our minds, of what a relief, O Jupiter, are we deprived! How pure, how free from all tumults, was the region of Daphne! how much ftill purer was the fhrine! like a haven formed by nature within a haven; both being tranquil, but the inner affording the moft tranquillity. Who did not there lofe his difeafes, his fears, his forrows? Who there wifhed

---

* Julian. The Pagans ufed religioufly to kifs the images of their Gods, if they could, and putting their hands to their mouths, they wafted kiffes to them at a diftance. From this cuftom fome derive the word *adoro*. Thus Job, xxxi. 27. *If my mouth hath kiffed my hand,* &c. WOLFIUS.

† The remains of Babylas. See the Mifopogon, Vol. I. p. 247.

for

for the ifland of the blefled? Ere long will be the Olympic games *; that annual feftival will convene the cities; thefe cities too will come, bringing oxen as victims to Apollo. What then fhall we do? Where fhall we fecrete ourfelves? Which of the Gods will open the earth for us? What herald, what trumpet, but will excite tears? Who now will ftyle the Olympic games a feftival, as this late misfortune fuggefts fo dire a lamentation?

Bring me my bow of horn †,

fays the tragedy. I add, a little in the fpirit of prophecy,

That thus I may attack, and thus deftroy,
The vile incendiary,

O impious deed! O facrilegious foul! O daring hand! Surely this was another Tityus ‡, or Idas §,

---

* Of Antioch. In the adjacent fields a ftadium was built by a fpecial privilege, which had been purchafed from Elis; the Olympic games were regularly celebrated at the expence of the city; and a revenue of thirty thoufand pounds fterling was annually applied to the public pleafures.
GIBBON.

In three of his Epiftles Libanius urges three of his friends to fupply thefe games with wreftlers; and in his Life, pp. 59 and 68, he mentions two orations which he compofed on that folemnity, which are not now extant. A third is in his works, Vol. II. p. 538.

† Δος τοξα μοι κερουλκα. Euripides in Orefte, 268.

‡ Struck by Jupiter with a thunderbolt, for attempting to ravifh Latona. See Odyff. xi. 575. and Æn. vi. 595.

§ — matchlefs Idas, more than man in war.
The God of day ador'd the mother's charms,
Againft the God the father bent his arms.
POPE, Il. ix. 672.

Let us not imitate that daring Idas, who bent his bow, it is faid, againft the God; for this is waging war with Apollo.
LIBANIUS.

R 4

the

the brother of Lynceus, not an archer, indeed, like
the one, or a giant, like the other, but a proficient in
nothing save frenzy towards the Gods.   The sons of
Aloëus *, while they meditated mischief against the
Gods, you, Apollo, quieted by death; but him, bringing fire from afar, your arrow did not arrest, trans-
fixing his heart.   O wicked hand of Telchin † !
O injurious fire ! What did it first catch ? Where
did the evil begin? Seizing the roof, did it descend
to the inferior parts, to the head, the face, the cup ‡,
the tiara, or the flowing robe ? Vulcan, the dif-

* Othus and Ephialtes, who being of a gigantic stature,
and threatening to make war against the Gods, were trans-
fixed and slain by the darts of Apollo and Diana.   See
Æn. vi. 582.

† The Telchines, who inhabited Rhodes, were the inven-
tors of several arts and other things beneficial to mankind.
They are also said first to have made images of the Gods,
and some of the ancient statues were surnamed from them.
Thus among the Lindians Apollo was called Telchinius.
Juno was also styled Telchinia. . . They were called en-
chanters ; and were said to produce, when they pleased,
clouds and rain, and to generate hail, and to be invidious
in teaching their arts.   Diodorus Siculus.
Thus it appears that the Telchinians were a people of
great ingenuity, by which they got a bad name, like our
Roger Bacon, and the German Faustus, who is supposed at
this very day to have dealt with the Devil ; so that this
exclamation, Ω δεξιας Τελχινος, standing in immediate con-
nection with the preceding sentence, Telchin here must be
Apollo.   And perhaps he means to give Apollo a rap here,
as he did Neptune [and Apollo too] in the other Monody. B.
‡ The colossal figure of the deity almost filled the ca-
pacious sanctuary.   He was represented in a bending atti-
tude, with a golden cup in his hand, pouring out a libation
on the earth ; as if he supplicated the venerable mother to
give to his arms the cold and beauteous Daphne.   Gibbon.

                                                penser

penfer of fire, though indebted to the God for his former obliging difcovery *, did not rebuke this wafting flame. Nor did Jupiter, who has the command of rain, pour water on it, though for the unfortunate king of Lydia he extinguifhed the funeral pile †.

What was the firft fuggeftion of him who undertook this enterprife? whence this rafhnefs? how could he retain his fury? how could he avoid abandoning his purpofe through reverence for his beauty of the God? My fancy, O my countrymen, prefents me with the form of the God, and fets before my eyes his image, the complacency of the afpect, the tendernefs of the fkin expreffed in the marble, the fafh over his breaft confining the golden robe, fo that fome parts of it fubfided, and others rofe. What mind had fuch fervour that the whole appearance of the ftatue could not calm? For the God feemed in the act of finging; or as when he was once heard playing on his harp at noon. The fong was in praife of the Earth, on whom, gaping to receive the virgin, and then contracting to con-

---

* Alluding to that paffage of Homer, Odyffey VIII, where, in the loves of Mars and Venus, fung by Demodocus,

> Warn'd by the God who fhed the golden day,
> Stern Vulcan homeward treads the ftarry way,
>   BROOME.

† Crœfus, being placed by Cyrus on a funeral pile, praying to Apollo was fayed by a fhower of rain, which extinguifhed the flames, See Herodotus, I. 87. Julian afcribes this miracle to Jupiter.

ceal

ceal her, he feemed to pour a libation from the golden cup.

At the eruption of flames the traveller exclaimed; the guardian of Daphne, the domeftic prieftefs of the God, was alarmed; the beating of bofoms, and fhrill fhrieks, echoing through the fpacious groves, foon reached the city, diffufing univerfal grief and horror. The prince *, whofe eye had fcarce yet yielded to fleep, at the dreadful intelligence fprung from his bed. Tranfported with fury, and wifhing for the wings of Mercury, he rufhed forth to inveftigate the caufe. Inwardly he burnt no lefs than the temple. The rafters now fell, fcattering the fire below, which deftroyed all that was within its reach; [the ftatue of] Apollo immediately, being near to the roof; then-other ornaments of the temple, the Mufes, the ftatues of the founders, the fplendid marbles, the beautiful pillars. Crowds of fpectators ftood by lamenting, but unable to affift, like thofe, who from land beholding a fhipwreck, can afford no relief but their tears. The Nymphs, leaving their fountains, loudly exclaimed; fo did Jupiter, who fat not far diftant, lamenting, as became him, the tarnifhed honours of his fon; fo did alfo an innumerable throng of Dæmons who inhabit the foreft. Nor lefs was the lamentation of Calliope, in the middle of the

* Julian.

city,

city *, when the high-prieft of the Mufes was injured by the flames * * * * †.

As propitious may'ft thou now be to me, Apollo, as Chryfes rendered thee, when he imprecated vengeance on the Greeks, full of indignation, and " dark as night ‡." Since while we were offering facrifices to thee, and were reftoring whatever had been purloined from thy temple, the objeɛ of our worfhip has been fnatched away from us; like a bridegroom, who, while the garlands are weaving for his nuptials, dies.

* I have an idea that there was a ftatue of Calliope in the middle of Antioch, to which Libanius here alludes; and alfo in one of his Epiftles. See Vol. I. p. 324. And from a paffage in his DCCXXXVIIth Epiftle, to Rufinus, it feems to have been erected to that chief of the Mufes by the great-great-grandfather of that friend.

† Something here is wantlng.

‡ Νυκτι εοικωα. Hom. Il. I. 47.
Breathing revenge, a fudden night he fpread.   Pope 65.

THE

HISTORY

OF THE

EMPEROR JOVIAN.

From the French

Of the Abbé de la BLETERIE.

——— *Infelix brevitate regendi.*

THE
AUTHOR's PREFACE.

AS the empire and religion are at the death of Julian in a kind of crisis which interests the curiosity of the reader, the Life of that prince would remain in some degree imperfect, if the History of Jovian were not annexed to it. Though he reigned only a few months, and though, in our age, when singularity alone may supply the place of merit, his character may be less interesting than that of his predecessor, I may venture to say, that his history presents some memorable facts, and suggests more reflections than the long reigns of many other sovereigns.

It is characterised by two remarkable events, one good, the other bad : I mean the re-establishment of Christianity, which is seen to re-ascend the throne of the Cæsars never again to leave it ; and that fatal treaty of peace, which announces and begins the fall of the Roman greatness. It is thus that *he who dwelleth in the heavens laughs* at the designs of his enemies. Julian flattered himself with restoring his empire to its ancient splendor.

He

He had, or feemed to have, moft of the talents
neceffary for the execution of this plan ; yet the
imprudence of Julian muft have been the caufe,
or, at leaft, the occafion, of the ruin of the empire.
Julian made no doubt of fuppreffing the Chriftian
religion : but Providence had decreed that he
fhould be the laft Pagan Emperor. The war which
he waged with Sapor was preparatory to that
which he meditated againft us [the Gauls]. He
thought that the conqueft of Perfia would give him
fufficient leifure and authority to complete by force
of arms the work which his cunning and his artifices
had only fketched ; yet it was really that war
which preferved the Chriftians. from the other
which he was preparing againft them ; it was that
war which took him out of the world; and gave
the Romans an Emperor who was zealous enough
to make Chriftianity triumph by means worthy; of
the true religion.

Hitherto the reign of Jovian has remained loft,
as it were, in general hiftory. I fhall be thanked,
perhaps, for fnatching it from oblivion. I have
treated it with all the care of which I am capable,
and I dare not fay how much it has coft me.
Hiftory is not a compilation of facts collected at
random, a brilliant collection of pretty thoughts, a
tiffue of learned differtations. It is neither a panegyric, nor a fatire ; it ought to be an impartial
and difinterefted narration, fimple and natural,
though fentimental, always eafy in its ftyle, even
when

when it offers the refult of many refearches and difcuffions. It ought, if I may fo fay, to render the reader contemporary with the events, to inftruct without fatiguing him, to enlighten without dazzling him, to make him think, and to give him the pleafure of believing that he thinks for himfelf, not faying every thing, and leaving nothing to be wifhed, allowing neither too much nor too little to conjecture, and removing apparent contradictions by lucky difcoveries; in a word, it fhould fupply the place of original authors to thofe who have it not in their power to read them, and enable thofe, who can confult them, to read them with more pleafure and emolument. I have endeavoured to write in this manner the Hiftory of Jovian. I do not flatter myfelf with having fucceeded; happy if connoiffeurs find fome marks of refemblance between the execution and the idea.

HISTORY

OF THE

EMPEROR JOVIAN.

A. D.
363. IT may be seen, in the Life of Julian, that that prince, after paſſing the Tigris above Cteſiphon, by an extravagance which even ſucceſs could not excuſe, burned his fleet and proviſions *. He was deſirous

* He deſtroyed, in a ſingle hour, the whole navy, which had been transported above five hundred miles, at ſo great an expence of toil, of treaſure, and of blood. Twelve, or, at the moſt, twenty-two ſmall veſſels were ſaved, to accompany on carriages the march of the army, and to form occaſional bridges for the paſſage of the rivers. A ſupply of twenty days proviſions was reſerved for the uſe of the ſoldiers; and the reſt of the magazines, with a fleet of eleven hundred veſſels, which rode at anchor in the Tigris, were abandoned to the flames, by the abſolute command of the Emperor. The Chriſtian biſhops, Gregory and Auguſtin, inſult the madneſs of the apoſtate, who executed, with his own hands, the ſentence of divine juſtice. Their authority, of leſs weight perhaps in a military queſtion, is confirmed by the cool judgement of an experienced ſoldier [Ammianus], who was himſelf ſpectator of the conflagration, and who could not diſapprove the reluctant murmurs of the troops. Yet there are not wanting ſome ſpecious, and perhaps ſolid, reaſons, which might juſtify the reſolution of Julian. The navigation of the Euphrates never aſcended above Babylon, nor that of the Tigris above Opis. The diſtance of the laſt-mentioned city from the Roman camp was not very conſiderable; and Julian muſt ſoon have renounced the vain and impracticable attempt of

forcing

firous of penetrating into the heart of Aſſyria; but at the end of ſome days march, finding neither corn nor forage, becauſe the Perſians had laid all the country waſte, he was obliged to approach the Tigris. Being unable to paſs it for want of boats, he took for the model of his retreat that of the ten thouſand *, and reſolved to gain, like them, the country of the Carduci, called in his time

forcing upwards a great fleet againſt the ſtream of a rapid river, which in ſeveral places was embarraſſed by natural or artificial cataracts. The power of ſails and oars was inſufficient; it became neceſſary to tow the ſhips againſt the current of the river; the ſtrength of 20,000 ſoldiers was exhauſted in this tedious and ſervile labour; and if the Romans continued to march along the banks of the Tigris, they could only expect to return home without atchieving any enterpriſe worthy of the genius or fortune of their leader. If, on the contrary, it was adviſeable to advance into the inland country, the deſtruction of the fleet and magazines was the only meaſure which could ſave that valuable prize from the hands of the numerous and active troops which might ſuddenly be poured from the gates of Cteſiphon. Had the arms of Julian been victorious, we ſhould now admire the conduct, as well as the courage, of a hero, who, by depriving his ſoldiers of the hopes of a retreat, left them only the alternative of death or conqueſt. Recollect the ſucceſsful and applauded raſhneſs of Agathocles and Cortez, who burnt their ſhips on the coaſts of Africa and Mexico. GIBBON.

* ——————————————— the martial throng,
Up Tigris' banks who wound their march along;
O'er wilds and mountains held their toilſome way,
By hoſts aſſaulted, and the ſolar ray;
By thirſt, by famine, by eternal ſnows —
Whom heaven and earth united to oppoſe.
Unconquer'd ſtill the Greeks each peril meet,
Regain their ſhores, and dignify retreat. IRWIN.

                    Corduenne,

Corduenne, a name which is ſtill found in that of Curdes and Curdiſtan. Corduenne, then ſubjeċt to the Romans, is ſituated on the north of Aſſyria. Thus marching on that ſide, Julian had the Tigris on his left, and went up towards the ſource of that river.

Superior in every attack to the lieutenants of Sapor, whether they waited for him in line of battle, or contented themſelves with inſulting him on his march, he was ſtill advancing, when on the 26th of June, 363, repulſing the enemy with too much ardour, he received a wound, of which he died the night following *.

At the death of Julian the Roman army was in a ſtrange ſituation; victorious, but in want of every thing. Corduenne, its only reſource, was ſtill far diſtant. To reach this province it muſt traverſe without proviſions, beneath a burning ſky, a ruined country, ſuſtain in this march the continual at-

* The defeċtion of this great man from the pureſt of all religions cannot be defended, though it may be accounted for; and his averſion and diſcountenance to Chriſtians ſuit not the informed and liberal mind of Julian in other points. It will ſuffice to ſay, that his life ſeems to have belied the name of Apoſtate, which he brought upon himſelf by his deviation from the faith in which he was educated. If the paths of Virtue lead to the temple of Truth, he invariably trod them; and may charitably be ſuppoſed to have arrived, by an indirect courſe, at the divine goal. The circumſtances of his death are ſo ſimilar to thoſe of Epaminondas, that we muſt be rejoiced to find their lives were equally dignified by purſuits that rendered their end immortal.   IRWIN.

tacks

tacks of the Perſians, always formidable though vanquiſhed, becauſe they were as ready to rally as to fly, and, beſides, as the death of Julian had raiſed the hopes of king Sapor.

It ſeemed difficult to remain without a chief; the moments were precious. On the 27th of June, therefore, at break of day, the officers met to chooſe a ſucceſſor to Julian, who had juſt expired. The creatures of that prince *, and thoſe who ſtill remained of the old court †, having neither the ſame intereſts, nor the ſame views, all earneſtly deſired an Emperor of their own faction; but as neither of the two factions had had time to concert among themſelves, all their ſuffrages, not one excepted, were united in favour of Salluſt the ſecond, Præfect of the Prætorium of the Eaſt. This illuſtrious Pagan, whoſe virtue cannot be ſufficiently admired and lamented, completed the juſtification of that choice by the firmneſs with which he refuſed to load himſelf with a burthen too oppreſſive, he ſaid, both for his age and infirmities. A ſubaltern officer ‡, then ſeeing the embarraſſment into which the perſevering refuſal of Salluſt had thrown the aſſembly, ſaid to the generals, " What

* Nevitta, Dagalaïphus, and the Gallic officers.   B.

† Arintheus, Victor, &c.   B.

‡ Thus I tranſlate that expreſſion, *honoratior aliquis miles.* I ſuſpect that Ammianus thus deſcribes himſelf.   B.

The modeſt and judicious hiſtorian deſcribes the ſcene of the election, at which he was undoubtedly preſent (xxv. 5.)
GIBBON.

" would

" would you do, if the prince, inftead of march-
" ing in perfon, had given you the command of
" the army? You would only think of extricating
" yourfelves from this dilemma. Act, as if he
" were ftill living; and when we have once reached
" Mefopotamia, in concert with the army of ob-
" fervation we will choofe an Emperor, whofe
" election cannot be contefted." This perhaps
would have been the beft advice; but fome on a
fudden exalted their voices in favour of Jovian, and
by their tumultuous clamours drew away all the
reft, without giving them time to confider.

Flavius Claudius Jovianus, aged about 33
years, was the firft of the Emperor's guards *. He
had conducted the corpfe of Conftantius to the im
perial city; and as, according to cuftom, fitting in
the funereal car, he received in fome fort the
honours which were paid to that prince, it was
imagined, after the event, that this honourable, but
tranfient and mournful, employment had been the
prognoftic and image of his future grandeur †.

The

---

* Jovian was not captain of the guards, as fome have
thought; but only what was called *domefticorum ordinis primus*. What rank this was we know not. *Domeftici*, or *pro-
tectores domeftici*, are certainly the body-guards.   B.

The *primus*, or *primicerius*, enjoyed the dignity of a fenator, and though only a tribune, he ranked with the military dukes. *Cod. Theodofian. l.* vi. *tit.* xxiv. Thefe privileges
are perhaps more recent than the time of Jovian. Gibbon.

† Wherever the Emperors paffed, deputies were fent
to them: they were harangued, famples of the provifions
intended for the troops were prefented to them, the horfes
were

The nobility of his family afcended no higher than count Varronian, his father, born in the territory of the city of Singidon in Myfia, and probably a foldier of fortune, who, for his merit, had been appointed to the command of the Jovians: Such was the appellation of a body of troops formed by Diocletian, who, it is known, had taken the fur-, name of Jovius. It was owing perhaps to his regard for the troop of which he was chief, that Varronian made one of his children bear the name of Jovian. This officer, full of years and glory, ftill enjoyed his high reputation in retirement. Some even pretend that it conftituted the prin- cipal merit of his fon. But to refute them it is fufficient to fay, that though Jovian had declared that he would rather quit the fervice than renounce the Chriftian religion, Julian did not ceafe to keep him near his perfon, and to take him with him, when he fet out on his fatal expedition. Julian was well acquainted with his talents. A confeffor of the faith, whom an apoftate and intolerant monarch thought worthy to retain a place of con- fidence, was certainly no ordinary fubject. The Pagans themfelves do juftice to his valour, and if

were fhewn to them, &c. which the public maintained for the ufe of thofe who travelled by order of the court. The fame ceremonial was obferved with regard to the Emperors after their deaths. On that occafion he who attended the corpfe acted and fpoke, without doubt, in the name of the late Emperor. It was a kind of fovereignty which expired on the tomb of the prince. See Amm. *l.* xxi. *c. ult.* B.

 they

they sometimes speak of him as a timid prince, this reproach falls rather on the politician than the warrior.

To finish his portrait, without copying the Christian authors, who might here perhaps seem less credible, I will chiefly confine myself to the testimony of Ammianus and Eutropius, both Pagans, who were in the Persian war, and of whom the former served in the guards with Jovian. With the sentiments of a generous and beneficent soul this prince united affable manners, a fund of gaiety which induced him to joke with those who approached him, sufficient application and activity, but too little experience. He had such a knowledge of mankind as promised discernment in the distribution of employments; some literature *, and great regard for men of learning; an extreme attachment to his religion, but a great respect to conscience, which he thought accountable only to God. Zealous without bitterness, and moderate without indifference, he professed orthodoxy; but he persecuted neither heretics, nor even Pagans. It is said, that these excellent qualities were accompanied with some faults. Ammianus accuses him of loving wine and the table, and some other pleasures still more unbecoming a Christian. Men are apt to be inconsistent, and their belief has not always a sufficient influence on their morals.

---

* This seems to me the sense of those words of Ammianus, *Mediocriter eruditus, magisque benevolus.*   B.

" But,"

" But," fays the fame author, " the refpect which
" he owed to his purple would have corrected
" them *." Jovian was in ftature much above the
common ftandard, and large in proportion, fo that
it was difficult to find an imperial habit that would
fit him. He was round-fhouldered, as he appears
alfo on his medals, and had a majeftic air, but a
heavy walk. The gaiety of his mind fparkled on
his face and in his eyes. He is ranked among the
good princes. Perhaps he would have been placed
among the greateft, if he had afcended the throne
at a juncture lefs fatal, and if he had reigned
longer.

The army was ftill ignorant, it feems, of the
death of Julian. It was beginning to leave the
camp, in order to march, when the new Emperor
appeared, and, invefted with the marks of his
dignity, repaired to the different quarters to fhew
himfelf to the foldiers. The name of *Jovian* refounded on all fides; but the refemblance of this
name to that of *Julian* caufing a miftake, fome
cried, JULIAN AUGUSTUS. Their cries, foon approaching by degrees to the vanguard already at a
diftance from the camp, were repeated with the
moft lively tranfports. It was imagined that the
wound of Julian was not dangerous, and that he
was leaving his tent, according to cuftom, in the

* Thefe are the hiftorian's own words, *Edax tamen et
vino venerique indulgens; quæ vitia imperiali verecundiâ forfitan
correxiffet.* B.

4   midft

midſt of acclamations. But this tranſient joy was immediately ſucceeded by affliction and tears, as ſoon as the preſence of Jovian announced what had juſt happened.

Such is the recital of an eye-witneſs, a Pagan indeed, but an impartial writer; I mean Ammianus Marcellinus. His teſtimony does not allow us to underſtand literally what Theodoret wrote about half a century after him, of the perfect unanimity with which all the army demanded Jovian for Emperor, while the officers were aſſembled for the election. Nothing, however, obliges us to reject what the ſame father adds: " Jovian," he ſays, " was placed on a tribunal prepared in haſte ; the " names of Auguſtus and Emperor were given " him. The prince then ſaid to the ſoldiers, with " his uſual frankneſs, that, being a Chriſtian, he " could not command Pagans, and that he ſaw the " wrath of the living God ready to fall on an army of " idolaters." " You command Chriſtians," exclaimed with one voice thoſe who heard him. " The reign " of ſuperſtition has been too ſhort to efface from " our minds and our hearts the inſtructions of the " great Conſtantine and his ſon Conſtantius. Im- " piety has not had time to take root in the ſouls " of thoſe who have embraced it *."

While Jovian received the homage of the army,

* Ammianus, calmly purſuing his narrative, overthrows this legend by a ſingle ſentence : *Hoſtus pro Joviano extiſque inſpectis, pronuntiatum eſt*, &c. XXV. 6.   .GIBBON.

an

an enfign of whom he had reafon to complain *, fearing his refentment, deferted to the enemy. He found Sapor, who had juft joined his troops, at the head of a confiderable reinforcement. This fugitive, admitted to an audience of the great king, told him, that " Julian was no more; and that the fervants " of the army had tumultuoufly fupplied his place " with the phantom of an Emperor, one only of " the body-guard, a man without vigour, without " courage, without capacity." At this unexpected news the monarch ftarted with joy. The valour of Julian, and the rapidity of his conquefts, had fo alarmed him, that he paid no attention to his hair, and ate on the ground as in the greateft calamities. The Perfians, even after the death of that formidable enemy, reprefented him, in their hieroglyphical paintings, under the emblem of thunder, or of a lion vomiting flames; fuch was the terror with which he had impreffed them. Sapor, who faw himfelf at the fummit of his wifhes at the very time when he thought himfelf on the brink of deftruction, flattered himfelf that the Romans would no longer ftand before him, and detached a body of cavalry † full fpeed to fall on their rear-guard, with the troops that had fought the preceding day.

Sapor had no doubt that the Romans were on their march; but the election of Jovian had fuf-

---

* He was an enemy of Varronian. By mangling the reputation of the father, he deferved the hatred of the fon. B.
† Perhaps the ten thoufand *Immortals*.   GIBBON.

pended

pended their departure; and this prince thought of deferring it till the next day. The Pagans, for all were not converted, having offered some sacrifices of thankſgiving for his election to the empire, the augurs found in the entrails of the victims that all would be loſt, if they remained in the camp, but that they ſhould gain some advantage, if they began their march. As the Emperor knew how much ſuperſtition can affect courage, he did not heſitate to purſue the latter. The Romans had ſcarce left their entrenchments when they ſaw themſelves attacked. Their cavalry was at firſt put into diſorder by the elephants which preceded that of the Perſians; but the legionaries ſo vigorouſly ſuſtained the ſhock of the hoſtile ſquadrons, that they forced them to retire. On the ſide of the Barbarians, beſides ſome elephants, a great number of ſoldiers were left on the field. The Romans, however, paid too dearly for that advantage, as it coſt them three of their braveſt officers *.

After having paid them the laſt duties, as well as the time and place would permit, they encamped near a caſtle named Sumera † ; and on the next day, for want of a better defence, they entrenched

---

* Tribunes.

† On the banks of the Tigris, about one hundred miles above Cteſiphon. In the ninth century, Sumere, or Samara, became, with a ſlight change of name, the royal reſidence of the Khalifs of the houſe of Abbas. The obſcure villages of the inland country are irrecoverably loſt; nor can we name the field of battle where Julian fell.

GIBBON.

them-

themfelves in a valley, furrounded by eminences which left only one outlet. From the top of thofe hills, covered with trees, the Perfians rained on the camp a. fhower of arrows, which they accompanied with the bittereft taunts, calling the Romans " traitors, and the murderers of their " Emperor." Thofe reproaches originated from the frivolous difcourfe of fome deferters, and the endeavours which the great king ineffectually employed to difcover who had delivered him from Julian. Sapor having offered a reward proportioned to the importance of the fervice without any one appearing to claim it, he concluded that Julian had been killed by one of his own fubjects; as if it were impoffible for that rafh prince to have been ftruck either by a dart thrown at random *, or that the horfeman, who wounded him, might himfelf have loft his life.

Libanius indeed has difplayed all his rhetoric to give fome colour to this accufation. This fophift abfolutely infifts that the fatal blow, which fhortened the days of Julian, came from a Chriftian hand directed and employed by the chief of the Chriftians †. By this Libanius probably means some

---

* Thus Ahab was killed by *a certain man who drew a bow at a venture.* 1 Kings xxii. 34.

† Εϊολην πληρων τω σφωι αυἱωι αρχοϊϊ. *Implens acceptum ab eo qui præeft illis mandatum.* Perhaps it fhould be tranflated *præerat*; as the oration of Libanius was not compofed till the reign of Theodofius. I have retained in the

French

some distinguished bishop, whom he makes the author of a conspiracy formed against the life of Julian. He pretends that he was privately acquainted with all the particulars of that dreadful tragedy, and that there needed only public authority to unravel and ascertain its horrors. Libanius, however, utters only conjectures that are easily confuted by other conjectures as probable as his; and as to the pretended conspiracy, the profound silence of all writers of the same religion is a proof either that they had not heard it mentioned, or at least that they considered it as a fable *. Those authors, and Zosimus himself, say expressly, or plainly suppose, that Julian was wounded by a soldier of Sapor. The malignity of Zosimus is well known: all the evil which he has not said of the Christians, and which others have said of them, has much the air of a calumny.

French the equivocal expression of the Greek. It is impossible to know what bishop Libanius had in view. It is surmised that it might have been either St. Basil or St. Gregory of Nazianzus. For my part, I think that in the time of Julian there was no bishop in the East who deserved the name of " chief of the Christians" better than St. Athanasius.   B.

* Above sixteen years after the death of Julian, the charge was solemnly and vehemently urged in a public oration, addressed by Libanius to the Emperor Theodosius. The suspicions are unsupported by fact or argument, and we can only esteem the generous zeal of the sophist of Antioch for the cold and neglected ashes of his friend.

        GIBBON.

After

After all, that a rhetorician, like Libanius, a Pagan even to madness, should think the Christians capable of attempting the life of Julian, is not surprising. That it is possible for an ignorant and fanatical Christian to think that he shall, immortalise himself both in this world and the next, by delivering the church from an implacable persecutor, history unhappily affords too many examples. But that an ecclesiastical historian, like Sozomen, should be tempted to canonise so detestable an action, might perhaps not be credited on my assertion. Let him speak for himself: "It is not "improbable," says that writer, "that one of "those who then served in the army might have "reflected, that the destroyers of tyrants were "highly extolled, not only by the ancient Greeks, "but by others even to our times, as men who for "the common liberty of all did not hesitate to die, "having chearfully assisted their countrymen, "friends, and relations. No one certainly," continues Sozomen, "can easily blame him, who, for "the sake of God and his religion, has acted such "a manly part *." Sozomen, it seems, had studied profane antiquity more than the morality of the gospel and the spirit of true Christianity. Let it be observed, that this historian was not a father

---

* *Sozom. Hist. Ecclef. l.* VI. *c.* 2.

Sozomen applauds the Greek doctrine of *tyrannicide*; but the whole passage, which a Jesuit might have translated, is prudently suppressed by the president Cousin.

GIBBON.

of

of the church, that he has no authority in matters of doctrine, that his language is here contrary to all tradition, that he wrote towards the middle of the fifth century ; and that he is the firſt in whom we perceive ſome marks of that anti-chriſtian fanaticiſm. But it is time to reſume the thread of the hiſtory.

While their enemies, poſted on the heights, were inſulting the army, a detachment of cavalry forced the gate of the camp, called the Prætorian gate ; and were very near penetrating even to the imperial tent : but they were repulſed with loſs. The Romans afterwards encamped at Carche ; from whence on the ſucceeding day, July 1, they arrived near the city of Dura *, which muſt not be confounded with another of the ſame name, ſituated in Meſopotamia. Four days were there loſt by the obſtinacy of the Barbarians. As ſoon as the army was on the march, they harraſſed it by continual ſkirmiſhes, ſometimes in rear, ſometimes in flank. If it faced about to receive them, by degrees they gave ground, being only deſirous of retarding its march, and leaving to famine the care of fighting for them.

The fear of the worſt misfortunes makes men credulous and ready to adopt the moſt hazardous expedients. On a ſudden a report being ſpread that the

* Dura was a fortified place in the wars of Antiochus, againſt the rebels of Media and Perſia. (Polybius, *l.* v. *c.* 48. 52.)   Gibbon.

frontiers

frontiers of the empire are not far distant; on this false suppofition the foldier will no longer coaft the Tigris, but clamoroufly infifts on being allowed to pafs it. The Emperor, with the principal officers, oppofes this rafh project in vain. In vain, fhewing this river always fo rapid, and then fwelled by the melting of the fnows of Armenia, he reprefents that moft of them cannot fwim, that the enemy is mafter of the two banks, and that, if they gain the other fide, it will only be to fall into his hands. Thefe fage remonftrances are difregarded. The clamours increafe, threats are added; every thing breathes fedition. It was neceffary to allow a number of Gauls and Germans * to attempt the paffage. Jovian flattered himfelf that if they perifhed, the reft would become more tractable; or, if they were fo lucky as to fucceed, he might reafonably make an attempt to tranfport the army.

By favour of the night, five hundred able fwimmers crofs the Tigris with more eafe than could have been expected, and find the Perfians, who guarded the oppofite bank, buried in a profound fleep. They make a great flaughter, and as foon as the day begins to break, they raife their hands, and throw their cloaths into the air, to announce their fuccefs. The army, anxious to follow them, urges the engineers to conftruct a kind of [floating]

---

* The text of Ammianus gives *Sarmatis*; but it is probably faulty. Soon after, the fame author calls them Germans.   B.

bridge, which they propofed to make of fheep
fkins faftened together *. They laboured on it
two days; but it was impoffible to fix it on
account of the violence and rapidity of the ftream.
The foldiers, having confumed the provifions that
they had left, became defperate, and rather chofe
to perifh fword in hand than languifh under the
horrors of a flow and cruel death.

Ths Perfians, on their fide, had alfo much to
lament. The intoxication of Sapor was already
difpelled; from the moft prefumptuous confidence,
he relapfed into an extreme perplexity; he faw his
country laid wafte, his towns taken by affault, his
troops, always defeated when they dared to wait
for the enemy, having no refource but in flight,
and confiderably diminifhed by the lofs of an innumerable multitude of men, and almoft all the
elephants. Every day fome new check made him
perceive that the valour of the Romans was not
buried † with Julian. Animated with the genius
of that conqueror, they feemed to think as much,
and perhaps more, of revenging him than of fur-
viving him. Famine itfelf could not force from
them the leaft propofal of peace. Was Sapor
certain of avoiding a battle? And if he muft fight,

---

* Covered with a floor of earth and fafcines. A fimilar
expedient was propofed to the leaders of the ten thoufand,
and wifely rejected. It appears, from our modern travellers, that rafts floating on bladders perform the trade
and navigation of the Tigris.　　　　　GIBBON.

† *Enfeve[lie]*. A flight inaccuracy. Julian was not then
" buried."

what

what had he not to fear from men refolved to determine their fate, either by gaining a complete victory, or at leaft by rendering their defeat fatal even to the conquerors? Could he flatter himfelf with annihilating the Roman army, he was not ignorant that Julian had left in Mefopotamia 40,000 men, under the command of his relation Procopius: at length the vaft provinces of the empire might eafily furnifh other legions, who, by attacking Perfia when exhaufted and terrified, might overthrow the throne of the Artaxerxides already tottering.

Amidft thefe melancholy reflections, he was informed of the fuccefsful temerity of the Gauls and Germans. This exploit of a handful of determined men alarms him, and makes him fenfible of what a whole army of defperadoes will be capable. Immediately he turns all his thoughts towards an accommodation with the Romans; he does not hefitate to make the firft advances, proceeding to effentials, and defiring, at any rate, to commence a negociation, which, in the prefent circumftances, muft infallibly terminate to his advantage. Thus, contrary to their expectations, the Romans faw the Surena (he was the general of the Perfian cavalry), arrive in their camp, with another lord *. " The " Great King our mafter," faid the deputies to

---

* Sextus Rufus (*de Provinciis, c. 29.*) embraces a poor fubterfuge of national vanity. *Tanta reverentia nominis Romani fuit, ut à Perfis primus de pace fermo haberetur.*

GIBBON.

T   Jovian

Jovian and the principal officers, " is not dazzled
" by profperity; he knows the fituation to which
" fortune has reduced you; but he knows ftill
" better the uncertainty of human affairs. Sapor
" refpects unfuccefsful virtue, even in his enemies.
" He efteems you enough to feek your alliance,
" and to offer you peace on equitable terms."

As the Romans were fupported only by defpair,
the hope of peace weakened them at once, and
made, it may be faid, their arms fall from their
hands. Jovian, in particular, was eager to enjoy
the empire, and to infure to himfelf its poffeffion
by repairing fpeedily to the capital. How did he
know, but that, in his abfence, fome ambitious
leader, Procopius for inftance, then at the head
of an army, might feize the diadem? At that time,
thofe who affumed the purple did not even deign
to feek pretexts to colour their enterprife; and
Procopius, as he was related to Julian, might
allege the rights of confanguinity. The propofals
therefore of Sapor were embraced with eagernefs.
They were vague, embarraffed, equivocal, and liable
to great difcuffions. At all events, this able politician defigned to protract the negociation, in order
to famifh the Romans more and more.

The Emperor, on the contrary, impatient to conclude it, difpatched, without lofing a moment,
Salluft, with Arintheus *, to draw from Sapor
himfelf

* Libanius puts the general Victor in the room of
Arintheus. The latter was reckoned one of the greateft
captains

himfelf fomething determinate. They had many conferences equally long and intricate by the management of the old monarch, who negociated peace as he waged war. The more the Romans advanced, the more he retreated. He formed fuppofitions upon fuppofitions, and raifed difficulties upon difficulties. Now he required time, then he would no longer grant what he had promifed, and promifed what he had refufed. Befides, he feemed to think it ftrange that the death of Julian was not revenged; for he ftill thought that that prince had been killed by a Roman * ; and as the deputies probably did not allow the fact, " if one " of my generals †," added he, " had loft his

captains of his age. Prodigies are related of his valour. He was of an extraordinary ftature, yet fo well made, that, St. Bafil fays, he was confidered as the model of a man. His ftrength was equal to his courage. His looks alone had made him gain fome battles. He received baptifm before his death. We have a confolatory letter written by St. Bafil to the widow of Arintheus, who had been the protector of the churches, and the friend of St. Bafil. We have alfo a letter from the fame faint to this general, in which he praifes him for his generofity and liberality, of which every one perceived the effects. See M. de Tillemont on the Emperor Valens, *Hiftoire des Empereurs*, tom. V. p. 100.   B.

* For the Perfians alfo had heard this report, and, in confequence, before Jovian made peace with them, the common foldiers reviled the Romans as traitors and murderers of the greateft of princes, as we learn from Ammianus, xxv. 6.   OLEARIUS.

† Libanius heard thefe words of Sapor to the Roman ambaffadors, no doubt, from Salluft himfelf, with whom he was extremely intimate, as four of his epiftles to Salluft fufficiently atteft.   *Ibid.*

" late

" life in a battle, thofe, who, being near his
" perfon, had the cowardice not to die with him,
" fhould not efcape my juft refentment. I would
" inftantly fend their heads to the family of that
" officer." We here difcern the ideas and lah-
guage of an Eaftern monarch. Sapor, by affecting
to intereft himfelf in revenging Julian, was alfo
defirous perhaps of teftifying his efteem for that
prince, with a view to infinuate, that he had little
regard for his fucceffor, and that he no longer
feared the Romans.

They became lefs formidable every moment. A
devouring famine confumed them, while by chi-
canery and affected delays he trifled with their
deputies. " We paffed four days," fays Ammianus, " in a ftate more cruel than the fevereft
" punifhments. During that time, if the Emperor,
" difcovering the artifices of Sapor, before he
" fent deputies to that prince, had continually
" gained ground, he would certainly have arrived
" at the ftrong places of Corduenne, which then
" belonged to us; and which would have fupplied
" us with provifions in abundance. We were but
" a hundred miles diftant *."

* About thirty leagues.   B.
It is prefumptuous to controvert the opinion of Amni-
anus, a foldier and a fpectator.   Yet it is difficult to underftand, how the mountains of Corduenne could extend over
the plain of Affyria, as low as the conflux of the Tigris
and the great Zab: or *how* an army of fixty thoufand
men could march one hundred miles in four days.
                                             GIBBON,

I wifh

I wish Ammianus had clearly explained the possibility of this march. If I am not mistaken, this is his idea. Sapor himself had occasion for a peace, and only offered it to his enemies because he feared to encounter them. Jovian therefore should have opposed craft to craft, should have expressed less eagerness for peace, should, however, have given good words to the envoys of Sapor, should have pursued his route, should have sent deputies to that prince, and have treated on his march. Sapor, from the fear of being forced to a battle, or of thwarting the accommodation, would not have attacked the Romans, and would have been taken in his own snare. Ammianus was a soldier: he understood his profession, and knew the country. He saw things near, and he saw them with reflection; to be convinced of this we need only read him. The judgement of an historian like him must embarrass the defenders of Jovian.

When Sapor thought he had subdued the Romans by famine, he threw off the mask, and, speaking with authority, he declared, first, that he insisted on their restoring to him, for so he expressed himself, the five provinces beyond the Tigris *, formerly conquered by the Emperor

---

* Most of these provinces were on this side the Tigris with regard to the Romans. In calling them " beyond the " Tigris" they conformed to the language of the Persians, whom they were on the other side of that river. As to the particular names of the provinces, they are not the same in all authors.   B.

Maximian-

Maximian-Galerius from King Narseus, his grandfather; viz. Arzanena, Moxoënia, Zabdicenia,
Rehimenia, and Corduenne. Secondly, that besides
these, there should be ceded to him fifteen castles,
the city of Nisibis, that of Singara in Mesopotamia, and another important place called the Castle
of the Moors (*Castra Maurorum*). Thirdly, that
they would engage to interfere no more in the
affairs of Armenia, and even refuse king Arsaces
the assistance which he might demand against the
Persians.

"It would have been a thousand times better,"
says Ammianus, "to have tried the chance of
" arms than to have accepted any one of these
" conditions." In fact, under pretence of a resti-
tution, which is not honourable but when it is
voluntary, to cede five provinces, annexed to the
empire for about seventy years, was to pay a
ransom the more humiliating as there were added
to it almost all Mesopotamia, and even Nisibis,
which had been possessed by the Romans ever since
the wars of Mithridates; Nisibis, the bulwark of
the East, and the rock which wrecked the pride of
Sapor *.

By

* He acquired, by a single article, the impregnable city
of Nisibis, which had sustained, in three successive sieges,
the effort of his arms.   GIBBON.
The treaty of Dura is recorded with grief, or indignation, by Ammianus (xxv. 7.) ; Libanius (*Orat. Parent.*
c 142. p. 364.) ; Zosimus (l. iii. p. 190, 191.) ; Gregory
Nazianzen (*Orat.* iv. p. 117, 118. who imputes the distress

to

By binding his hands with regard to Armenia, Jovian surrendered at discretion, to a revengeful, perfidious, and cruel prince, Arsaces *, the faithful ally of the Romans, to whom he was connected by the nearest and most honourable ties, as Constantius had made him espouse Olympias, daughter of the Præfect Ablavius, who had been contracted to his brother the Emperor Constans. Sapor was the declared enemy of the Christians; and, what must personally affect Jovian, Arsaces, by his attachment to Christianity, had merited, like Jovian himself, disgrace from Julian. King Arsaces had been essentially serviceable to the empire. He had just ravaged the provinces of Persia bordering on Armenia. That was his crime in the sight of Sapor, and the secret reason, but easy to be guessed, for which he required them to refuse him assistance.

These considerations could not escape Jovian; but he was besieged by a crowd of flatterers, who

to Julian, the deliverance to Jovian); and Eutropius (x. 17.) The last-mentioned writer, who was present in a military station, styles this peace *necessariam quidem, sed ignobilem.*
Ibid.

* See p. 186. The unsuspicious Tiranus was persuaded by the repeated assurances of insidious friendship to deliver his person into the hands of a faithless and cruel enemy. In the midst of a splendid entertainment, he was bound in chains of silver, as an honour due to the blood of the Arsacides; and, after a short confinement in the Tower of oblivion at Ecbatana, he was released from the miseries of life, either by his own dagger, or by that of an assassin. The kingdom of Armenia was reduced to the state of a Persian province. *Ibid.*

incessantly

inceffantly reprefented to him Procopius as an enemy more dangerous than Sapor *. . . His fear of Procopius was well grounded ; and it may be faid that his revolt † juftified it two years after, if, neverthelefs, this fear itfelf did not occafion his revolt. Befides, there is the greateft probability, that the irreparable lofs of four days, imprudently confumed in inactivity, had rendered the army utterly incapable of fighting, and reduced Jovian to the indifpenfible neceffity of accepting the peace. Thus the treaty was perhaps lefs the work of his timid policy than of his inability.

Be that as it may, to the difgrace of the Roman name, this prince received the law from Sapor, and agreed to all the articles propofed. All that he obtained, and that with difficulty, was, that the garrifons of the places ceded as well as the inhabitants of Nifibis and Singara, fhould retire into the territories of the Romans. Arfaces was included in the treaty, of which he did not fail to be foon after made the victim. On both fides a peace, or rather a truce, of thirty years was fworn, and in the mean time hoftages ‡ were given for the performance of the treaty.

* La Bleterie has expreffed, in a long direct oration, thefe fpecious confiderations of public and private intereft.
GIBBON.

This harangue being imaginary, I have omitted it.

† For an account of his revolt and death, fee p. 221. note

‡ Remora, Victor, and Bellovædius, tribunes, on the part of the Romans ; and Bineſes, with three other fatraps, on that of the Perfians.   AMMIANUS.

Rufinus

Rufinus and Theodoret, deceived by probability, pretend that Sapor furnished the Romans with provisions *. Nothing was more natural; but without doubt, the Persians had no magazines, and subsisted themselves with difficulty in an exhausted country. At least, it is certain that the Romans gained by that disgraceful peace not even the permission to deviate from the banks of the Tigris †, where the roads were rough and craggy, in order to cross the country to the place where they intended to pass that river. Thither they proceeded by long marches, continually tormented by famine, to which was also added want of water. Many, collecting their expiring strength, withdrew from

* Such a fact is probable, but undoubtedly false. See Tillemont, *Hist. des Empereurs*, tom. iv. p. 702. GIBBON.

† In the neighbourhood of the same river, at no very considerable distance from the fatal station of Dura, the ten thousand Greeks, without generals, or guides, or provisions, were abandoned, above 1200 miles from their native country, to the resentment of a victorious monarch. The difference of their conduct and success depended much more on their character than on their situation. Instead of tamely resigning themselves to the secret deliberations and private views of a single person, the united councils of the Greeks were inspired by the generous enthusiasm of a popular assembly; where the mind of each citizen is filled with the love of glory, the pride of freedom, and the contempt of death. Conscious of their superiority over the Barbarians in arms and discipline, they disdained to yield, they refused to capitulate; every obstacle was surmounted by their patience, courage, and military skill; and the memorable retreat of the ten thousand exposed and insulted the weakness of the Persian monarchy. GIBBON. See p. 256. note *.

the

the body of the army, and endeavoured to fwim
crofs the Tigris.   Moſt of them periſhed ; the reſt
fell into the hands of the Perſians and Saracens
poſted on the other ſhore.   Theſe Barbarians, in-
cenſed by the maſſacre of their companions whom
the Gauls and Germans had ſlaughtered, put to
death all who eſcaped the waters, or if they ſpared
ſome of them, it was only to ſell them, and ſend
them to ſuch a diſtance that the Romans could
never reclaim them.

When the Emperor and the army were arrived
at the place of paſſage, which no author, not even
Ammianus, has taken care to point out to us, after
ſome ſlight preparations, the trumpet gave the
ſignal.   It is impoſſible to expreſs with what pre-
cipitation every one, caring only for himſelf,
haſtened to outrun his companions, and braved
danger, to eſcape, as ſoon as poſſible, from that
fatal country.   Some on bad hurdles, by way of
rafts, drew after them their horſes ſwimming ;
others were carried on bladders ; all availed themſelves of what was offered them by chance, or of
what neceſſity, ever fruitful in expedients, made
them contrive.   Twelve ſmall flat boats, the remains of the fleet of Julian, ſerved to tranſport
the Emperor, with the principal officers, and made,
by his order, as many voyages were neceſſary to
complete the tranſportation. " Thus," ſays Ammianus, " by the divine goodneſs, we all paſſed
                                      " ſafely,

" safely, excepting some who had the misfortune
" to be drowned."

Immediately after, advice was received that the
Persians, out of the fight of the Romans, were
constructing a bridge, no doubt that they might
intercept the stragglers and the baggage; but seeing themselves discovered, they did not dare to
execute their perfidious design. Thus the Persians, it appears, had materials for a bridge. Why
then did not Jovian insist, as a preliminary, that
they should facilitate his passage? Sapor was too
great a gainer by the treaty to have made a difficulty
of a condition which he could with ease perform.
This seems worth remarking, as another proof of
the inability of Jovian.

The Roman army, continuing its march with
extreme diligence, encamped some leagues from
the Tigris, near the town of Hatra *, situated on
a hill in the midst of a vast desert, formerly inhabited by the Scenites Arabians: it had been
reckoned impregnable, but had now been long
abandoned. Perhaps the Romans, when they saw
Hatra, consoled themselves a little on their disgrace, by recollecting that which had befallen,
under the ramparts of that place, the two greatest

* So called by Ammianus, by Dio, (*lib. ult.*) Τα Ἄτρα,
and by M. de la Bleterie, *Atra*.

M. d'Anville (see his maps, and *l'Euphrate et le Tigre*,
pp. 92, 93.) traces their march, and assigns the true po-
sition of Hatra, Ur, and Thilsaphata, which Ammianus
has mentioned. GIBBON.

general

generals that had filled the throne of the Cæfars. Trajan had made the taking it a point of honour, but nature abfolutely armed againft him, in defence of the befieged; and what may be confidered as a prodigy of another kind, Severus, who, after having raifed the fiege, attacked it a fecond time, called back his foldiers very unadvifedly, when they were juft ready to ftorm the place, and when he ordered them to return to the affault, he could never make himfelf obeyed. This prince, as well as Trajan, thought he fhould have perifhed before that town with all his army. Artaxerxes, the founder of the fecond monarchy of the Perfians, was not more fuccefsful, and Providence * feemed conftantly to declare in favour of Hatra. However, the frequent attacks of the Romans, and the danger to which the town was expofed, efpecially in the laft fiege, might make the Scenites Arabians think, that the liberty, of which they were always fo jealous, and which they ftill preferve, was lefs endangered in their tents than under the fhelter of the ftrongeft walls. They abandoned Hatra We no where read that it was taken, and yet it had been long deferted when Jovian arrived there. The Romans were now informed, that they had a plain

* In this Dr. Delany, a learned Englifh divine, thinks he difcovers the marks of the vifible protection of God to the defcendants of Ifhmael, agreeably to the promifes made to Hagar and Abraham, Gen. xvi. and xvii. See the work, entitled, *Revelation examined with Candour*, vol. II. differt. IV.

of thirty leagues to traverse, where nothing was to be found but wormwood and such kind of herbs, with a little putrid and brackish water. They provided therefore some fresh water, and killed some of the camels and other beasts of burden, whose unwholesome flesh prolonged their lives at the expence of health.

In about six days march they met, near the castle of Ur, a place dependent on the Persians, a convoy of some provisions, which Jovian, immediately after his election, had sent the tribune Mauricius to seek in Mesopotamia. This weak supply, the fruit of the oeconomy of the two generals Procopius and Sebastian, enabled the Emperor to recover breath, and to take measures to make himself acknowledged through the whole empire. He might even consider this assistance as an act of obedience on the part of Procopius and his collegue, whose submission necessarily drew after it that of the Eastern provinces. But who could insure to him the West, till Illyricum and Gaul had acknowledged him? The troops of Illyricum and Gaul had often disposed of the purple, and occasioned great revolutions. They were indeed less formidable since the time of Constantine. That prince, more on his guard against civil wars than against the invasions of the Barbarians, had, by good or bad policy, weakened the authority of the generals by dividing it. He had also dispersed in the inner part of the provinces the legions long stationed on

the

the frontiers, where the proximity of their quarters placed them within the reach of keeping up
correspondences, of secretly forming and suddenly
executing conspiracies. Nevertheless, in spite of
these precautions, the recent examples of Vetranio *
in Illyricum, and of Magnentius † and Julian in
Gaul, did not allow a doubt that the legions might
again make Emperors there ; and the distance must
increase the uneasiness of Jovian.

He dispatched therefore, with the necessary
orders to secure to him those important provinces,
two confidential men, Procopius, secretary of state,
who must be distinguished from the relation of
Julian, and Memoridus, a tribune. The whole
family of Jovian was in Illyricum ; his wife, his
son yet in the cradle, Count Varronian his father,
and his father-in-law Count Lucillian. Both, after
having quitted the service, enjoyed the repose of a
quiet life. But the infirmities of age without doubt
rendered Varronian incapable of acting, as the
orders of the Emperor were addressed to Count
Lucillian. The messengers carried him the com-

* Vetranio, an aged general, beloved for the simplicity
of his manners, who had long governed the martial countries of Illyricum, assumed the purple in 350. But Constantius, having seduced his troops, and undermined his
throne, at an interview with the usurper, appointed at Sar-
dica, by the defection of his followers, Vetranio was de-
posed and banished to Prusa, where he lived six years in the
enjoyment of ease and affluence. *Abridged from* GIBBON.

† For an account of the usurpation of Magnentius, see
Vol. I. p. 175. note *.

mission

miffion of mafter-general of the horfe and foot *. Thus invefted with two employments which were ufually feparated, he was to take with him fome officers of merit and known fidelity, whofe names were mentioned in a private difpatch, and to repair immediately to Milan, from thence to watch over the remainder of the Weft, and to refort, in cafe of commotions, where-ever the exigence of affairs might require his prefence. The Emperor took from Jovinus the command of the troops in Gaul, and conferred it on Malarich, by nation a Frank, long attached to the fervice of the Romans. Thus he freed himfelf of a man whofe fuperior talents rendered his fidelity fufpected, and put in his place a foreigner, who, not being able to have any pretenfions to the empire, would always confider the good fortune of his benefactor as the foundation of his own, and would confine his ambition to ferving him well. The meffengers had alfo orders to announce on their journey the death of Julian and the election of his fucceffor, to convey to the governors of the provinces the letters of Jovian, and to publifh every where that he had terminated the war by an advantageous peace. They travelled night and day, without ftopping ; but, more expeditious and more fincere than they, Fame outftripped them, and declared the truth.

* In M. de la Bleterie, *le brevet de généraliffime de l'infanterie et de la cavalerie:* in the original of Ammianus, *magifterii equitum et peditum codicillis.* For obvious reafons I prefer the latter.

Jovian wrote, without doubt, at the fame time to the fenate of New Rome, and efpecially to that of the Old, which ftill retained fome kind of pre-eminence, praying them, at leaft for form-fake, to confirm what the army had done in his favour. It was at that time probably, that he nominated himfelf conful for the enfuing year, with his father Count Varronian, who had learned, in a dream, if we credit Ammianus, that he fhould be appointed to the confulfhip, but who certainly knew not that death would prevent his taking poffeffion of that high dignity *.

If the Pagans of the army had been fenfibly affected by the lofs of Julian, it was no lefs diftreffing to the others, of whom there were fuch numbers throughout the empire ; and, without doubt, the latter, not being conftrained by the prefence of their new prince, abandoned themfelves to their grief with more freedom. " This intelligence," fays Libanius, " was a ftroke that pierced me to " the heart. I caft my eyes on a fword, and wifhed " to rid myfelf of a life that would henceforth be " more cruel to me than death. But I recollected " the prohibition of Plato, and the punifhments re-" ferved in hell for thofe who difpofe of themfelves

---

* Count Varronian thus dying foon after he had heard of his fon's good fortune, and before he had feen him, Jovian declared his infant-fon Varronian conful with himfelf, in the room of his grandfather; " becaufe," adds Ammianus, " the old man was foretold in his fleep that " the higheft magiftracy fhould be borne by that name."

" without

" without waiting for the command of God. Be-
" fides, I reflected that I owed that hero a funeral
" oration *."

Libanius acquitted himfelf of that duty by con-
fecrating to the memory of Julian two difcourfes,
which have been tranfmitted to us. The firft †,
which feems to have been compofed immediately,
is only a very fhort and yet fufficiently tedious lamentation, with more wit than fentiment, and more
pedantry than wit. The fecond ‡ is an hiftorical
elogium, laboured at leifure, in which the orator
follows Julian ftep by ftep, and always fhews the
bright fide of him. This piece, perhaps the beft
of his works, and worthy, almoft in every refpeft,
of the pureft antiquity, makes, on the whole, a remarkable contraft to the eloquent difcourfe of St.
Gregory of Nazianzus §.

At Carrhæ in Mefopotamia, a city entirely devoted to Paganifm, the meffenger who brought
the firft account of the death of Julian, was near

---

* *De vitâ fuâ.*

† Ιυλιανος, η Επιταφιος επι τω Ιυλιανω. (" A funeral ora-
" tion on Julian.") This difcourfe was publifhed imper-
fectly by Morell; but more correctly, with Latin tranflation
of Olearius, by Fabricius, Bibl. Græc. Vol. VII. p. 223.

‡ Υπερ τυ Ιυλιανυ τιμωριας. (" On revenging Julian.")
Spoken before the Emperor Theodofius, 379, firft publifhed
by Olearius, 1701, and afterwards, with his tranflation and
notes, by Fabricius. See p. 224. note ‡.

§ Though in the editions of this Father the work is divided into two, it is, however, only one and the fame
difcourfe, as is proved by the judicious writer who has
given a French tranflation of it, printed at Lyons, in 1735.

being ftoned to death, and really was fo, according to Zofimus. Such was the defpair of the Pagans. They faw their reign vanifh like a dream, the flattering hopes which they had conceived from the youth and zeal of Julian pafs away in fmoke, Hellenifm ready to be buried in the tomb of its reftorer, and the Chriftian religion again invefted with the purple, and more ftrengthened than ever, at the very time when, thinking it arrived at its fatal period, they only waited the return of Julian to give the laft blow. Many had perfecuted it without difcretion, and had been betrayed into the greateft exceffes. What probability that the moft moderate Chriftian prince would let crimes, at which Julian himfelf had been forced to blufh, pafs with impunity !

On the other fide, the Church, in the tranfports of a fudden deliverance, bleffed by its canticles the God ever faithful to his promifes, whofe arm had exterminated the new Sennacherib. But the Chriftians, it muft be owned, did not all confine themfelves to the legitimate fentiments which this kind of refurrection planted in their hearts. Inftead of a Chriftian joy, pure in its motives, humble and modeft in its effects, mixed with compaffion for a perifhing enemy, and with fear at the profpect of profperity ; many gave themfelves up to the merely human emotions of a proud and outrageous joy, and feemed already to threaten the vengeance

givenefs. Thofe of Antioch, perfonal enemies to Julian on fo many accounts, infulted at once the memory of the Pagan, the philofopher, and the author. In this great city, fo voluptuous, and which thought itfelf fo Chriftian, there was nothing but public entertainments, nothing but facred and profane feftivals. In the churches and oratories of the martyrs were feen dances, and the tumult of public fhews; and the theatres refounded with religious exclamations. There was publifhed the victory of the crofs; there was apoftrophifed, though abfent, the philofopher Maximus, the oracle and the perverter of Julian. " Foolifh " Maximus," they exclaimed, " what is become of " thy predictions? God and his Chrift have con- " quered."

But if the Church triumphed, the empire was covered with difgrace, and had received a deep wound, of which it never recovered. Thus the tranfports with which the intereft of religion, efpecially when joined with animofity, at firft infpired the people, were no fooner abated, than the public rejoicings gave place to uneafinefs and alarms. To inveigh againft Julian, to impute the calamities of the ftate to his apoftacy and fenfelefs conduct, publickly to expofe the fhocking remains of the human victims which he was accufed of having facrificed in his abominable myfteries, this might be a kind of confolation, but it was not a refource. Jovian alone gained by it, becaufe he

U 3

had

had the advantage of succeeding a prince that was hated, and confequently refponfible, in the opinion of the multitude at leaft, for the firft faults of his fucceffor.

By the ceffion of the provinces beyond the Tigris, and of Nifibis, Syria was going to become almoft a frontier, and the city of Antioch remained expofed, with the reft of the Eaft, to the incurfions of the Barbarians. Whoever had ftill a Roman heart muft confider, that for the fpace of about eleven centuries, neither the annals of the republic, nor thofe of the monarchy, furnifhed an example of an event fo grievous, fo ignominious, all things confidered, as the treaty of Jovian; that if, in former times, fome generals had fubfcribed to difhonourable conditions, the fupreme authority, which then refided in the people, by declaring thofe treaties null, had made all their infamy fall on their authors; that the majefty of the empire, after it was concentered in a monarch, had been no doubt deeply humiliated by the captivity of Valerian, who had grown old in the chains of another Sapor; but that this majefty had degraded and annihilated itfelf in the perfon of Jovian, who had forfaken the fundamental principle of the policy of the Romans, who yielded nothing by force, nor were ever more haughty, or more intractable, than when they feemed crufhed; that this precious maxim, efcaped from the wreck of the republic and of ancient manners, had fupported

to

to the prefent day the empire which it had formed; but when that was once abandoned, the Emperors would in future be feen fucceffively to cede the provinces, to difmember the ftate, under a pretence of faving it; in fhort, that it was eafy to forefee the fall and total ruin of that vaft body.

Without extending their views fo far, the inhabitants of Nifibis, fufficiently occupied with their own calamity, trembled to fee themfelves at the mercy of Sapor, and of Sapor provoked. They retained, neverthelefs, fome hopes founded on the importance of their fortrefs, their paft fidelity, and their recent fervices. They could not believe that Jovian would deliver them to Barbarians; and they flattered themfelves, that if, from a regard to his oaths, he did not dare directly to infringe the treaty, fenfible at leaft of the juftice of their remonftrances, he would not deprive them of the liberty of defending themfelves againft an enemy, whom they had already fo often repulfed.

The army, however, after having confumed the little provifions that it had received, again endured fo ftrange a famine, that they were on the eve of eating human flefh. If a bufhel of corn was found by chance, " which happened," Ammianus fays, " but feldom," it was fold for at leaft thirteen pieces of gold. By degrees, as the horfes were killed, the arms and baggage were abandoned; fo that there is perhaps lefs exaggeration than malignity in the picture which Libanius draws of the

ftat-

ftate of the troops at their return: "Our foldiers,"
fays he, " returned without arms, without cloaths.
" They afked alms, being as naked, for the moft
" part, as people who efcape from fhipwreck.
" If any one retained half his buckler, a third
" part of his fpear, or even one of his boots, which
" he carried on his fhoulder, he confidered himfelf
" as a hero. All thought themfelves fufficiently
" juftified, by faying, that Julian was dead, and
" that it was not furprifing that the Romans fhould
" appear in the deplorable ftate in which the Per-
" fians would have been, if that conqueror had
" lived."

It is fuppofed, that the army re-entered the territories of the empire at a place named Thifal-
phata. It was there, at leaft, that Procopius and
Sebaftian, with the officers of the troops of Mefopotamia, came to pay their duty to the Emperor,
who received them gracioufly. Jovian foon repaired to the gates of Nifibis, and encamped under
the walls, without liftening to the prayers of the
inhabitants, who conjured him, with reiterated intreaties, to lodge in the palace, like his prede-
ceffors. He was afraid to fhew himfelf, and was
ftill more afraid, no doubt, to confine himfelf in a
Roman colony, of which he had put the Barbarians
in poffeffion.

That very evening he committed an act of de-
fpotifm more fuitable to the fufpicious character
with which he is reproached, than to the delicacy

of

of confcience on which he piqued himfelf. At the beginning of the night, on his rifing from table, an officer, who had diftinguifhed himfelf in the laft war at the taking of Maogamalcha *, was put to death. He was dragged out, and thrown into a dry well, where ftones were heaped over him. He was named *Jovianus*, like the Emperor, and had had fome votes to fucceed Julian. To remain a fub-ject, after having appeared worthy to reign, is a fituation fo delicate, that the greateft circum-fpection is fcarce fufficient to ward its dangers. Of this Jovianus was not aware. Ambition or vanity made him utter fome expreffions the more fufpicious, as he occafionally invited fome officers to his table ; and " to this," fays Ammianus, " his deftruction, " was certainly owing." The tragical end of this unfortunate man, who feems to have been more imprudent than culpable, is related by none of the modern writers who mention Jovian †. I queftion whether they would have omitted a fimilar paffage in the hiftory of his predeceffor.

On the next day Binefes, a lord of the Perfian court, who attended Jovian, to ferve as an hoftage, and at the fame time to urge the execution of the

* Whilft the Barbarians defended themfelves, finging, according to their cuftom, the praifes of their king, and braving the Emperor, faying, he might fooner fcale the walls of heaven than take Maogamalcha, the legions en-tering by the mouth of the mine, furprifed them, maffacred them, and threw down the ramparts. B.

† A fubfequent hiftorian, Mr. Gibbon, ironically ftyles it " a *royal* act."

treaty

treaty of peace, efcorted, no doubt, by a guard which the Emperor gave him, entered Nifibis, and difplayed on the citadel the ftandard of the Great King. The fight of this fatal flag, and the order which the inhabitants received to retire fomewhere elfe, threw them into the utmoft confternation. At firft they had imagined, that Jovian had engaged to deliver up the city with all its inhabitants. One would think therefore that it muft have been fome abatement of their grief to learn that their perfons would not fall into the hands of Sapor. But befides their not being able, as I have faid, to perfuade themfelves entirely that this engagement would take place, the banifhment, to which they faw themfelves condemned, appeared to them as terrible as flavery. Several perhaps would even rather have chofen to live flaves in the bofom of their country, that is, fubjects of the kings of Perfia, than to preferve in exile, in poverty, in the miferies of a new eftablifhment, a chimerical liberty under the Roman Emperors, princes as abfolute in fact * as thofe who bore the fceptre of Arfaces and Artaxerxes pretended to be by right.

It is very ufual with hiftorians, when they relate the ruin of illuftrious cities, to recount in few words their origin and the principal events which rendered them diftinguifhed. May I therefore be allowed to fay fomething here of the famous Nifibis,

----

* Witnefs the inftance juft related.

o as

as the Romans then loft it for ever, and as it in a
a manner even perished itfelf by the total tranfmi-
gration of its citizens? Nifibis, if we may credit
the oriental hiftorians, is the fifter and contemporary of Babylon, Nimrod alfo being its founder.
According to fome, he gave it the name of *Chalya* ;
according to others, that of *Achad*; and it is, fay
thefe, the fame city of Accad which is mentioned
in Genefis, among thofe of which the fon of Cufh
laid the firft foundations in the land of Shinar.
It took afterwards the name of Nifibis; and if we
had a right to infift on an uncertain etymology *,
we might conjecture that it was already, or then
became, a place of ftrength. One of the kings of
Syria who fucceeded Alexander, gave it the name
of Antioch of Mygdonia, and certainly it was fo
called, as may be feen in Polybius, (*l.* v.) in the
reign of Antiochus, furnamed the Great. It was
fituated in the north part of Mefopotamia, two
days journey from the Tigris, near mount Mafius,
in a pleafant and fruitful plain, watered by the
river Mygdonius, which interfected the city. Not-
withftanding its antiquity, Nifibis does not begin
to figure in hiftory till towards the latter time of
the Roman republic.

Tigranes, king of Armenia, having taken it
from the Parthians, being himfelf attacked by

* נצב fignifies, it is faid, in Phœnician, " columns,
" heaps of ftones." It means in Hebrew, " a monument,
" a ftatue," &c. but it alfo fignifies in the Bible " a gar-
" rifon, ftationary foldiers." 1 Sam. xiii. 12.   B.

Lucullus,

Lucullus, there lodged his treasures. He thought them safe in a city surrounded by two walls all of brick *, of a prodigious thickness, which a broad and deep ditch secured from being undermined, and also put out of the reach of machines. Thus it despised Lucullus, when he ventured to appear before Nisibis in the depth of winter. But by the favour of this contempt, and of a tempestuous night, he carried the place by scaling, sixty-eight years before the Christian æra. After the defeat of Crassus, it again became subject to the kings of Armenia. Occupied by their civil wars, the Romans did not think of retaking it; and the policy of Augustus, who fixed the limits of the empire to the banks of the Euphrates, was a law to his successors till Trajan. Thus for more than a hundred and fifty years the Romans saw without jealousy Nisibis and its territory in the hands of the kings of Armenia, their vassals, or of the kings of Adiabena, vassals of the Parthians. Trajan, the most warlike of the Emperors after Julius Cæsar, exploded the state-maxim introduced by Augustus, and carried his victorious arms far beyond the Euphrates. The taking of Nisibis was one of the first exploits on that side; but Hadrian soon abandoned it, with the

* Nisibis is now reduced to one hundred and fifty houses; the marshy lands produce rice, and the fertile meadows, as far as Mosul and the Tigris, are covered with the ruins of towns and villages. See Niebuhr, Voyages, tom. ii. p. 300—309. GIBBON.

new provinces which Trajan had conquered in the
East.

Lucius Verus, the brother and collegue of Marcus Aurelius, retook it; and in the time of Severus besieged twice, once by the people of Mesopotamia revolting against the Romans, and the other time by Volagesus king of Parthia, it defended itself with such vigour and success, that Severus, who first firmly established the Romans in Mesopotamia, not contented with fortifying Nisibis, and making it the capital of a particular province, raised it even to the dignity of a colony, and made it take the name of *Septimia*. In the time of Alexander the son of Mammea, Artaxerxes, who had just dethroned Artabanes, the last king of Parthia, and restored to the Persian nation the sceptre which she had lost for about 555 years, endeavoured, but ineffectually, to make himself master of Nisibis.

Under one of the succeeding Emperors it was taken either by the same Artaxerxes, or his son Sapor I.; but by taking it he only procured the younger Gordian the honour of re-conquering it. Julius-Philip, the murderer and successor of Gordian, deserved by some benefactions to be considered as a new founder of the colony, as on a medal which she caused to be struck in honour of Philip, she took the name of *Julia* with that of *Septimia*. The captivity of Valerian, and the effeminacy of Gallienus his unworthy son, ceded to Sapor I. most of the Asiatic provinces. It

was neceſſary for another Barbarian, named Odenathus, the chief of ſome Saracens, more Roman
than the Emperor himſelf, to take care of the intereſts of the empire; and he ſaved, it in the Eaſt.
Niſibis firſt ſubmitted to that prince, whoſe ſervices Gallienus rewarded with the title of Auguſtus.
It ſeemed again ſeparated from the empire in the
reign of Zenobia, the widow of Odenathus; but
it was re-united by Aurelian. The Perſians having
made themſelves maſters of it after the death of
Carus, the terror of the arms of Diocletian forced
them to abandon it.

In ſhort, the æra of the glory of Niſibis, and
the moſt brilliant parts of its hiſtory, muſt be
ſought in the IVth century after Jeſus Chriſt. In
the reign of Conſtantius, Sapor II. as has been
ſaid, was thrice foiled before its ramparts. Of
thoſe three ſieges, the moſt memorable is that of
the year 350 *, deſcribed by Julian with no leſs
elegance than energy, in his two firſt orations,
which the orator has found the ſecret to render
intereſting in a certain degree, though they are
panegyrics, and the panygyrics of Conſtantius. To
give an idea of that ſiege; I will add, that Sapor
having learned that the revolt of Magnentius, and
the progreſs of that uſurper, called Conſtantius into
the Weſt, deſirous of availing himſelf of that
juncture, invaded Meſopotamia at the head of an

* The other two ſieges were in 337, and 359, according to   nheim. Mr. Gibbon, though he refers to this

innumerable army, and that, after having taken
some castles, he on a sudden invested Nisibis. At
first he besieged it in form ; but neither the ram,
nor the mine, nor the tortoise, having any effect, he
turned the course of the river Mydonius, hoping to
reduce the inhabitants by drought. From this, happily, the springs and the wells preserved them. The
Great King then conceived a design worthy of Darius and Xerxes. He surrounded the place with a
high and strong mound, and stopped the river below
it.. The waters ebbing filled a bason that was prepared for them, and rose almost as high as the
rampart, which was not more above their level than
was necessary to prevent the city from being
overflowed. Sapor then equipped on this lake a
fleet of barks filled with machines to batter and
scour the walls, and with soldiers to assault them.
This new mode of attack continued several days
with an amazing lofs on the side of the Barbarians,
and with prodigies of intrepidity on the side of the
Romans, till a weak part of the bank breaking,
buried in the waters great numbers of the besiegers.

Sapor, seeing his reputation endangered, stopped
the Mygdonius above the city, and discharged the
river against the walls, of which it threw down a
hundred cubits, 152 feet. Though he played incessantly on the breach, the inhabitants raised a new
wall some paces from the old one, with such expedition, and defended it with such vigour, that they
repulsed all the assaults. The king, in the violence

of

of his paffion, fhot an arrow into the fky to revenge
himfelf, as far he could, of the deity himfelf.   But
he made that impious prince ftill more fenfible of
his power by an army of gnats, whofe ftings fo
enraged the horfes and elephants, that they crufhed
in pieces feveral thoufand foldiers.   At length,
after lofing 20,000 men, he burnt his machines,
and raifed the fiege, which had lafted more than
four months.   Count Lucillian, who commanded in
the city, and St. James, its bifhop *; divided the honour of having faved it; the former by his courage
and military talents, the latter by his fervent
prayers, which he interrupted only to animate his
people to fight for their liberty and religion; for
they all profeffed Chriftianity, of which Sapor was
the perfecutor.

Such was the city of Nifibis, which the fon-in-
law of Lucillian ceded to the fame Sapor. Thofe,
whom he ordered to leave it and give place to Barbarians, were in general the fame, who, thirteen
years before, had fo well defended it. The fenate,
in a mournful filence; and the people uttering lamentable cries; repaired to the camp of the Emperor; and, proftrate at his feet, faid to him every
thing that grief and the love of their country fug-

*. The miracles which Theodoret (*l.* 11. *c.* 30.) afcribes
to St. James, bifhop of Edeffa, were at leaft performed in
a worthy caufe, the defence of his country.   He appeared
on the walls under the figure of the Roman Emperor, and
fent an army of gnats to fting the trunks of the elephants,
and to difcomfit the hoft of this new Sennacherib. GIBBON.

gested to them most affecting. As the whole answer that he opposed to their supplications, to their
arguments, to their sighs, was the sanctity of an
oath; " Sire," said they, " if necessity constrains
" you to cede your rights to Nisibis, do not forbid
" us, at least, to support ours, sword in hand.
" We ask of you neither stores, nor troops, nor
" money. By conquering Sapor we are all be-
" come soldiers. Consider us as foreigners. Aban-
" don us to ourselves, or rather to Heaven, the
" protector of justice and innocence. That will
" continue to render invincible such Romans as
" shall fight for their altars, for their hearths, for
" those walls which they have cemented with their
" own blood. After we have repulsed Sapor, the
" only use that we wish to make of our liberty is
" to give ourselves back to you."

Jovian answered, that he had expresly sworn
to deliver up the city, and that he was incapable
of eluding an oath by vain subtleties. Then
Sabinus, to whom his birth and riches gave a distinguished rank among his fellow-citizens, said to
him with equal spirit and boldness: " Constantius,
" always at war with the Persians, was almost al-
" ways unfortunate; he shivered at the name of
" Sapor, and this terror embittered all the mo-
" ments of his life. Constantius, however, over-
" whelmed with misfortunes, Constantius, reduced
" to the necessity of escaping almost alone, and of
" eating a morsel of bread in the cottage of a

" poor woman, ſtill preſerved Niſibis. What do
" I ſay? He never ceded to the enemy an inch
" of ground; but Jovian no ſooner comes to the
" empire than he ſurrenders the bulwark of the
" Eaſt." Jovian heard theſe reproaches unmoved,
ſtill intrenching himſelf in arguments drawn from
a point of honour and conſcience.

It was cuſtomary for every city to offer new
princes a crown of gold. In the critical ſituation
to which the inhabitants of Niſibis were reduced,
they were particularly careful to perform that duty.
The Emperor, who did himſelf juſtice, being very
ſenſible that he did not deſerve the crown, eſpecially
from them, refuſed that which they preſented to
him. But the inhabitants, with a perſeverance proof
againſt all refuſals, conjured him to receive it,
thinking, without doubt, that he would allow himſelf to be affected by that mark of attachment and
reſpect, and that, if he accepted their homage, he
would contract a kind of engagement with them.
Jovian, in order to extricate himſelf from their im-
portunity, ſeemed at length to accept it; and in-
ſtantly a lawyer, named Silvanus, exclaimed, with
a loud voice, " In like manner, great Emperor,
" may you be crowned by the other cities!" At
this ſpeech he was ſo exaſperated, that he immediately ordered the inhabitants to evacuate the city
in three days, and ſent ſome troops to haſten them,
with orders to p t any to death who ſhould remain
there after the time preſcribed.

This

This terrible decree filled Nisibis with consternation. Instantly nothing was heard but groans, cries, imprecations against the government, and frightful howlings. To see some women of rank forced by their sovereign to banish themselves from the scenes of their birth, from the places where they had happily passed their days in the bosom of opulence, forced, I say, to abandon all their possessions, and, what was more distressful, to remove for ever from the tombs of their husbands, their parents, their children, whose ashes remained at the discretion of the Barbarians, was a sight capable of moving Sapor, if he had been present. Sometimes they tore their hair and their faces, sometimes they clasped in their arms the doors of their houses, bathing them with tears, and bidding them a last farewell. In a word, there was seen the image of a city taken by assault, and all the symptoms of grief and despair which great calamities produce among the orientals, whose passions were always more expressive than ours. But who could describe the anguish of heart which must be felt by those brave men who had sustained three sieges, and who would have thought themselves happy to shed the remainder of their blood for a country, which they considered not only as the place of their birth, but also as the theatre of their glory, and the monument of their valour! Every one seized in his haste, and as if he had stolen it, any thing, that he could carry away, of his own effects;

X 2

for,

for, to complete their misfortunes, beaſts of burden were wanting, ſo that a large quantity of valuable furniture was obliged to be left.

The roads were ſoon covered with theſe poor fugitives, who, groaning under their burdens, and ſtill more oppreſſed by the weight of their affliction, were going to ſeek the firſt aſylum that providence ſhould be pleaſed to offer them. Moſt of them retired under the walls of Amida, where Jovian ordered a walled ſuburb to be built for them, which was called the town of Niſibis. Amida, founded by Conſtantius, and almoſt ruined by Sapor, thus increaſed by the ruins of this ancient city, and repaired its loſſes with ſo much advantage, that it became the capital of what the Romans retained in Meſopotamia. As ſoon as the inhabitants of Niſibis were departed, Jovian diſpatched the tribune Conſtantius to expell thoſe of Singara, another Roman colony, and to deliver the five provinces to the officers of Sapor. Thus this famous treaty was literally executed, a treaty, which may be regarded as the epocha of the fall of the empire, and whoſe execution expoſed Jovian, more than the treaty itſelf, to the reproaches not only of Pagan, but of ſome Chriſtian authors. Are their reproaches well founded? This is a problem, whoſe diſcuſſion will be more properly placed at the end of this hiſtory *.

After

---

* The Abbè de la Bleterie, though a ſevere caſuiſt, has pronounced, that Jovian was not bound to execute his
promiſe;

After having fulfilled his engagements with the
Persians, the Emperor ordered Procopius to convey to Tarsus in Cilicia the corpse of Julian, agreeably to the laft will of that prince. In the funeral proceffion, which muft have been a fortnight
at leaft on the road, the cuftoms of the Pagans
were obferved, of which the moft fantaftic was, to
enliven the funeral pomp of the great, and even
of the Emperors, at the expence of thofe whom
they pretended to honour. They added humour
and fatire to the demonftrations of grief. Here
were heard mournful fongs and lamentations, and
tears were feen to flow : there drolls and buffoons
danced and acted fome jocofe fcenes, or one of
the troop, in a mafk which reprefented to the
life him whofe obfequies were celebrated, imitated
his gefture and his voice *, and made him utter,
in a ludricrous ftrain, the language moft proper to
characterife him. The inferior perfonages loaded

promife ; fince he *could not* difmember the empire, nor
alienate, without their confent, the allegiance of his people.
I have never found much delight or inftruction in fuch political metaphyfics.   GIBBON.

Not being convinced or edified by the Abbè's reafon-
ing, I have not tranflated his differtation.

* Of this we are informed by Suetonius in the following
remarkable paffage : " At the funeral of Vefpafian, Favo,
" the chief of the comedians, who played his part, and imi-
" tated, as is cuftomary, his words and actions while alive,
" afked the managers of the folemnity aloud, " What
" would be the expence of the funeral pomp ?" and they
" anfwering, ' a hundred millions of fefterces,' the pretended
" Vefpafian exclaimed, " if they would give him but a
" hundred fefterces, they might throw him into the river." B.

this principal performer with railleries and affronts. The pretended Julian muſt have been highly ridiculous, as the copy was always more extravagant than the original. Neither the faults of that unfortunate prince, nor perhaps his good qualities, were ſpared. He was reproached in the bittereſt terms for his apoſtacy, his temerity, his defeat, his death. To conceive how far the licentiouſneſs was carried, it muſt be remembered that the actors revenged themſelves on the enemy of the ſtage, and that they were ſure of the applauſe of the Chriſtians.

As ſoon as Procopius had acquitted himſelf of this commiſſion, alarmed at the fate of Jovianus, and at the falſe report that was ſpread, that Julian, his relation, had wiſhed, at the point of death, to have him for his ſucceſſor, he thought that his life was in danger. He therefore ſecreted himſelf, and had the art to elude the ſearches of Jovian, and afterwards thoſe of Valens. About two years after the death of Julian, he appeared again in order to aſcend the throne, from which he fell almoſt the ſame inſtant *.

From Niſibis Jovian took the road to Antioch, and came to Edeſſa, which ſhould have been dear to him for the ſame reaſon † that had made it odious to his predeceſſor. He was in that city on the 27th of September, according to the date of a

* See p. 221. note †.

† Julian would not paſs through Edeſſa, becauſe that city was ſtrongly attached to Chriſtianity.   B.

law,

law *, which excuses the soldiers from going to forage more than twenty miles, or one day's journey, from the camp. Julian, the restorer of military discipline, had obliged them to go in search of it to that distance; but perhaps some officers sent them still farther. Jovian, interested in conciliating the affection of the troops, delivered or preserved them from that fatigue, to which there was no right to oblige them; and the spirit of his law agrees exactly with that of Julian.

The Emperor continuing his march by long stages, and received very sorrowfully on his route, entered Antioch in the month of October, and could not dispense with making some stay there, notwithstanding his impatience to go and shew himself at Constantinople, and afterwards, no doubt, in the provinces of the West. His troops were in extreme want of repose. Antioch, the abode of plenty, and the centre of all the conveniences of life, was the properest place in the world to recover them; and prudence did not yet allow Jovian to separate himself from an army, whose suffrages were the only right that he had to the empire.

During six weeks, more or less, that he passed in the capital of the East, he applied himself chiefly to regulate what concerned religion. That

---

* This law is dated in the consulship of Jovian and Varronian, and consequently the date is false, at least in that respect. It is well known, that the dates marked in the Theodosian code are so faulty, that scarce any stress can be laid on them.　B.

　　　portion

portion of public affairs, fo effential and always fo delicate, then required extreme difcretion. Julian, with his pretended toleration, which had been no more in fact than a perfecution aukwardly difguifed, in which the injuftice of oppreffion was aggravated by the infolence of difhonefty, had in a manner fet all the fubjects of the empire at variance. The people were incenfed againft the people; cities were divided; families were difunited; the ferment of minds was fo violent, that it feemed as if it could not be calmed but by the extinction of one of the parties. The unexpected revolution, which again gave the Chriftians a prince of their religion, was not fufficient to reftore tranquillity. There was room to fear, that, under the appearance of zeal, the animofity of fome ill-informed Chriftians, indulging itfelf in fome unworthy reprifals, might drive the Pagans, with whom patience was founded on no religious principle, to extremities. Already the temples were every where * fhut; the blood of victims flowed no longer; the priefts of the idols abfconded; the philofophers trimmed their beards, and quitted the cloak, to refume the common drefs. This was not a panic fear: they had unworthily abufed their credit. St. Gregory of Nazianzus, at the conclufion of his difcourfe againft Julian, exhorts to the for-

---

* Τα ιερα των Ελληνων παντα απικλυσθ. Suppofing that Socrates is not miftaken in faying that the temples were

givenefs of injuries in a manner that would induce a belief, that, on that occafion, he confidered obedience to the precept as a great effort of virtue. One would be apt to think, that, though he inveighs with fuch warmth againft the Pagans, and againft the memory of Julian, it is a ftroke of Chriftian policy; and that by taking, as it were, in the name of the church, and by public authority, a lawful vengeance, he means to prevent and difarm that of individuals.

The war kindled between the Chriftians and Pagans was not the only one of which religion was either the pretext or the caufe. Not to mention fome fects that were obfcure or of little account *, every thing that bore the Chriftian name was divided between the faith of Nice and the herefy of Arius. The moft vehement controverfies are often no more than difputes on words. Here, under the appearance of difputes on words †, and even on letters, there were real divifions as to fundamental tenets ; and the difputes were managed with as much animofity, as if incomprehenfible truths had been in queftion. The Arians, whom the favour of Conftantius had put in poffeffion of the churches of Conftantinople, and of the principal

* Such as the Valentinians, the Marcionites, the Montanifts, the Manicheans. B.

† The terms ομοουσιος, " confubftantial," " of the fame fubftance," confecrated by the council of Nice, and ομοιουσιος, " like in fubftance," which moft of the Arians admitted, only differ an iota more or lefs. B.

fees of the Eaft, fubdivided into pure Arians and demi-Arians, agreed only againft the Catholics. In lefs than fifty years they had made fixteen formularies of faith *, and it was doubted whether they had made the laft. Arianifm was a cruel fect, and even by that, according to St. Athanafius †, bore on its front a mark of reprobation. To cruelty it knew how to add cunning and artifice. Deceived by its equivocal forms ‡, under Conftantius the whole world was furprifed to find itfelf Arian without thinking of it; but error did not long enjoy this imaginary triumph. A reunion founded on duplicity had only produced a more cruel divifion.

On the other fide, thofe who acknowledged the divinity of the Word, did not all agree as to the reft. Some, by an excefs of delicacy, rejected the term " confubftantial," as not being in fcripture; and though they admitted the tenet meant by that word, all had not, like Athanafius §, equity enough to compaffionate their weaknefs, and to reckon them among the orthodox.

An obftinate fchifm, formed by miftake, and perpetuated by imprudence, rent the city of

---

* The enumeration of them may be feen in the Ecclefiaftical Hiftory of M. Fleury, l. xiv. 23.   B.

† *Ath. Hift. Arian. ad Monachos*, t. 1. p. 382. *Edit. Bened.*   B.

‡ At the Council of Rimini.   B.

§ *Athan. de Synodis*, l. 11. p. 755.   B.

Antioch.

Antioch *.   There were seen two Catholic bishops,
besides one Arian.   At Constantinople, and elsewhere,

* In the year 330, under the reign of Constantine, having succeeded in deposing and banishing St. Eustathius,
bishop of Antioch, the most zealous of the Catholics began
to hold their separate assemblies.   As they still acknowledged Eustathius, the name of Eustathians was given them.
The see was successively filled by several bishops, more or
less attached to the Arian cabal, with whom the great
number of Catholics of Antioch, either through love of
peace, or from weakness, did not fail to communicate. Things
remained in this state during the reign of Constantius.   But
in 361 (the last year of that prince) Anianus, the Arian bishop,
having been banished, and, besides, Eustathius having died in
his exile, they were desirous to elect a bishop who might
re-unite the church of Antioch.   The Arians and the
moderate Catholics cast their eyes on Meletius, the most
amiable and most peaceable of men.   Every one thought
him of his own party.   But in that the Arians were mistaken.   Meletius was no sooner elected than he declared
for the Catholic faith.   The Eustathians, however, ob-
stinately resolved not to acknowledge him, because the
Arians had had great share in his election.   On the other
side, the Arians, enraged at being deceived in him,
caused him to be banished a month after, to the great regret of the moderate Catholics, who, retaining an inviolable
attachment to the holy bishop, would no more assemble, as
they had hitherto done in the churches of the Arians, and
offered to unite themselves with the Eustathians, or zealous
Catholics.   But these refused to admit them to their communion.   There were then at Antioch therefore three
parties; the Arians, the Eustathians, and the Meletians.
After the death of Constantius, in 362, Lucifer, of Cag-
liari in Sardinia, whom that prince had banished into Syria,
a man celebrated for his courage, and his sufferings in the
good cause, but whose views were too confined, ordained
as bishop the priest Paulinus, whom the Eustathians already
considered as their head.   Lucifer thought that the Meletians, more pacific than the others, would accept Paulinus, who, besides, was very worthy of the prelacy;
                                                    but

where, the Macedonians *, orthodox, at leaſt in appearance, as to the conſubſtantiality of the Son, denied that of the Holy Ghoſt. The Donatiſts, thinking that there was no church, or even ſacraments, out of their ſociety, carried fanaticiſm in Africa to a decree of madneſs. The Novatians †, whoſe hereſy was to erect a deſperate rigour into an article of faith, kept up ſome good underſtanding with the Catholics, who diſtinguiſhed them extremely from the other ſectaries; and it may be ſaid, that they merited that diſtinction by the purity of their manners, and by their attachment to the ancient doctrine as to the divinity of Jeſus Chriſt. They had ſupported with heroic courage the Arian perſecutions: but ſome had ſhewn ‡, that for the defence of their faith they knew how to employ other arms than thoſe of true Chriſtians.

As the moſt natural effect of a foreign war is to ſuſpend civil diſſentions; in ſpite of the artifices of

but this imprudent ſtep only ſerved to put an end to the ſchiſm. Thus there were ſeen in the ſame city three biſhops, Euzoius the Arian, Meletius, returned from his exile, and Paulinus, both Catholics. This diviſion did not terminate till long after, under biſhop Alexander, to whom the Euſtathians re-united themſelves in 415.   B.

* So named from Macedonius, archbiſhop of Conſtantinople.   B.

† The Novatians did not admit to penitence thoſe who had fallen after baptiſm.   B.

‡ Under Conſtantius the Novatian peaſants of Mantinium in Paphlagonia, armed with ſcythes and axes, cut in pieces four companies of ſoldiers, who had been ſent to oblige them to embrace Arianiſm.   B.

Julian

Julian to foment the flame of difcord, there appeared in his reign between the moft oppofite communions a kind of truce refembling peace. Excepting only the Donatifts, who committed exceffes againft the Catholics, for which the magiftrates thought it their duty to account to the Emperor; excepting, I fay, thofe madmen, the Chriftians had feemed to forget their domeftic divifions, and to employ themfelves in concert in offering up prayers for their common deliverance. But as foon as the election of a Chriftian prince was known, the flumbering difputes began to awaken, and the chiefs of the different communions were eagerly defirous of going to meet the Emperor as foon as he was in the Roman territories; either to engage him, or at leaft to render him favourable to their party.

Amidft fuch a diverfity of opinions, Jovian, as I have already faid, had the happinefs to know the truth. He had preferred Chriftianity to his fortune, and openly profeffed the Catholic doctrine. If the purity of his manners did not perhaps anfwer to that of his faith, at leaft he ardently wifhed, it cannot be doubted, to fee all his fubjects re-united in the bofom of the true religion. But Jovian was too well inftructed in the nature of religion itfelf to offer violence to any one. A confeffor of the faith become a perfecutor would have been a kind of prodigy. Who fhould be better acquainted with the rights of confcience than he

who himself had been obliged to claim them ? He
was convinced that faith perfuades, but does not
command ; that to employ fire and fword, in the
progrefs of the gofpel, is to combat at once the
fpirit of the gofpel, and the principles of reafon ;
that fear only makes hypocrites ; that God rejects forced homage, and that if he difapproves
error, he detefts perjury ; that the excellence of
the end propofed cannot fanctify unlawful means ;
that, befides, in order to fucceed, the means muft
be fuited to the end, and thus that confciences can
no more be carried by force of arms than ramparts
by arguments *.

But, befides, if Jovian had thought it lawful and poffible to convert men by the dread of
punifhments and death, it would have been rifking
too much at the beginning of a new reign to irritate
the Arians, who ftill retained, among the Chriftian
communions, that air of fuperiority which had
been given them by the protection and favour of
Conftantius. It would have been ftill more dangerous to attack Paganifm in front, which, under
Julian, had recovered ftrength, and had even become again the religion of the ftate. It muft be
fuppofed, that the Pagans, feeing themfelves at the

---

* Thefe truly Proteftant doctrines flow from the pen of
a nominal Papift, but are as different from thofe of the
murderers of Cranmer in former times, and of thofe of
Calas in the prefent, as light from darknefs. Such liberal
fentiments in fome ages and countries would have configned
the author to the Inquifition.

difcretion of a prince who was a zealous enemy to idolatry, were extremely alarmed, and that many expreffed fo much uneafinefs as to occafion fome to that weakly eftablifhed prince. With a view therefore to confirm them, and alfo to confirm himfelf, he haftened to make a law, by which he maintained them in the free exercife of their religion, and permitted them to re-open the temples, where, by forcible means, and without the authority of the prince, they had been fhut fince the death of Julian.

"You underftand," fays Themiftius, a Pagan philofopher and fenator of Conftantinople *, in a panegyric on Jovian, which he pronounced before him, " that there are fome things which a fo-
" vereign cannot reftrain. Among thefe are the
" virtues, and efpecially religion. A prince,
" who fhould make an edict to enjoin his fubjects
" to love him, would not be obeyed. Could he
" flatter himfelf with being fo for commanding
" them to have fuch or fuch a religious perfuafion?
" Fear, without doubt, will effect tranfient meta-
" morphofes. But fhall we confider as men con-
" vinced, thofe men more changeable than Eu-
" ripus †, perfuaded by their variations to be the
" adorers of the purple, and not of the divinity,
" thofe ridiculous Proteufes who difhonour human
" kind, and who are fometimes feen in the temples

---

* See the Epiftle to him, Vol. I. p. 4.

† This narrow fea, between Bœotia and Eubœa, ebbed and flowed feven times in 24 hours, or oftener, or feldomer, as the wind fat.

" at

" at the feet of the statues and altars, and some-
" times at the holy table in the churches of the
" Christians ? Thus, instead of using violence, you
" have made a law which allows every one to pay
" to the Deity the worship which he shall think
" the best.   As the image of the Supreme Being,
" you imitate his conduct.   He has placed in the
" heart of man a natural inclination which leads
" him to religion ; but he does not force him in
" the choice.   Thus the coërcive laws, which
" tended to deprive man of a liberty which God
" leaves him, have lasted at most during the lives
" of their authors ; instead of which, your law,
" or rather that of God himself, subsists in all
" ages.   Neither confiscations, nor exiles, nor
" punishments can annull it.   The body may be
" imprisoned, tormented, destroyed ; but the soul
" takes her flight : she escapes from violence, bear-
" ing in herself this indelible law, this liberty of
" thinking, of which it is impossible to deprive
" her, though the tongue should be forced
" to articulate some words. . . . . . The wisdom
" of your edict allays our cruel divisions. This,
" Emperor, beloved by God, you know better
" than any one : The Persians were less formidable
" to the Romans than the Romans themselves ; the
" incursions of those Barbarians less dangerous than
" the accusations suggested by the spirit of party
" to destroy citizens. Continue to hold the ba-
" lance even. Allow all mouths to address prayers
" to heaven for the prosperity of your empire. . .
                                        " A law

"A law so just must penetrate all the subjects of
"our divine monarch with respect and love, those,
"among others, to whom not contented to restore
"liberty, he explains the tenets of their religion
"as well as the ablest of their teachers."

Thus, in the presence of Jovian himself, spoke
Themistius, one of the most illustrious magistrates
of his age, and deputed by the body to harangue
the Emperor. His authority sufficiently authen-
ticates the law of Jovian, though it no longer exists,
and though other writers seem to have been ignorant of it. The panegyrics of princes sometimes
praise them for virtues which they do not possess,
but never for laws which they have not made. It
cannot be denied that Themistius, in the discourse,
part of which I have just quoted, lays down, on
occasion of that law, some very philosophical and
even very Christian maxims. But as truth is very
seldom found in the mouths of Pagans without any
mixture of error, to the solid arguments which
condemn cruelty and violence he adds the pretended impossibility of knowing how the Deity
would be adored, and the imaginary honour which
redounds to the Supreme Being from the variety
of worships which divide the world. This philosopher confounds political toleration with indifference, while Jovian, by the light of the gospel,
perfectly distinguishes them.

The same edict, which permitted the temples to
be re-opened, ordered the abominable sanctuaries

of impoſtures and witchcraft to be ſhut. It ſuffered the public ſacrifices, and the worſhip formerly authoriſed, to remain ; but it forbade enchantments, magic, and all worſhip viſibly founded on impoſture. Though the Roman laws had always condemned theſe practices, the fooliſh ſuperſtition and credulity of Julian had brought them extremely into faſhion. The wiſeſt among the Pagans muſt greatly praiſe his ſucceſſor for the care which he took to proſcribe what they deemed foreign to their religion, and likely to do it diſcredit. It ſeemed to them, no doubt, performing a legitimate act of the pontifical power, which they ſtill aſcribed to the Chriſtian Emperors, and of which Conſtantine had uſefully availed himſelf, to effect the deſtruction of idolatry.

Properly ſpeaking, the Pagan religion had no dogmas ; it conſiſted of a heap of practics, and the Sovereign Pontiff had a right to ſuppreſs ſuch as he thought abuſive *. Conſtantine therefore having formed the plan of diſſolving it by little and little, and of deſtroying it by degrees, without ſhocking the Pagans, had confined it within very narrow bounds, by retrenching ſometimes a worſhip contrary to good manners, ſometimes a ſuſpicious practice ; here ſubverting a temple that was become the ſchool of libertiniſm, there inter

* See the Diſſertation of the Baron de la Baſtie, on the Sovereign Pontificate of the Roman Emperors (Part III.) in the *Memoirs of the Academy of Inſcriptions and Belles Lettres*, t. XV. B.

diſting

dicting an oracle whose priests manifestly abused the public credulity. It appears that Jovian did not pretend to tolerate Paganism but in the state to which Constantine had reduced it. On that footing only it could in fact be suffered, and the moderate Pagans required nothing more.

The political toleration of Jovian was effective and sincere. Instead of seeking pretences to disturb the Pagans, he did not avail himself of the most natural occasions. He might, without injustice, have abandoned to the severity of the laws several priests of the idols, and the philosophers who had abused the confidence of Julian. Nevertheless, it is not to his reign that the rigours which, Libanius says *, were exercised against them, must

be

---

* As Libanius did not pronounce his second funeral oration on Julian till eighteen months after the death of that prince, and consequently more than ten months after the death of Jovian, I know not why M. de Tillemont applies to the reign of the latter the bitter complaints of that orator. "At present," says that orator, (*Orat. Parent.* 148, *et seq.*) " those who declaim against the Gods are treated
" with respect, while the priests, those who are only guilty
" of serving the Gods, undergo unjust trials. That which
" they have employed in divine worship, that which the
" flame has consumed on the altars, they are forced to
" surrender. Are they unable to pay? They languish in
" fetters. The temples have been destroyed, or remain
" half-built, to serve as a ridicule for Christians. The
" philosophers are put to the torture. To have received
" something from the Emperor is to have contracted a
" debt. What do I say? It is to have committed a theft.
" In the midst of summer, at noon-day, a man is exposed
" quite naked to the heat of the sun. Besides what he

Y 2
" has

" has received, he is afked what every one fees he has not
" received. It is well known that this is to require an
" impoffibility ; but it is a pleafure to burn him ; he muft
" expire in this horrible torture. The profeffors of elo-
" quence, accuftomed to live with the great, are driven
" from their doors, like infamous murderers. That nu-
" merous fwarm of young difciples who always accom-
" pany them, feeing their mafters thus treated, conceive
" that knowledge is good for nothing, and feek a better
" protection. In every city the members of the public
" council unjuftly difpenfe with the fervice, which their
" country has a right to expect from them ; and no one
" checks fo outrageous a diforder. Nothing is every where
" feen but exactions, forced fales, confifcations, indigence,
" poverty, tears. The labourer choofes rather to beg than
" to cultivate the earth. He who to-day gives alms, to-
" morrow will be obliged to afk them. The Scythians, the
" Sarmatians, the Celts, in a word, all the Barbarians be-
" gin again to infult us on all fides," &c.

The odious ftrokes of this picture do not relate to Jovian.
Indeed, during his reign, the bifhops, and other Chriftian
preachers, were in great efteem, and fpoke againft Paganifm with full liberty. It is alfo very poffible, that at
the news of his election, in places where the Chriftians
were the ftrongeft, the populace might deftroy fome temples.
Thofe which Julian was building remained unfinifhed, becaufe Jovian would not furnifh the expence, and the zeal
of idolaters cooled. I alfo fuppofe that Libanius, and his
fellows, did not find the fame accefs to the great : fome magiftrate might have refufed him admittance ; a very fenfible
affront to that fophift, who treated Julian as an equal. But
this is all that can reafonably be afcribed to the reign of
Jovian. According to Libanius, it was " the height of
" fummer," ($\mu \epsilon \sigma \upsilon \theta \epsilon \rho \upsilon \varsigma$) when the philofophers were perfecuted. Now Jovian did not enter on the territories of the
empire till towards the beginning of autumn, and died before the end of winter. Befides, the philofopher tormented fo cruelly is plainly the famous Maximus. But
Prifcus and he were brought to trial at the beginning of the
reign of Valentinian and Valens.

As to what Libanius fays of the venality of exemptions,
and of the oppreffion of the people, no author reproaches
Jovian with any thing like it ; on the contrary, the patrician
Petronius,

be afcribed. It is true, that, after the death of
Julian, their protector and their dupe, fome philofophers were called to a fevere account for the
immenfe fums, which, it was faid, they had drawn
from him; and this perhaps is the only time that
the royal treafure has purfued men of letters. But
thofe enquiries were not made till the reign of Valens. Eunapius, alfo a Pagan, and as plaintive
as Libanius, affirms that Jovian continued to honour the philofophers * who were in the train of
his predeceffor. We may at leaft conclude, from
that expreffion, that he had fome regard for them.
Themiftius reckons as a merit in him his protecting
philofophy at a time when almoft every one elfe
declared againft it, and recalling it to court in a
lefs difgraceful habit. Fear had at firft driven the
philofophers from it; but they foon recovered
their courage; and Jovian allowed them to appear
there again, but in the common drefs. It may,
however, be prefumed, that they were not feen
there with a very gracious eye, and that they muft

Petronius, the father-in-law of Valens, a monfter of avarice and cruelty, rendered immediately the government of
his fon-in-law highly odious, and ruined a multitude of
families, by enquiring what was due to the treafury for
near a century paft. See Amm. xxvi. 6. In fhort, the
two brothers reigned when the Barbarians, being no longer
reftrained by the fear of Julian, again took up arms. Thofe
people had fcarce had time to hear of his death, and to
make fome preparations, during the reign of Jovian. B.

* Τιμων τους ανδρας διαλελιοιν. *Illos viros honore profequi non
deftitit.*

fuffer

suffer some mortifications, and perhaps insults, from the courtiers, which the Emperor did not take the trouble to avenge; and that, if I mistake not, is the meaning of what Themistius says, in a discourse addressed to Valens; that " it is a stain to " the glory of Jovian to have suffered insults to " be offered them, though, as to himself, he offered " them none."

Libanius continued incessantly to bewail Julian, and to praise him in his writings. Some would have made it a state crime, and Jovian was advised to send him to console himself with his hero. But he thought it beneath an Emperor to trouble himself with what a sophist might write. He was sensible also that by putting an author to death, his works, instead of being suppressed, are assured of immortality. As Jovian spared a Maximus and a Libanius, we may judge what tranquillity was enjoyed by such Pagans as could be reproached with nothing but their religion. It is certain, that at Constantinople sacrifices were publickly offered for the solemnity of the consulship of Jovian.

If this prince, in quality of common father and chief of the body politic, thought himself obliged not to restrain the consciences of his subjects, he did not forget that he owed a striking protection to the religious society of which he was a member. It appears by his medals that he replaced in the

Labarum

Labarum * the monogram of Jesus Christ. Not content with having thus declared that Christianity was the religion of the empire, he formally declared by a letter †, which he wrote to the gover-

nors

---

* The principal standard which displayed the triumph of the cross was styled the *Labarum*, or *Laborum*, an obscure though celebrated name, which has been vainly derived from almost all the languages of the world. It is described as a long pike intersected by a transversal beam. The silken veil, which hung down from the beam, was curiously enwrought with the images of the reigning monarch and his children. The summit of the pike supported a crown of gold, which inclosed the mysterious monogram, at once expressive of the figure of the cross, and the initial letters of the name of Christ. The safety of the Laborum was entrusted to fifty guards of approved valour and fidelity.   GIBBON.

Julian had replaced in the standards the antient Latin letters, S. P. Q. R.

† This letter, mentioned by Sozomen, is, I fancy, the very law of which Themistius gives the elogium. He says, plainly enough, that this law was the first of those of Jovian; and Sozomen asserts, that Jovian did not defer a moment (ωδεν μελλησας) to write to the generals of the provinces. It is probable, that the law contained two heads. The Emperor there declared, first, that the Christian religion was that of the state, &c. Secondly, that he did not pretend to deprive any one of the liberty of following and exercising any other, &c. The Pagan philosopher dwells only on the second head, which was advantageous to the Pagans: the ecclesiastical historian mentions only the first, which favoured the Christians. Each of them comments in his own way on the article which interests him, and gives it too much latitude. In reading Themistius, one would think that Jovian had put all religions on the same level; but Sozomen, whose text I am far from understanding rigorously, says, that this prince declared Christianity the only religion of his subjects. M. de Tillemont did not know how to reconcile the law that Themistius mentions

Y 4

with

nors of the provinces, all Pagans no doubt, as they had been put or left in place by Julian; enjoining them to act so that the Christians might assemble in the churches: for in several places they had either been destroyed or converted to profane uses. He recalled all who had been banished on account of religion, restored to the clergy, to virgins, and to widows the privileges granted by the Christian Emperors, and re-established the distribution of corn which the demesne allowed to every church for the subsistence of widows and orphans. The famine which then afflicted the empire obliged him to reduce to one-third that pious donation of Constantine; but he promised to give the remainder at the first return of plenty.

He made also a law, which we still have; addressed to Sallust the Second, Præfect of the prætorium of the East, denouncing capital punishment to those who should dare to steal away, or even solicit in marriage, the virgins consecrated to God *.

Thefe

with that referred to by Sozomen. I flatter myself that this learned writer would have approved the method of agreement here proposed.   B.

The Abbé de la Bleterie judiciously remarks, that Sozomen has forgot the general toleration, and Themistius the establishment of the Catholic religion. Each of them turned away from the object which he disliked, and wished to suppress the part of the edict the least honourable, in his opinion, to the Emperor Jovian.   GIBBON.

* The following are the very terms of the law. *Imp. Jovianus A. ad secundum P. P. Si quis, non dicam rapere, sed vel atten-*

Thefe fcandalous marriages had grown common under Julian. To accomplifh them, fome had employed violence, and others feduction. An officer, named Magnus, the fame who was, under Valens, and perhaps from the time of Julian, treafurer of the Emperor's houfhold *, had burned, by his private authority, the church of Beryta in Phœnicia. Ecclefiaftical hiftory reprefents Count Magnus † as

unprin-

attentare, matrimonii jungendi caufa, facratas virgines vel invitas aufus fuerit, capitali fententiâ feriatur. Dat. XI. Kal. Mar. Antiochiæ, Joviano A. et Varroniano Coff. Inftead of *invitas,* we fhould perhaps read *invitare.* Sozomen feems to have read *intueri,* as he tranflates the Latin word by thefe; αχολαςως ωροσ*ɓλεποɴa, impudicè afpicientem.* There is no probability that this was the fenfe. The date of this law is alfo falfe, like a number of others. Jovian did not take the confulfhip till a month at fooneft after his leaving Antioch ; and, befides, he was no longer in this world on the 19th of February, 364, as he died between the 16th and 17th of that month.   B.

The new law which condemned the rape or marriage of nuns, is exaggerated by Sozomen ; who fuppofes that an amorous glance, the adultery of the heart, was punifhed with death by the evangelic legiflator.   GIBBON.

* Thus, I think, *Comes largitionum comitatenfium* fhould be tranflated.   B.

† It was he who, in the time of Valens and of the governor Palladius, perfecuted by an inferior order the Catholics of Alexandria, to oblige them to receive the bifhop Lucius. Having caufed nineteen, as well priefts as deacons, to be apprehended and brought before his tribunal, fome of whom were more than fourfcore years of age, he faid to them, " Embrace, wretches, embrace the opinion of " the Arians. If your religion be true, God will pardon " you for having yielded to neceffity. You will pleafe the " moft clement, auguft Valens." After having put them

in

unprincipled, a slave to the court, ardent to distinguish himself in all persecutions, and committing with the baseness of a subaltern some crimes of supererogation. He was very near being beheaded by Jovian. Powerful intercessions obtained his pardon; but he was condemned to re-build the church of Beryta at his own expence.

Athanasius, the personal object of the hatred and persecution of Julian, hearing of the death of that prince, had on a sudden re-appeared in the midst of his people, who were agreeably surprised. As the orders of Julian had not then been revoked, a Pagan or an Arian might have made an attempt on the person of the holy prelate. How was it known whether the new Emperor would not be displeased that Athanasius should shew himself publickly in Alexandria, without the leave of the same authority which had banished him from all Ægypt? But his fears were immediately dispelled by a letter from Jovian, conceived in these terms: " To the most religious friend of God, Athanasius, " Jovian. As we admire beyond all expression the " sanctity of your life, in which shine forth the

in prison, and caused them to be scourged and tormented, he banished them into an idolatrous country, made them set out immediately, urging them himself, sword in hand, without giving them time to take necessaries, without waiting till the sea became calm, without being moved by the cries and tears of the whole Catholic people. *Epistola Petri Alexandrini apud Theodoret.* l. IV. 22. B.

" marks

" marks of refemblance to the God of the uni-
" verfe *, and your zeal for Jefus Chrift our Sa-
" viour, we take you now under our protection,
" moft refpectable bifhop. You deferve it by that
" courage which has made you reckon as nothing
" the moft painful labours, and regard as an ob-
" ject of contempt the rage of perfecutors and
" menacing fwords. Holding in your hand the
" helm of faith, which is fo dear to you, you ceafe
" not to combat for the truth, nor to edify the
" Chriftian people who find in you the perfect
" model of all virtues. For thefe caufes, we re-
" call you immediately, and we order you to return,
" to teach the doctrine of falvation. Return there-
" fore to the holy churches ; feed the people of his
" God. Let the paftor, at the head of the flock,
" offer up prayers for our perfon : for we are per-
" fuaded that God will diffufe on us, and on thofe
" who are Chriftians like us, his moft fignal favours,
" if you grant us the affiftance of your prayers."

It appears by the order contained in this letter,
that the Emperor was ignorant, or chofe to be
ignorant, that Athanafius had refumed the public
exercife of his functions †. Be that as it may,

---

* The word " celeftial" faintly expreffes the impious
and extravagant flattery of the Emperor to the archbifhop,
τῆς πρὸς τὸν Θεὸν τῶν ὅλων ὁμοιώσεως.　　　　　GIBBON.

† He might be ignorant of it ; for St. Gregory of Na-
zianus fays, that the order for the recall of Athanafius was
difpatched the firft of all. *Greg. Naz. or.* XXI.　　　B.

Jovian wrote to him again, to afk inftruction of him
as to the tenets which were then the fubject of
difputes. Not that he was not a confirmed catholic.
The letter juft quoted would alone prove it *;
and, befides, thus to confult the great Athanafius,
the man of the church and the bulwark of the
faith, was loudly to declare himfelf for the doctrine
of Nice. But not to mention the difpute which
had been raifed concerning the divinity of the Holy
Ghoft, the Arians, by their fophifms and captious
formularies, fome of which were rather infuffi-
cient than erroneous, had introduced into a con-
troverfy, fimple in itfelf, more difficulties than
were neceffary to embarrafs a foldier like Jovian.
Thinking himfelf then obliged by the ftate to
labour on the great work of the re-union of Chriftians, and refolved to employ only perfuafion, he
had need of fome palpable but decifive and keen
arguments to convince the fectaries, without en-
tering into thorny difcuffions, which would have
been above his reach, and in one fenfe beneath his
dignity.

Athanafius entered fully into his views; convened fome intelligent bifhops, and anfwered him

* Theodoret (l. iv. c. 2.) fays, that he ordered thofe,
who had adhered to the faith of Nice in its purity, to be
put in poffeffion of the churches. If that be true, the
order was not rigoroufly executed. It appears, however,
that Jovian gave a church new-built to the Catholics of
Antioch (of the communion of St. Meletius) ; which feems
to prove that under Julian the Chriftians might build
churches.   B.

in the name of the whole patriarchate of Alexandria. After congratulating the Emperor on the care which he took to inform himself of the truth *, the holy teacher proves that he must attach himself to the faith of Nice. It is the faith of the Apostles and martyrs. They were in possession of that doctrine when Arius came to sow his errors. All the churches have received, and still receive, the decision of Nice; the small number of Arians that oppose it cannot form a prejudice against the rest †

of

---

* We have this letter in the History of Theodoret, and among the works of Athanasius. In the letter, as it is quoted by Theodoret, is a half phrase in which Athanasius seems to promise Jovian a long and tranquil reign, as the reward of his desire to be instructed in heavenly truths: Και την βασιλειαν μετ᾽ ειρηνης πολλαις ἐων περιοδοις επιλελιτοις: "and "you will govern the empire many years in peace."

As Jovian reigned a very short time, Baronius imagines, that these words are an addition of some Arian, who was willing to make Athanasius pass for a false prophet; but in authors who are not inspired such sort of expressions ought to be regarded as wishes, and not as promises, much less as prophesies. B.

Before his departure from Antioch ‡, he assured Jovian that his orthodox devotion would be rewarded with a long and peaceful reign. Athanasius had reason to hope, that he should be allowed either the merit of a successful prediction, or the excuse of a grateful, though ineffectual, prayer. In some MSS. this indiscreet promise is omitted; perhaps by the Catholics, jealous of the prophetic fame of their leader. GIBBON.

† Συμψηφοι τυγχανεσιν αι κατα τοπον εκκλησιαι . . . παρεξ ολιγων των τα Αρειου φρονειων . . . και τοις αντιλεγων ταυτη τη πιστει ε δυνατιαι προκριμα ποιειν πασι τη οικυμιη. "All the churches "every where agree . . . a few excepted, who embrace

‡ This letter was rather previous to his coming to Antioch, and indeed occasioned it. See p. 334.

"the

of the world. At length Athanafius, willing to guard Jovian againft the herefy of Macedonius, obferves, that the fame council of Nice has fufficiently eftablifhed the confubftantiality of the Holy Ghoft, by faying, that it is " glorified with the Fa-" ther and the Son." Thus this able divine adapts himfelf to the neceffity and capacity of the prince, and does not omit to fupply him with peremptory arguments, drawn from prefcription, and the confent of the churches as to a formal and determined tenet.

The Emperor was fo well fatisfied with the letter of Athanafius, that he wifhed to converfe with him, and ordered him to repair to Antioch. The holy bifhop obeyed the more willingly, as he had already refolved to go to court; not from tafte (for no bifhop was ever lefs a courtier), but for the interefts

" the opinion of Arius *, and though fome contradict this " faith, we know that they cannot prejudice the whole " world." Athanafius, by reducing the Arians to fo fmall a number, feems to differ from the common opinion; but it muft be obferved, 1. That the bifhops who had fub-fcribed to the council of Rimini, had recovered their fall after the death of Conftantius. 2. At the very time when herefy feemed to prevail, many of thofe who received the forms propofed by the Arians, received them in a Catholic fenfe. 3. As the moft determined of the Arians did not fcruple to fay, that Jefus Chrift is God, the Chriftian people, who knew only the Supreme God, underftood that Jefus Chrift was the only and fame God with his Father, and underftood in a good fenfe the ambiguous expreffions with which the error was envelopped. This occafioned the faying of a father of that time: " The ears of the people " are more holy than the hearts of the priefts."   B.

* This affertion was verified in the fpace of thirty or forty years.

GIBBON.

of

of the church, and from deference to the advice of his intimate friends. However advantageous his reputation was, he always gained by a perſonal acquaintance. Jovian liked him extremely, and gave him his confidence. It is honourable for that prince to have placed it ſo well. Athanaſius was the greateſt man of his age; and perhaps, taken all together, the church has never had a greater. God, who deſtined him to combat the moſt dreadful of hereſies, armed at once with the ſubtleties of logic and the power of the Emperors, had endued him with all the gifts of nature and of grace, which could render him proper to fill that high deſtination.

He had a juſt, quick, and penetrating mind; a generous and diſintereſted heart; cool courage, and, it may be ſaid, uniform heroiſm, always the ſame, without impetuoſity or extravagance; lively faith; unbounded charity; profound humility; a chriſtianity, ſtrong, ſimple, and noble, like the goſpel; a natural eloquence, abounding with penetrating ſtrokes, ſtrong in ſubſtance, going directly to the point, and of rare preciſion in the Greek writers of that time. The auſterity of his life rendered, his virtue reſpectable; the gentleneſs of his manners made him beloved. The calmneſs and ſerenity of his ſoul were painted on his face. Though he had not an advantageous perſon *, his external appearance had ſomewhat majeſtic and ſtriking. He

* See note *. p. 141.

was not ignorant of the profane sciences, but he avoided making a parade of them. Skilled in the letter of the scriptures, he also possessed their spirit. Neither Greeks, nor Romans, ever loved their country so much as Athanasius loved the church, whose interests were always inseparable from his. Long experience had inured him to ecclesiastical affairs. Adversity, which enlarges and refines when it does not crush the genius, had given him admirable penetration to discover resources, even human, when every thing seemed desperate. Threatened with exile when he was in his see, and with death when he was exiled, he struggled for near fifty years against a league of men subtle in arguments, profound in intrigues, acute courtiers, masters of the prince, arbiters of favour and disgrace, indefatigable calumniators, barbarous persecutors. He disconcerted, confounded, and always escaped them, without giving them the consolation of seeing him make one false step; he made them tremble even when he was flying before them, and when he was buried alive in the tomb of his father *. He read hearts and futurity. Some Catholics were persuaded that God revealed to him the designs of his enemies; the Arians accused him of magic; and the Pagans pretended that he was

---

* Under Valens he concealed himself in the sepulchre of his father, and remained there four months. Among the ancients, particularly in Ægypt, sepulchres were buildings in the open country, so considerable that there were apartments in them. *M. Fleury*, l. XVI. 10. B.

verfed

verfed in the fcience of auguries, and that he u derftood the language of the birds *; fo true it is that his prudence was a kind of divination. No one difcerned better than he the feafons to difclofe or to conceal himfelf; thofe of fpeech or filence; of action or repofe. He knew how to fix the inconftancy of the people (the Alexandrians, which is faying all), to find a new country in the places of his exile, and the fame credit at the extremity of Gaul, in the city of Treves, as in Ægypt, and the very bofom of Alexandria; to keep up correfpondences; to procure protections; to unite the orthodox; to encourage the moft timid; of a weak friend never to make an enemy; to excufe weakneffes with a charity and goodnefs of heart, which fhewed, that, if he condemned rigorous methods in matters of religion, it was lefs from intereft than principle and character.

* This we learn from Ammianus: "It was faid, that "being thoroughly fkilled in foothfaying, and in what "was portended by augural birds, he fometimes foretold "future events." It is related on this fubject, that as Athanafius was paffing through the ftreets of Alexandria on the eve of a feftival which the Pagans were to celebrate with great feftivity, a raven was heard to croak. "What "fays that bird?" exclaimed the Pagan populace. Athanafius anfwered fmiling, "He fays, *cras*" (which fignifies in the Roman language, "to-morrow)," "and declares to "you that the Emperor of the Romans forbids you to cele- "brate your feftival." On the morning after, the prohibition of the Emperor did not fail to arrive. SOZOMEN. B.

A prophecy, or rather a joke, is related by Sozomen, (l. iv. c. 10.) which evidently proves, if the crows fpeak Latin, that Athanafius underftood their language. GIBBON.

Julian, who did not perfecute the other bifhops, at leaft openly, confidered the taking away his life as a piece of great policy, thinking that the fate of Chriftianity was attached to that of Athanafius. This honourable diftinction feemed to have completed the glory of the holy bifhop, when he repaired to Jovian. He was then about feventy years old; but his career was not ready to clofe. After having made him triumph over three former Emperors *, God deftined him to gain other victories over Valens †. _

We are ignorant of the particulars of the advice which Athanafius gave to Jovian; but we may be certain, that he confirmed him in the defign of labouring only in a Chriftian manner to re-unite Chriftians; and that he made him underftand that it was previoufly neceffary to infpire all parties with principles of kindnefs; to teach them to bear with one another; to defire and to feek peace, till it fhould pleafe God to accomplifh it. At the fame time he difclofed to him the fnares of the fectaries, fome of whom at leaft had formed projects of conqueft on a prince who was not fufficiently inftructed in theological matters to diftin-

---

* That is; of Conftantine (in the latter years of his reign deceived by the Arians), Conftantius, and Julian. B.

† The Janfenifts have often compared Athanafius and Arnauld, and have expatiated with pleafure on the faith and zeal, the merit and exile, of thofe celebrated doctors. This concealed parallel is very dexteroufly managed by the Abbé de la Bleterie.   GIBBON.

guifh

guish by himself what characterises error, when it borrows the features of truth.

Arrian and Candidus, pure Arians, ordained bishops by the famous Ætius *, both relations of the Emperor, were gone to meet him at Edessa ; and Jovian, if we may believe Philostorgius, had, in speaking to them, expressed a kind of neutrality which might give them some hope, though his answer might be only the effect of his moderation. They had followed him, without doubt, to Antioch ; and it is also known that Euzoïus, bishop of that great city, and some other Arians, already practised upon the eunuchs of the palace, having not forgotten that, by that method, they had gained the favour of Constantius, and reigned in his name. All the leaders of parties besieged Jovian to obtain his permission to persecute their enemies. We may judge of their respective pretensions by the petition of the Macedonians, who demanded to be put into possession of the churches which were occupied by the pure Arians. The Emperor contented himself with replying, " I hate disputes : I love and honour those who have peaceable views, and who " concur in union." These words, proceeding from the mouth of the sovereign, and coming from the bottom of his heart, were an effectual stroke, and immediately chilled the warmest disputants. They held a council in Antioch, where the Arians of the party of Acacius of Cæsarea in Palestine

* See Vol. I. p. 2. note *.

com-

communicated with Meletius, one of the two Catholic bifhops of that city, and fubfcribed to the form of Nice. The fincerity of their fignature is queftioned ; but if they betrayed their confcience, it was not the fault of Jovian, who declared plainly that he would not conftrain any one, and who faid it fincerely. He was not fo fuccefsful in terminating the fchifm of the Catholics of Antioch, divided between Meletius and Paulinus. Fraternal diffenfions are always the moft obftinate.

Though Jovian fhewed very great regard for Athanafius, the Arians of Alexandria, fupported clandeftinely by Euzoïus, made fome attempts to prevent his returning to his church. After the tragical death of their bifhop, George of Cappadocia, which happened in the time of Julian *, they had caft their eyes on a prieft named Lucius, a man of very bad looks, and of a ftill worfe character, who did not fail to juftify their choice by the cruelties which he committed in the perfecution of Valens. The Arians of Alexandria, for fome reafon that is not known, had not yet caufed him to be ordained. They fent deputies to Jovian, and Lucius at their head; wifhing to have him for their bifhop, or, at leaft, any other that the Emperor would give them to the exclufion of Athanafius. The Catholics of Alexandria fent deputies alfo on their part, to oppofe the efforts of the Arians; the latter addreffed the Emperor feveral

* See the IXth and Xth Epiftles of Julian, p. 17—23.

times.

tines. We have the original relation of the different audiences which he gave them *. It is a
curious remain in many refpects. Above all, Jovian is there feen drawn to the life: he there
fhews firmnefs, fenfe, judgement, and equity, fomething blunt and military, a lively difpofition, and,
if I miftake not, a tafte rather than a talent for
raillery. But I am wrong to foreftall the reader;
let him judge for himfelf †.

[The Emperors, who originally were only generals of the army, were accuftomed to exercife
with their foldiers. There was near every city a
place for exercife, called, " The field of Mars,"
or, " The field.]" One day, when Jovian [at-
tended by his guard] was going on horfeback
through the Roman gate to the field of Mars,
Lucius, Berniccus, and the other [deputies of
the] Arians, approached him, faying, " We beg
" your power, your majefty, your piety, to give
" us audience." ' Who, and whence are you?'
faid Jovian. They anfwered, " Sir, we are Chrif-
" tians." ' Whence, and of what city?' added
the Emperor. " Of Alexandria," replied the Arians.
' What do you defire of me?' faid the Emperor.
" We befeech your majefty," faid they, " to give
" us a bifhop." ' I have ordered Athanafius,' re-

---

* *Petitio Arianorum ad Jovian. inter opera Athan. t.* I.
p. 782. B.

† I give this account entire, having taken care to inclofe
within crotches all that is not in the acts themfelves, and
yet was neceffary to facilitate the underftand.ng them.

                    plied

plied Jovian, ' to return to his fee.' " Sir," faid
the Arians, " Athanafius has been banifhed many
" years for crimes of which he is not cleared."
Then a foldier [a Catholic, of the Emperor's
guard] in the tranfport of his zeal, took the
liberty to fay, ' Sir, give yourfelf the trouble
' to examine who are thefe people, and whence
' they come.   They are the miferable remains
' of the faction of Cappadocia, the agents of
' George, of that villain, who defolated the city
' of Alexandria, and the whole world.'   At thefe
words, the Emperor fpurred his horfe, and went
to the field.

They prefented themfelves a fecond time, and
faid, ' We have feveral heads of accufation againft
' Athanafius, which we are able to prove. It is
' thirty years fince he was banifhed by Conftan-
' tine and Conftantius, of immortal memory. He
' has been banifhed lately by the beloved of God,
' the moft philofophical * and moft happy Julian.'
" The accufations of ten, twenty, thirty years,"
faid the Emperor, " are obfolete. Speak no more
" to me of Athanafius. I know why he was ac-
" cufed, and how he was banifhed."
[So firm an anfwer did not repulfe the Arians.
They returned to the charge a third time.] " We

---

* It is difficult to conceive that perfons who profeffed
Chriftianity, and, befides, were fpeaking to a Chriftian
Emperor, fhould have been fo irreligious, fo abfurd, as to
give Julian thefe epithets.

· Muft there not have been fome interpolation here ?   B.

" have,"

" have," faid they," " new complaints againſt Atha-
" naſius." [The deputies of the Catholics of Alexandria beginning, as it ſeems, to ſpeak at the ſame
time], " Jovian ſaid, ' When all ſpeak together, it
' is impoſſible to underſtand who is in the right.
' Chooſe two perſons on each ſide ; for I cannot
' anſwer both of you.' The Catholics began. " Sir,"
ſaid they, " theſe men, whom you ſee, are the re-
" mains of the deteſtable George, the ſcourge of
" our province. They do not ſuffer in the cities any
" ſenator" . . . The Arians [wiſhing to cut ſhort an
account which would have covered them with confuſion, and perceiving, beſides, that Lucius, a crea-
ture of George, would never be approved by the Emperor, interrupted the Catholics by ſaying], ' Be ſo
' kind, Sir, as to ſet over us whomever you pleaſe,
' except Athanaſius.' " I have already told you," replied the Emperor, " what concerns Athanaſius is
" ſettled ;"—and in an angry tone, he ſaid to his
guard in Latin, " *Feri, feri*," that is to ſay, " Strike,
" ſtrike *." [The order, without doubt, was noᵗ
executed, as the Arians perſiſted.] ' Sir,' ſaid
they, ' if you ſend back Athanaſius, our city is
' ruined ; and, beſides, no one aſſociates with him.'
" I have, however,' ſaid Jovian, " made en-
" quiries ; and I am aſſured, that he thinks well,
" that he is orthodox, and that he teaches ſound

* Jovian ſpoke Greek to the Alexandrians. It is probable that the Emperors always ſpoke Latin to their
guard.   B.

Z 4   " doctrine."

" doctrine." ' It is true,' replied the Arians, ' that
' he speaks well; but he thinks ill.' The Emperor said, " I require no other testimony than that
" which you have given him. If he thinks ill, he
" must give an account of it to God. We men
" hear words; God alone knows the bottom of the
" heart." ' Sir,' said the Arians, ' allow us to
' hold our assemblies *.' " Ah!" replied Jovian,
" what hinders you?" ' But, Sir,' added they,
' Athanasius declares us heretics and dogmatists.
" His place obliges him," said Jovian. " It is the
" duty of those who teach the truth." ' Sir,'
proceeded the Arians, ' he has taken away the lands
' of the churches †.' " You would make me be-
" lieve," said Jovian, " that you are brought
" hither by other views than those of the faith.
" Retire, and live in peace. Go to church; you
" have an assembly to-morrow." [This was on
a Saturday, or the eve of some festival.] " After
" the assembly, every one shall subscribe his pro-
" fession of faith. You have here some bishops
" and Nemesinus ‡. Athanasius also is here. Those
" who are not instructed in the faith have only to
" apply themselves to him. I give you to-morrow,
" and the day after. I am now going to the field

* Συναγισθαι.

† This perhaps is the meaning here of the word τα
τιμενη.　　　B.

‡ This Nemesinus is not known; he might be an officer
employed by the Emperor to effectuate the re-union. Under
Constantius we find *Nemesianus*, intendant of the finances,
eames largitionum.　　　B.

" of

" of Mars." A lawyer, a Cynic philosopher, then
said to Jovian, ' Sir, on account of the bishop
' Athanasius the treasurer-general has taken some
' houses from me.' Jovian answered him, " If the
" treasurer-general has taken some houses, is Atha-
" nasius responsible for it?" Another lawyer,
named Patalas, then said to him, ' I have a charge
' against Athanasius.' " What business," said the
Emperor, " has a Pagan like thee to trouble him-
" self with Christians?"

[During this time Lucius kept behind the other
deputies. The bad situation in which he saw his
affairs was likely to increase the confusion which
his disadvantageous person might already have occasioned in him. He would have mingled in] the
crowd of the people of Antioch, who were collected round the Emperor. But some seized him,
and having made him advance, against his will,
' See, Sir,' said they, ' what a subject they wish to
' make a bishop!' [It must be remembered that
Athanasius had a countenance full of nobleness
and dignity *.]

Nevertheless the same Lucius [depending perhaps on some private recommendation] ventured
to appear again before the Emperor at the
gate of the palace, and begged an audience.
Jovian stopped, and said to him, ' Lucius, is it
' thou to whom I am speaking? How camest thou
' hither? By sea or by land?" " By sea, Sir," replied Lucius. ' May the God of the universe, may

* See p. 141, note.

' the

' the fun * and the moon,' faid the Emperor,
' punifh the companions of thy voyage, for not
' having thrown thee into the fea! May the fhip
' be eternally the fport of outrageous waves, and
' never arrive in port!' [Thus he delivered himfelf from that odious man by an ironical impre-
cation, in which the learned editors of Athanafius
difcover much wit †. I queftion whether every one
difcovers as much; nor do I know whether they will
not be furprifed at this fantaftic affemblage of the
fun and moon with the God of the univerfe in the
mouth of a prince in other refpects fo religious.]

The Emperor, having learned that the Arian
cabal were ufing indirect meafures at court, and
that Euzoïus had engaged Probatius, the great
chamberlain, and the other eunuchs of the palace, to fpeak to him in favour of the Arians
of Alexandria, was enraged to fee that the fucceffors of Eufebius and Bardion ‡, who had made
a traffic of the favours of Conftantius, fhould pretend to fucceed to their credit. He made his
eunuchs undergo the torture to difcover the
bottom of the intrigue; and faid, " that he would
" treat in the fame manner the firft [of his do-
" mefticks] who fhould dare to folicit him againft
" the Chriftians." After having begun the work

* It is in the Greek Κομήτης ηλιος, " the blazing fun." B.
† See the Latin Life of Athanafius, which is prefixed to
the new edition ; *et facetè quidem.*   B.
‡ Eruadion in the French ; but in the Greek, Βαρδιων.

of re-union, as far as time would permit, under the eyes and direction of Athanasius, he allowed him to return into Ægypt, and remained impressed with esteem for his virtues and talents *.

With such zeal for the Christian religion, Jovian, one would think, must have succeeded at Antioch better than his predecessor. But the city was filled with Arians, or with persons who thought themselves such; and the Arian sects deemed themselves persecuted when they could not persecute. Besides, the inhabitants of Antioch remained in possession of the faculty of despising all their sovereigns, or at least of turning them into ridicule. What prince could have found favour in their sight? They did not spare Marcus Aurelius. Some Emperors had punished those insolent people. Most had connived at their insults.

* Athanasius at the court of Antioch is agreeably represented by La Bleterie. He translates the singular and original conferences of the Emperor, the primate of Ægypt, and the Arian deputies. The Abbé is not satisfied with the coarse pleasantry of Jovian; but his partiality for Athanasius assumes, in his eyes, the character of justice.

GIBBON.

As soon as Athanasius had gained the confidence, and secured the faith, of the Christian Emperor, he returned in triumph to his diocese, and continued, with mature counsels and undiminished vigour, to direct, ten years longer, the ecclesiastical government of Alexandria, Ægypt, and the Catholic church. The true æra of his death is perplexed with some difficulties. But the date (A. D. 373, May 2.) which seems the most consistent with history and reason, is ratified by his authentic life (*Maffei Osservazioni Letterarie*, tom. III. p. 81.)

Ibid.

3   Julian

Julian had lately revenged himself with his pen. But Antioch was a city that was incorrigible, was reckoned such, and abused its reputation. Jovian was not well received. The treaty of peace, and the cession of Nisibis, furnished the jokers with a thousand sarcastic strokes. They had ridiculed Julian for his beard, his diminutive stature, his temerity. As for Jovian, he was treated as a second Paris: " he has," it was said, " the good looks and per- " son of the Trojan prince. He has, like him, " ruined his nation. O that he had perished in " the war! He should be sent back into Persia " to commence another treaty. His person was " formed at the expence of his mind. The measure " of his stature is that of his folly." The walls were covered with abusive bills, the streets and squares were strewed with verses of Homer, applied, or parodied, in the most insulting manner *. In the Hippodrome a man of the dregs of the people made the spectators laugh by repeating, with a loud voice, some low jests on the stature of the Emperor; and at the idea of this wretch being ap- prehended, the people revolted. This sedition might have had dreadful consequences, if the præfect Sallust the second had not quelled it ; and that required all his authority.

* The libels of Antioch may be admitted on very slight evidence.   GIBBON.

These

Thefe facts, though taken from. the fragments
of a Greek monk *, an hiftorian little known, are
no more than probable and fuitable to the character
of the inhabitants of Antioch. But what the
fame writer adds merits no belief. " There was,"
fays he, " in Antioch, a fmall temple, of very
" elegant architecture, built by Hadrian, in ho-
" nour of his adoptive father, Trajan. Julian had
" converted it to a library, and entrufted the. care
" of it to the eunuch Theophilus. Jovian, at the
" inftigation of his wife, reduced it to afhes, with
" all the books that it contained." But, what is
more furprifing, the author makes Jovian march to
this expedition at the head of his feraglio, with a
torch in his hand †, juft as Alexander formerly,
with the courtefans of Greece, burned the palace
of Perfepolis.

I am far from fufpecting the Greek monk of in-
venting fo ridiculous a ftory, and of intentionally
blackening Jovian. He copied, without difcern-
ment, fome enemy of that prince, Eunapius perhaps, an hiftorian very envenomed against the
Chriftian Emperors. That the morals of Jovian

* John of Antioch, whofe hiftory began with the cre-
ation of the world, and clofed with the reign of Phocas. B.
† Αυ]ων των παλλακιδων υφαπ]υσων μϊα γελωῖος την πυραν.
" The harlots themfelves with laughter lighting the pile."
SUIDAS.
He might be *edax, et vino Venerique indulgens.* But I agree
with La Bleterie in rejecting the foolifh report of a Bac-
chanalian riot (*ap. Suidam*) celebrated at Antioch, by the
Emperor, his *wife,* and a troop of concubines. GIBBON.

were

were not very regular we may believe, if we please, on the word of Ammianus Marcellinus, though according to the judicious reflection of Ammianus himself, on the subject of another Emperor, the malignity, or corruption, of mankind, is accustomed to lend frailties to princes who have them not *. However, if Jovian had lived in a public and scandalous irregularity, the Christians would not have loaded him with praises at a time when no one had any thing more to hope or fear from him. The concurrence of the Empress with the mistresses of the Emperor is also something very singular. But by what caprice could the wife of Jovian, Cariton, to whom her father, Lucillian, had, without doubt, given a Roman education, suitable to the rank which he himself held in the state, have wished to burn a temple, which was no longer a temple, but a library? To annihilate the remains of profane literature is a Mussulman taste, which never prevailed among Christians, especially in the fourth century, when the most celebrated men in the church were at the same time the most conversant with the sciences of the Greeks. Besides, we shall presently see that the wife of Jovian was not then with him. In short, the silence of Ammianus and Zosimus completes the destruction of this calumny, and even renders what I have just

---

* It is supposed that they would do all that they can with impunity. *Quod crimen etiamsi non invenit malignitas, fingit in summarum licentiâ potestatum.*　　　B.

mentioned,

mentioned, of the ribaldry of Antioch againſt Jovian, in ſome degree ſuſpicious.

Neither of them ſay a word of what happened during his reſidence in that city. Ammianus contents himſelf with relating ſeveral natural events which the Pagan ſuperſtition conſidered as fatal preſages. The ſtatue of Maximian, placed in the veſtibule of the palace, loſt on a ſudden the [brazen] globe (a ſymbol of the empire) which it held in its hand. A dreadful noiſe was heard in the council-room. Comets were ſeen in the day-time *. The Emperor, too intelligent to be alarmed by theſe pretended ſigns of the wrath of heaven, but filled with a thouſand anxieties on account of the provinces of the Weſt, of which he had received no intelligence, ſet out with his army in the month of December. Forced marches, and the rigour of the ſeaſon, deſtroyed a great number of men and horſes.

At Tarſus he paid the laſt duties to Julian, according to Socrates, and gave him a ſolemn funeral. Ammianus only ſays, that he ordered his

---

* Ammianus, who is very ready to diſplay his erudition, here relates the various ſentiments of the ancient philoſophers on comets, and concludes with the opinion of Pythagoras, which ſeems then to have had the preference: " that they are ſtars, like the reſt, but that we are igno- " rant of their revolutions." *Stellas eſſe quaſdam cæteris ſimiles, quarum ortus obituſque, quibus ſint temporibus præſtituti, humanis mentibus ignorari.* B.

tomb

tomb to be decorated *. This order was executed under Valentinian and Valens, with much attention, on their part, and even with sufficient magnificence. To give some idea of it, it is enough to say, that Libanius was satisfied. Thus three Christian Emperors, whom Julian had molested on account of their religion, concurred in granting him that frivolous reward of his frivolous virtues, or rather that prerogative annexed to the rank in which God had placed him in the world. Humanity, decorum, policy, and even religion authorised their conduct; and Jovian did not foresee, that, at the end of twelve centuries, his having buried the dead, and expressed some regard for the talents of the man, the Emperor, and the nephew of the great Constantine, would be imputed to him as a crime †.

Though we have no incontestible proofs of the apotheosis of Julian, there is no doubt that the

* Zonaras says the same in these words ; εξ Αντιοχιας δι εις Ταρσον γεγονως, και το μνημα κοσμησας τε Ιελιανε επαινει." " Going from Antioch to Tarsus, he honoured Julian by " adorning his tomb." He also relates that the corpse of Julian was afterwards removed from Tarsus to Constantinople ; which is confirmed by Cedrenus.   VALOIS.

† Baronius, in his Annals, considers the premature death of Jovian as the punishment of his having commanded the adorning the tomb of a wretch who deserved to be thrown into the highway, *hominis alioqui ne cæspititiâ quidem sepulturâ digni.*   B.

The Abbé de la Bleterie handsomely exposes the brutal bigotry of Baronius, who would have thrown Julian to the dogs.   GIBBON.

fenate of Rome, whofe members were ftill almoft
all idolaters, paid him an honour due by right to
the Emperors, unlefs a procefs was inftituted againft
their memory. Even the Chriftian princes were
deified. There was no medium: they muft be
ranked among the Gods, or numbered among the
tyrants. Many cities, in which Paganifm prevailed,
affociated Julian with their tutelar deities. Some
of his credulous adorers thought that they perceived fome effects of his power ; while it was faid
by the Chriftians, that the afhes of that apoftate
ftirred in the tomb. A report was even fpread
that the earth, by a violent fhock, had difcharged
them from her bofom. There, however, they remained, when, writing in the reign of Theodofius,
Ammianus judged the city of Tarfus little worthy
of fuch a treafure. This hiftorian, a foldier, wifhed
to have feen Julian on the banks of the Tiber
among the firft Cæfars * ; and Libanius, entirely
a man of letters, would have been better pleafed
with him in the Academy by the fide of the divine

* xv. 10. The paffage deferves to be tranfcribed:
*Cujus fuprema et cineres . . . non Cydnus videre deberet, quam-
vis gratiffimus amnis et liquidus ; fed ad perpetuandam gloriam
rectè factorum præterlambere Tiberis, interfecans urbem æternam,
divorúmque veterum monumenta præftringens.*   B.

" Whofe obfequies and afhes fhould not have been feen
" by the Cydnus, though a moft pure and limpid ftream,
" but, to perpetuate the glory of his good deeds, fhould
" have been laved by the Tiber, which interfects the
" eternal city, and chills the monuments of the ancient
" Gods."

Plato *. Either in the field of Mars, or in the Lyceum, Julian would have been placed with propriety. On the contrary, he would have been remarkably misplaced, if, as the modern Greeks pretend, he had been afterwards removed from Tarsus to Constantinople, and interred among the Christian princes in the church of the Holy Apostles. Who could have made that august temple so strange a present? This kind of digression will, I hope, be excused. To the history, that I am writing, nothing that relates to Julian is foreign.

Jovian, continuing to make long marches, passed through Tyana in Cappadocia, where Procopius, the secretary of state, and the tribune Memoridus, who had been dispatched into the West, brought him the following intelligence. Lucillian, his father-in-law, on arriving at Milan, had learned that Malarich, that confidential Frank appointed by the new Emperor to command the troops in Gaul, in the room of Jovinus, refused to accept that employment. Upon that, the Count had speedily passed the Alps, and repaired to Rheims, with Valentinian and the tribune Seniauchus. He

---

* *Orat. Parent.* c. 156. p. 377. Τετον εδεξατο μεν το προ Ταρσον της Κιλικιας χωριον, ειχε δ' αν δικαιοτερον το της Ακαδημιας πλησιον Πλατωνος.   B.

     " The suburb of Tarsus in Cilicia received him ; but " he had a greater right to be buried in the Academy near " the tomb of Plato."

     The history of princes does not very frequently renew the example of a similar competition.   GIBBON.

had

had found Gaul tranquil and submissive to Jovian.
But without considering that the authority of his
son-in-law was not sufficiently established, he undertook to proceed against some officers with a
premature severity. A criminal, apprehensive of
being punished for his misdemeanours, sought an
asylum among some troops of Batavians *, who
were probably quartered in the neighbourhood of
Rheims. To induce them to take him under their
protection, he assured them that Jovian was only
an usurper who had revolted against Julian ; but
that Julian was living, and would soon make that
rebel sensible of it, if he had not already ; and that
the most essential service which subjects could render to their lawful sovereign was to exterminate the
emissaries of a tyrant, who came to surprise the
fidelity of the people, and to engage them in their
revolt. This Roman, indiscreet as he was, found
credit among people that were simple, and besides
affectionate to Julian. They took arms, and massacred Lucillian and the tribune Seniauchus. Valentinian (who in a few months was to reign) owed
his life to the care which his host took to secrete
him. The Batavians, having soon discovered the

* Ammianus only says, *ad militaria signa confugit*, without mentioning the Batavians. Zosimus names them,
but extremely mutilates all this history, and places the
scene at Sirmium. It appears, however, by the *Notitia* of
the empire, that there were Batavians at Condren, in
the second Belgic, of which Rheims was the capital. *Præ-
fectus Læterum Batavorum Contraginensium, Noviomago Belgicæ
secundæ.*   B.

A a 2   imposition,

impofition, returned to their duty. As, on the refufal of Malarich, Jovinus had retained the command of the troops, he difpatched the principal officers to Jovian, to affure him of the fubmiffion of the army and himfelf *. Procopius and Memoridus, accompanied by Valentinian, proclaimed the approaching arrival of his deputies.

The Emperor, to reward the zeal of Valentinian, gave him the fecond [fchool, or] company of targetteers, of his domeftic guards, and fent Arinthæus immediately with a letter to Jovinus, by which he confirmed that general in his poft, and enjoined him to punifh the author of the impofition, and to fend the principal leaders of the fedition to court, loaded with irons.

At the little town of Afpuna †, in Galatia, the deputies from the army of Gaul met Jovian, who having given them a public audience with extreme fatisfaction, made them prefents, and ordered them to return immediately to their refpective employments.

He entered Ancyra ‡ at the end of the month of December; and on the firft day of January, 364, he there celebrated the folemnity of his confulfhip. In the room of Varronian, his father,

* The moderation of Jovinus, mafter-general of the cavalry, who forgave the intention of his difgrace, foon appeafed the tumult, and confirmed the uncertain minds of the foldiers. GIBBON.

† As he defcended from mount Taurus. *Ibid.*

‡ The capital of Galatia.

who

who died conful elect, he had chofen for his collegue young Varronian, his fon. He had been
brought from Illyricum to Ancyra, where the Emperor immediately conferred upon him the title of
Nobiliſſimus; a title invented for the brothers of
Conftantine, and afterwards given to the fons of
the Emperors *. They quitted it only to affume
that of Cæfar. Other princes had often raifed
their fons to the confulfhip before the time fixed
by the laws; but a conful in the cradle had never
yet been feen. Jovian thought it a debt to the
memory of his father to fubftitute to that illuftrious
veteran an infant who bore his name. After
all, this dignity, which was ftill called the fummit
of human grandeur, had no longer any functions.
It ferved merely to denominate the years, and to
perpetuate the form of the ancient government.
On the day of the ceremony, when the young
prince was to be placed, according to cuftom, in
the curule chair, he expreffed by obftinate cries a
reluctance, which feemed a bad omen, and which
was foon after confidered as a kind of forefight †.

* The fame is now the title of our dukes.

† *Cujus vagitus, pertinaciter reluctantis, ne in curuli fellâ
veheretur ex more, id quod mox accidit portendebat.* Ammian.
xxv. 10. Auguftus, and his fucceffors, refpectfully folicited
a difpenfation of age for the fons or nephews, whom they
raifed to the confulfhip. But the curule chair of the firft
Brutus had never been difhonoured by an infant. GIBBON.
See p. 290.

From

From Ancyra Jovian repaired to Dadaſtana, a ſmall city, or town, on the frontiers of Galatia and Bithynia, but which belonged to the firſt of theſe provinces *. There, if we credit Socrates, he received the deputies from the ſenate of Conſtantinople, who came to compliment him on his conſulſhip. Themiſtius, the chief of the deputation, there pronounced, according to the ſame hiſtorian, the panegyric of the Emperor, in which nevertheleſs are obſerved all the marks of a diſcourſe pronounced the very day that Jovian took poſſeſſion of the conſular dignity. The piece, however, is written with great elegance and dignity; but, like all that comes from the pen of Themiſtius, is rather too much loaded with learned alluſions. Some ſtrokes of flattery appear in it concerning the election of Jovian, and on the peace made with Sapor. The author extolls, with much more juſtice, the patronage with which the prince honours men of learning. The elogium principally turns on his mildneſs and equity with regard to matters of religion. The ſame orator gives him a commendation which is alone worth a panegyric; namely, that his elevation had made no change in his manner of treating mankind. He neither forgot nor ſlighted thoſe who had been his equals. He did not affect to make his ſuperiority perceived by thoſe who

---

* The Itinerary of Antoninus fixes Dadaſtana 125 Roman miles from Nice, 117 from Ancyra. Weſſeling, Itinerar. p. 142.　　　　　　　　　　　　　　　Gibbon.

might

might have made him senfible of theirs. His friends,
his benefactors, did not difcern the change of his
fituation, but by the effects of his gratitude and
liberality. He collected at his court the moft virtuous men in the empire: he invited thither, he
attached to his perfon, thofe whom difgrace, or
exile, had eftranged. "There were feen," according to the expreffion of Themiftius, "watching
"over the fafety of his reign, the wife Neftor, the
"free and generous Diomed, the Chryfantus of Cy-
"rus, and the Artabazus of Xerxes." I fufpect that
Salluft the fecond is the Neftor; Valentinian might
be the Diomed. I am not fufficiently acquainted
with the court of Jovian to guefs the two others.
It is not only in modern times that orators, by
way of being eloquent and figurative, exprefs
themfelves in a manner fometimes ænigmatical to
their contemporaries, and almoft always unintelligible to pofterity.

The endowments of Jovian, acknowledged by
the Pagans themfelves, his attention to find out
perfons of merit, and that talent, which in a prince
may fupply the place of all others, of knowing
mankind, of eftimating their worth, and properly
employing them, announced to the Romans a wife
government. Some faults, which I have not difguifed, he committed. Raifed on a fudden from a
ftation of little eminence to the fupreme power, to
which he had never afpired even in a dream, in a
manner dazzled and feduced by the fatality of cir-

A a 4

cumftances,

cumſtances, he made ſome ſlips on the moſt rugged and ſlippery ground in the world. But the faults of inexperience and ſurprife often turn to the advantage of thoſe who commit them, when they have good ſenſe and juſt intentions. Jovian was young : he might have acquired what he wanted. Ammianus could not have had a mean opinion of him, as, when he reproaches him with ſome vices, that author preſumes that he might have corrected them through reſpect to his diadem. Every thing may be hoped from a monarch who reſpects himſelf ſo far as to find motives to become virtuous even in independence, the uſual ſtumbling-block of virtue. The choice, which Jovian made, of his confidents and miniſters, gives room to believe, that he was capable of receiving advice ; and, as it is obſerved by one of the greateſt men of the laſt age, " ſtates " are generally better governed under a prince of " moderate abilities, who knows how to hear and " follow good advice, than by a ſovereign of a " ſuperior genius, who is attached to his undor- " ſtanding, and thinks himſelf infallible *."

The two capitals, the provinces, the armies, had acknowledged Jovian. The church was about to enjoy a profound peace : the ſtate, united within itſelf, hoped to repair its loſſes : Jovian ſeemed

* Grotius, in his hiſtory of the war of the Netherlands, *l.* vii. under the year 1598. *Uſu compertum . . . . multa ſæpè ſalubriùs geſta ſub principe qui aliorum benè repertis aures et juſſa commodaret, quàm ſi cui ſapiendi fiducia contumaciam addidiſſet.* B.

able

able to promife himfelf a long and glorious reign. Conftantinople was preparing to receive him magnificently, and, impatient to poffefs him herfelf, conjured him to get the ftart of the prince his fon. Rome, who alfo flattered herfelf with foon feeing the Emperor, was already ftriking medals to celebrate his arrival ; his wife was coming to meet him with the pomp of an emprefs ; when, in the night between the 16th and 17th of February [364], he was found dead in his bed, after having reigned only feven months and twenty days. This was the third Emperor who difappeared in lefs than three years and a half.

It is pretended that he was fuffocated by the fumes of charcoal that was lighted in his chamber, to warm it, and to dry the walls which had been newly plaiftered *. The danger to which Julian had been expofed at Paris †, might have put him on his guard againft a like accident. Others afcribe his death to indigeftion ‡, or to the attack of an apoplexy. The caufe was neglected to be afcertained ; without doubt, becaufe it was thought natural : but this very negligence made many imagine it to be the effect of the wickednefs of men. Am-

---

* See Ammianus Eutropius, who might likewife be prefent, Jerom, Orofius, Sozomen, Zofimus, and Zonaras. We cannot expect a perfect agreement, and we fhall not difcufs minute differences. GIBBON.

† See the Mifopogon, Vol. I. p. 236.

‡ Occafioned either by the quantity of the wine, or the quality of the mufhrooms, which he had fwallowed in the evening. GIBBON.

mianus,

mianus, by faying, that " his death, like that of
" Scipio Æmilianus, was followed by no enqui-
" ries," infinuates, that he loft his life by fome
fecret attack *. St. Chryfoftom fays exprefsly,
that " Jovian was poifoned by his domeftics."
Would the eunuchs of the palace have formed a confpiracy to deprive themfelves of a mafter who feemed
not to be of a temper to fuffer himfelf to be governed, or were they fet at work by fome ambitious man, fuch as Procopius, who, neverthelefs,
did not avail himfelf of that crime? Still it is certain, that the fufpicion could not fall on the fucceffor of Jovian. It was not till after having offered the empire to Salluft, born to deferve it, and
conftantly to refufe it †; it was not till after having caft their eyes on various fubjects, among others
on Januarius, a relation of Jovian, that the army
fuddenly determined [Feb. 26], in favour of Valentinian ‡, who was then abfent §. The Chriftians

---

* Ammianus, unmindful of his ufual candour and good
fenfe, compares the death of the harmlefs Jovian to that
of the fecond Africanus, who had excited the fears and
refentment of the popular faction.　　GIBBON.

† He enjoyed the glory of a fecond refufal; and when
the virtues of the father were alleged in favour of his fon,
the præfect, with the firmnefs of a difinterefted patriot,
declared to the electors, that the feeble age of the one, and
the unexperienced youth of the other, were equally incapable of the laborious duties of government.　　*Ibid.*

‡ Valentinian was the fon of Count Gratian, a native
of Cibalis, in Pannonia, who, from an obfcure condition,
had raifed himfelf, by matchlefs ftrength and dexterity, to
the military commands of Africa and Britain; from which
he

tians bitterly lamented Jovian, and thought that God had only shewn him to the world, because the world was not worthy of him *. A proof that it was not the spirit of party that caused their tears to flow, is the good that is said of him by the Pagans. Valentinian and Valens did not prevent the senate of Rome from placing him among the Gods †. His corpse was carried to Constantinople into the church of the Holy Apostles ‡, where, long after, his tomb was seen among those of the other Augusti.

His wife survived him several years; an instance as memorable, but still more striking, of the insignificance of what is styled grandeur. She had lost in a few months a father-in law, a father, a husband, of whose elevation she only heard to feel more poignantly his loss. That which is the resource of all other mothers, completed her unhappiness. She had a son; but a son deprived of the highest hopes, and suspicious to the government.

he retired with an ample fortune and suspicious integrity. The city of Nice in Bithynia was chosen for the place of election. Valentinian associated his brother Valens in the empire, in one of the suburbs of Constantinople, thirty days after his own elevation. GIBBON.

§ In his quarters at Ancyra.

* *Ostendunt terris hunc tantum fata, neque ultra*
Esse sinunt. VIRG.

† This seems to me the meaning of these words of Eutropius: *benignitate principum qui ei successerunt inter Divos relatus est.* B.

‡ The sad procession was met on the road by his wife Charito. GIBBON.

The

The empire was elective, and young Varronian not having been chosen Cæsar, had no right to pretend to it. Besides, Jovian had not had time to ingratiate many dependents. It was feared, however, that Varronian would sooner or later aspire to the place which his father had filled. He was still living in the year 380. A barbarous policy had already deprived him of an eye; and his mother constantly trembled for the life of that unfortunate child, who had no crime but that of being the son of an Emperor *. She was, without doubt, a Christian, and no one had ever more need of the solid consolations which Christianity alone can give. It is not certain that Jovian had conferred on her the title of *Augusta*. No medal of this princess now exists, though those of Jovian are not scarce. She was placed, after her death, in the tomb of her husband.

* Chryfoftom, *tom.* I. *p.* 336. 344. *edit. Montfaucon.* The Christian orator attempts to comfort the widow by the examples of illustrious misfortunes; and observes, that " of " nine Emperors (including the Cæsar Gallus) who had " reigned in his time, only two (Constantine and Con-" stantius) died a natural death." Such vague consolations have never wiped away a single tear. GIBBON.

An ABSTRACT of an ESSAY,

By the Abbé de la BLETERIE,

On the Rank and Power of the ROMAN EMPERORS, in the Senate *.

From *Les Memoires de l'Academie des Sciences et Belles Lettres*, at Paris, tom. XXIV.

THE object of this Memoir is to shew the error of those who. consider the imperial government as a monarchy, and to prove that it was in fact an aristocracy, the head of which, invested with the power of the civil and military magistrates, the consuls, tribunes, and generals of the ancient republic, was, after all, only the first magistrate; powerful enough indeed to oppress his country, when willing to expose himself to the risk of acting the tyrant, but also liable to be punished as such whenever she could assert her rights. Without admitting this point, the history of the Emperors must appear a heap of the grossest contradictions, a confused chaos of unaccountable facts and events, a downright school of fanaticism and rebellion; whereas, by adopting it, every obscurity vanishes, every difficulty is removed; and we

---

* The Abbé de la Bleterie delights to pursue the vestiges of the old constitution, and sometimes finds them in his copious fancy.　　　　　GIBBON.

are

are no longer furprifed at feeing the fenate proceed judicially againft a Nero, and other fuch
monfters, both before and after their deaths.

In the fenate the Emperor fat between the two
Confuls. His curule chair did not, by any thing
that appears, differ in any refpect from theirs.
The privilege, granted to Caius *, of fitting on a
tribunal fo high that it was impoffible to reach
him, did not defcend to his fucceffors. Neither
Tiberius nor Auguftus had ever any guards in the
fenate. Tiberius, indeed, in the twentieth year of
his reign, afked leave to introduce with him Macro,
Præfect of the Prætorium, accompanied by a fmall
number of other officers; and the fenate permitted
him to bring in as many military men as he thought
proper; but this conceffion, of which that prince,
as he never returned to Rome, never had occafion
to avail himfelf, became fo precarious, as to be renewed for Caius, and then for Claudius, after
whom the Emperors generally appeared in the
fenate with one or two Præfects of the Prætorium.

The meetings of the fenate were either ordinary,
the number of which was fixed to two for every
month, or extraordinary, being called, as the exigence of affairs feemed to require, by the Conful
in poffeffion of the *fafces*, the Prætor, in the abfence of the Confuls, or the Tribune, in certain

* Caligula.

cafes,

cafes, which it is not eafy to determine. The
Emperors, without being Confuls for the year, had
the privilege of calling extraordinary meetings of
the fenate; firft, as invefted with the tribunitian
power; fecondly, by virtue of the conceffion made
to Auguftus, A. U. C. 732; thirdly, as perpetual
Confuls. Moft of the Emperors, when at Rome,
were prefent in the fenate; and all, or almoft all
of them, acknowledged themfelves inferior to it,
at leaft in fome refpects. They addreffed it as
fuppliants or petitioners. " I pray you, I conjure
" you, I befeech you, confcript Fathers," are their
common expreffions. Some of them ftyle the fenators their lords and their patrons; others call
them the princes of the world, and give them the
title of " Your clemency, your majefty," &c. The
Emperors chofen by the army always applied to
the fenate to confirm their election. But what
were the prerogatives of the Emperor in this auguft
affembly?

Either the Emperor was Conful for the time
being, or Conful elect, or neither the one nor the
other. In quality of Conful for the time being,
he convened the fenate, prefided in it, propofed
the affairs upon which it was to deliberate, collected the fuffrages, and finally difmiffed it; all
functions attached to the confular dignity; but it
was only alternately with the other Conful, his
collegue, that he performed them. For a long
time, the Prince, when in the exercife of the confular

fular power, wore the fame kind of robes as the other Confuls *; which robes were kept in the capitol, to fhew that both one and the other held from Heaven, and their fellow-citizens, the powers of which thofe robes were the enfigns †.

As Conful-elect, the Prince performed the functions attached to that dignity. The Confuls elect gave their votes firft, and it appears that the Emperor fubmitted to this cuftom. In the early days of Rome, the Confuls for the time being never gave their votes in affairs of their own propofing; and if they fometimes voted during the Imperial goverment, it was never but in matters which the Emperor himfelf had laid before the fenate.

The Emperor feldom prefided in the fenate, though actually prefent, unlefs invefted with the ordinary confular dignity. This the Abbé de la Bleterie proves by a paffage in Pliny the younger, who, fpeaking of Marcus Prifcus, fays, that Trajan then prefided in the fenate, " for he was " Conful." The Prince was often prefent only in quality of fenator. We read that feveral Emperors reckoned it an honour to be members of the Senate, and to pay the tax called *glebæ fenatoriæ præftatio.*

* That drefs was a robe of purple, embroidered with filk and gold, and fometimes ornamented with coftly gems.
GIBBON.

† The Emperors themfelves, who difdained the faint fhadow of the republic, were confcious that they acquired an additional fplendor and majefty as often as they affumed the annual honours of the confular dignity. *Ibid.*

They

They never left the house till the Consul had dismissed the senators in the usual form, by the words " *Nihil vos moramur, Patres conscripti.*" There are many instances to prove, that the Emperor used to give his opinion in the senate; and that the Consul called upon him for it. This is sufficient to shew the error of Salmasius and Muret, who, from the Emperor's collecting the votes, concluded, that he never gave any himself; it being an established custom, that whatever member collected the votes never gave any himself, and the prince was, besides, superior to all the other magistrates. But, as the prince did not always preside, neither did he always collect the votes, nor was he superior to the state, of which the Consul was both the organ and the representative, when, as president of the assembly, he called upon the members for their votes. Accordingly, the senate often decided against the opinion of the Emperor, and its decrees were always considered as the voice of the state. Sometimes, it is true, the will of despotic princes was blindly followed by the senators; but even then the senate deliberated and decided sovereignly. On this occasion M. de la Bleterie observes, that authors, in general, are too apt to exaggerate the abuse which the Roman Emperors made of their authority. From the year of Rome 727, the epocha of the lawful authority of Augustus, to the first year of Diocletian, and U. C. 1037, there elapsed 310 years. Now let

us, on the one hand, add together the reigns of
all the bad Emperors, and, on the other hand, the
reigns of thofe who were fometimes good and
fometimes bad, and we fhall not be able to make
out above 120 years of oppreſſion for the Romans;
and even in this interval we fhall find proofs of the
Roman liberty fubfifting, at leaft *de jure*, though
oppreſſed *de facto*; fo that there remain 190 years,
during which the government was conformable to
law, and favourable to liberty. This learned
Academician has, befides, obferved, in order to
invalidate a fact related by Tertullian, that authors
are apt to infift too much on the flavifh fubjection
of the fenate to the will of Tiberius. That Emperor, having received from Paleftine an account
of the miracles performed by Jefus Chrift, wrote
to the fenate to propofe placing him among the
Gods; which propofal was rejected. It is true,
indeed, that the fenate was, at that time, both the
inftrument and the victim of that Emperor's cruelty,
and that, therefore, it would not have refufed to
comply with his defire, had he difcovered fuch
earneftnefs to have it granted as might have been
deemed an order. But the fenate, no doubt, was
aware, that, in order to amufe the people with a
fhadow of liberty, he afked, with little earneftnefs,
what he was not folicitous to have granted. Nor
was much refolution requifite to humour this gri-
mace.

But

But if, on the one hand, the senate had a right to decide against the opinion of the Emperor, the Emperor, on the other, by virtue of his tribunitian power, had a right, by his *veto*, to hinder the decisions of the senate from being carried into execution. Besides, he presided " extraordinarily," without being Consul, by virtue of a special concession, which constituted one of the most considerable branches of the Imperial power. This prerogative is known by the name of *jus relationis*, or " right of proposing matters in the senate." This was primitively the ordinary function of the Consuls, in the absence of the Prætors, and, in certain cases, of the Tribunes. When, in the year of Rome 731, Augustus divested himself of the Consulship, which he then exercised for the eleventh time, he likewise resigned that consular prerogative. Upon which, the senate confirmed to him, in perpetuity, the tribunitian power, with the privilege of proposing, at every sitting, any one subject that he thought proper ; whereas the Consul had an unlimited authority of proposing as many as he pleased. Soon after, the senate conferred upon him the right of convening it as often as he thought proper. In 735, the senate offered him, for life, the ordinary and extraordinary powers of the consulship, and he accepted them, but without assuming any title that indicated such perpetual consulship; without depriving the annual Consul of the right of performing the

B b 2

public

public ceremonies, and propofing affairs to the deliberation of the fenate, and perhaps too, without accepting the lictors and fafces, that were likewife offered to him. He accepted, however, firft, the precedence in the fenate; fecondly, a tribunal, with a right of trying caufes, and, probably, the general infpection of the finances; and, thirdly, the prerogative of acting as he thought proper in the preffing exigencies of the ftate, without waiting for the orders of the fenate.

Auguftus confined himfelf to the prerogative, that had been granted him, of propofing any one fubject he thought proper, at every meeting, fo that neither he, nor his fucceffors, unlefs they happened to be annual Confuls, ever enjoyed an unlimited right of propofing matters to the deliberation of the fenate. Accordingly we find this right conferred at every change, with fixed bounds, *jus tertiæ, quartæ, quintæ relationis*. As often as the Emperor propofed any affair to the deliberation of the fenate, he became Prefident of it, if he was not fo already in quality of annual Conful, and ufed to afk the votes as a mere Conful might have done, but with one remarkable difference. Originally, and even under the Emperors, the magiftrates in office never gave their opinion in affairs of their own propofing. The Conful who prefided, and propofed the bufinefs on which the fenate was to deliberate, did not call upon his collegue, nor the Prætors, nor any of the Curule magiftrates, magiſtrates, for their opinion. He firſt addreſſed himſelf to the Conſuls elect, to the Prince of the ſenate, or firſt ſenator, to the Prætors, and other magiſtrates, elect, in ſhort, to all the members of the ſenate not actually in office. He might indeed re-capitulate the arguments on both ſides, and weigh them one againſt another, but without pretending to conclude upon them; which precautions were, no doubt, employed to ſecure to all the members a proper liberty of ſpeech. But when the Emperor propoſed any affair, the Conſul and other magiſtrates were allowed to give their opinion. This is expreſsly obſerved by Tacitus, (*Ann.* III. 17.) in ſpeaking of the charge brought againſt Piſo, and his wife Placina, for the murder of Germanicus. The Abbé de la Bleterie is of opinion, that this conceſſion, to the Conſuls, of voting, was by way of compenſation for the two ſpecial privileges they had before, one, of propoſing any affair they thought proper, the other, of hindering the ſenate from deliberating upon it; and that this conceſſion extended by degrees to the other magiſtrates.

This entertaining and inſtructive Memoir is followed by another, containing " an anſwer to ſome " objections." The firſt objection is, that the deciſions of the Roman ſenate might be, and were ſometimes, actually amended, and even reſcinded, by the judgements of the Emperor; and that the Emperor continued in the poſſeſſion of this prerogative till the reign of Hadrian, which began 140 years after that of Auguſtus. This we find in the Digeſt, *ſciendum eſt appellari à ſenatu non poſſe principem; idque oratione Divi Hadriani effectum* *. Till then, therefore, the decrees of the ſenate were ſubject to the reviſion of the prince, whoſe authority, of courſe, muſt have been ſuperior to that of the ſenate, and the whole nation.

This prohibition of Hadrian, ſays the Abbé de la Bleterie, proves indeed that appeals uſed ſometimes to be made from the ſenate to the Emperor, and that the Emperor finally decided upon theſe appeals; but it does not prove, that theſe appeals, or the deciſions given upon them, were according to law. The legal authority of the Emperor reſulted entirely from his power as both Conſul and Tribune. Now, neither the ordinary power of the Conſul, nor even the extraordinary power, by virtue of which the Conſuls might act, in preſſing emergencies, without conſulting the ſenate, gave him any right to alter the decrees of the ſenate, not even while the republic ſubſiſted in its primitive form, when the ſenate was only the national council, and ſtill leſs under its new form, when the ſenate repreſented the whole nation. As Tribune, the Emperor had a right firſt, to interpoſe both judicially and by force in favour of the oppreſſed, and obſtruct the execution of all ſentences, even thoſe that were national: ſecondly, a

---

* *Lib.* XLIX. *Tit.* 2. *a quibus appellare.*

new

new right of trying all caufes brought into his court, either in the firft inftance, or by appeal, and of pardoning thofe who had been condemned at any other tribunal whatever. But the author has elfewhere proved, that the only appeals that could be made from the fenate to the Emperor, were thofe which preceded a final fentence. Befides, to pardon and to abfolve are different things, and, in general, inftead of giving it himfelf, he ufed to afk the fenate for the pardon of criminals.

Suetonius, it is true, feems to fay, that Tiberius cancelled fome decrees of the fenate, *conftitutiones quafdam fenatûs refcidit*; but, perhaps, thefe decrees had not as yet gone through the ufual forms. For example, a *fenatûs confultum* was confidered as little better than the project of a law, till it had been depofited in the *Ærarium.* In fuch cafes, therefore, the oppofition of the Emperor did not exceed the bounds of his authority as Tribune. Perhaps too the hiftorian means no more than that Tiberius engaged the fenators to alter fome of its decrees; an interpretation which no way clafhes either with the text or the ftyle of Suetonius. For example, he tells us, in another place *, that Vitellius, uncle to the Emperor of the fame name, " accufed Pifo of the murder of Germanicus, and " condemned him," *accufavit, condemnavitque*. Now, the fame perfon could not be both judge and accufer; and it is, befides, well known that Pifo was

* *In Vitell. c.* II. 2.

condemned by the senate on the accusation of Vitellius. This therefore must have been the meaning of Suetonius; and the word *rescidit* will admit of the same latitude. Besides, the passage of Suetonius can only be understood of the beginning of the reign of Tiberius, who not being as yet firmly seated on the throne, and being, besides, under apprehensions from Germanicus, would hardly have ventured to give any umbrage to the senate by annulling its decrees.

Suetonius, likewise tells us, that Vespasian cancelled the decree *, by which the senate had voted divine honours to Galba † : *decretum Vespasianus abolevit.* The Abbé de la Bleterie, by combining what Tacitus and Suetonius have said on this subject, proves, that, at the request of the younger Domitian, the senate by way of reparation for the

* Here we may observe that the superiority of the senate over the Emperor, if we may trust to Father Hardouin, is proved by the decrees of that body granting divine honours to these princes. *Neque enim consecrat,* says he, *aut in Divos reponit, nisi potestas superior eo qui consecratur*; a principle, from which he has drawn the following conclusion, which M. de la Bleterie has corroborated by so many other proofs: *Atque hinc intelligis id, quod multis aliunde constat argumentis, Imperatores Romanos senatui fuisse subjectos, a quo utique consecrabantur ii, qui hunc sibi post obitum deferri honorem in vitâ meruissent.* Note 18. on the xxxvith book of Pliny, Sect. 14.

This argument scarce proves the superiority of the senate to the living reigning prince. All that can well be deduced from it is, that the senate was superior to the Emperors when they were dead, according to the old adage, *A living dog,* &c.

† Galba, c. xxiii.

insults

insults offered to Galba, ordered, first, that his statues should be erected again; and, secondly, that a column and a new statue should be erected to him in the forum: that Tacitus mentions only the first of these orders, and Suetonius only the second. The first was executed; the second required time; and Vespasian, who suspected Galba of having formed a design upon his life, gave himself no trouble to hasten the execution of it; and the senate, being informed of the Emperor's suspicions, suffered the project of the statue and the column to drop; so that this part of its decree was abolished by the mere non-execution of it; and the term employed by Suetonius may signify no more, and not a formal abrogation.

By a short view, which our learned author takes, of all the Emperors before Hadrian, it appears that Caligula was the only one among them who can be proved to have made any encroachment on the jurisdiction of the senate; and it was, no doubt, in order to prevent such encroachments for the future, that Hadrian, who was perfectly well acquainted with the rights of the Roman people, and never decided any important question without the advice of the senate, whose interest he had very much at heart, brought in the law mentioned in the Digest. After all, this law only forbade appeals, after judgement had been formally given by the senate; till then, the parties might appeal from the senate to the Emperor, who, in quality

of

of Tribune, might interpose, of himself, *ex officio*, so as to hinder the senate from ever proceeding to judgement, though he had no right to judge himself, or call the affair to his own tribunal.

The second objection to this doctrine of the Abbé de la Bleterie is drawn from an epistle quoted by Julius Capitolinus. Macrinus, Præfect of the Prætorium, having caused Antoninus Caracalla to be assassinated, was chosen Emperor by the army *, who did not believe him accessary to that murder. This election required confirmation by a national act. The decree of the senate, as representing the nation, that conferred on the new prince all the prerogatives of which the Imperial authority was the result, was styled, first, *lex imperii*, and afterwards, under Justinian, *lex regia*. Macrinus, therefore, wrote to the senate, requesting them to ratify what had been done by the army. He says, in his epistle, that in conjunction with the troops, he had decreed divine honours to Caracalla, adding, " You will likewise decree them " to him, conscript Fathers : we have a right, as " Emperor, to command you to do it; neverthe- " less, we only request it of you." *Et vos, Patres conscripti, ut decernatis, cum possimus imperatorio jure præcipere, tamen rogamus.*

But this epistle bears so many marks of forgery, that it is surprising M. de Tillemont should have been the only one who has discovered the imposture;

* See the Cæsars, Vol. I. p. 163.

though

though Tillemont, nevertheless, for want of having narrowly examined the nature of the Imperial government, considered the Emperors as real monarchs.

Our learned Academician shews, that this pretended epistle is full of contradictions, and of expressions, which not only clash with probability, but custom, and even truth. He also proves, that it must have been forged by some friend of Elagabalus, an implacable enemy of Macrinus and his son Diadumenus. We likewise find, in the history of Augustus, two epistles ascribed to the last, though it is evident that they were forged with a design to blacken Diadumenus, and to make him pass for a monster, of which Elagabalus did well to rid the world.

For farther particulars the reader must be referred to the Memoir itself, in which he will meet with deep researches, solid reflections, and great purity of style.

ADDI-

ADDITIONAL NOTES.
VOLUME I.

P. 14. l. 18. Carterius. *

* Libanius, in his Life, p. 59, mentions a Carterius, who was in many respects notorious for his folly, particularly in daring to offend the august Emperors. The person above-named must probably have offended Constantius, or he would not have wanted the interest of Julian, and the assistance of Araxius. Libanius also mentions another Carterius, in his CCXLVIIIth Epistle (probably the son of the former) as an orator whom the senators of Arce in Phœnicia had enrolled among them. And in his DLXXth he apologises to Maximus for his deserting the Muses, and following Mars. Araxius was præfect of Palestine. Libanius has six Epistles to him.

P. 121. note †.

To the " Rhodian shower of gold" Libanius also alludes in his DCCCLXXIIId Epistle; and Ammianus, XVII. 7.

P. 149. To note * may be substituted this.

* Julian has here in view that passage of Homer, in the first book of the Iliad, [ver. 607.] where he says, that " every God has his mansion and throne † fabricated by " Vulcan with his own hands ;" and which he repeats in another place.   SPANHEIM.

Ib. l. 18. When therefore they rise at the entrance of their Father ‡ &c.

‡ This is also taken from a passage of Homer, in the same book [ver. 533.] to this effect; that " at the approach " of their Father Jupiter all the Gods rise from their " seats, and go to meet him, and that no one waits for " him." I find, however, that the poet says the same thing of Apollo, in the Hymn which is ascribed to him, in praise of that God.   Ibid.

---

† In this passage Homer mentions only their mansion, or house, δώμα.
—— their starry domes ——
The shining monuments of Vulcan's art.   POPE, 778.

The

The fhining fynod of th' immortals wait
The coming God, and from their thrones of ftate
Arifing filent, wrapt in holy fear,
Before the majefty of heaven appear, &c.   POPE, 696.
P. 151. To note † add.

† The authority of Julian, no doubt, is highly refpectable; but if a perfon in youth carry the marks of a bad difpofition, and deliberately commit atrocious actions, when his intereft required them, we are ftill warranted to queftion the fincerity of his converfion, though, in a different ftate of his intereft, even the whole tenor of his life fhould change.   FERGUSON.

P. 290. To note † add.
Thefe Abantes are alfo mentioned by Libanius in his Orat. xix.

P. 305. To note † add.
The Jupiter, who laments with tears of blood the death of Sarpedon, his fon, had a very imperfect notion of happinefs, or glory, beyond the grave.   GIBBON.

Libanius, " on hearing of the death of Julian," repeats this allufion, by faying, " I looked up to heaven, expecting " tears mixed with blood, fuch as Jupiter fhed upon Sar- " pedon ; but I did not fee them ; though perhaps he " poured them on the corpfe, and, like the duft and blood " attendant on a battle, they were feen by few." *In Jul. Imp. Necem.*

P. 312. note ‡.   Ουτ' εν λογω υτ' εν αριθμω.   Subftitute this.
Libanius quotes this oracle again in his MCXVJth Epiftle : " But now he who is ignorant of the laws is truly an " Ægian *, of no name or rank." On which the tranflator has the following note :

* Αιγιευς.] In the MS incorrectly Αιγιυς, called Αιγιυς, from Αιγιοι, a city of Achaia, as we learn from Stephens de Urbibus, p. 36, who quotes this oracle given to them,

Υμεις δ'Αιγιεες υιε τριτοι, υιε τιταρτοι,

to which others add the following,

Ουδε δυωδεκατοι, υτ' εν λογω, υτ' εν αριθμω.

Compare Th. de Pinedo on this paffage, p. 36.   To this our author refers.   Erafmus, in his Adages, p. 393, applies this to the Æginenfians, deceived by the fimilitude of the name.   WOLFIUS.

The fcholiaft on Theocritus applies it to the inhabitants of Megara.

Υμεις δ'ω Μεγαρεις, κ. τ. λ.

P. 316. note *.

Calliopius, it appears from several other Epistles, was also an assistant to Libanius in his instruction of youth, one of his ushers.

P. 324. l. 8. Calliope is also honoured, &c.

† See Vol. II. p. 251. note *.

VOLUME II.

P. 14. Epistle VIII. " You are come, Telemachus.'
Libanius begins his Legation to Julian (προσευτικος προς Ιυλιανον) with the same quotation.

P. 45. Epistle XXII. To LEONTIUS *.

* Consular of Palestine in 363, as appears by the title of a law, xii Cod. Theod. tit. 55. *De Decurionibus.*

This Leontius seems to be that governor of Palestine whom at that time, together with Alypius, Julian is said by Ammianus to have given a fruitless commission to re-build the temple of Jerusalem. [See p. 74. note.] To the same there are several Epistles of Libanius. He afterwards governed Palestine as Pro-consul under Theodosius the Great.
GODEFROI.

P. 46. Epistle XXIII. To HERMOGENES †.

† Libanius often mentions an Hermogenes, as Prætor of Syria, and styles him in his Life, p. 39, " the best of " magistrates."   He has also two Epistles to him, viz. the MDXLIXth of Wolfius, and the xiith of Zambicari, l. iii. By the latter he appears to have had a house at Corinth. Ammianus too mentions him, xix. 12. See Valois on the passage, and Godefroi in the prosopographia of his Theodosian Code, p. 365.

P. 69. l. 16. The garden *.

* The short description, which Julian here gives, of this Syrian garden, may be added to the few particulars of ancient gardens which Mr. Burgh has collected in a note on Mr. Mason's English Garden, p. 130. The extent is not mentioned, but by its comparison to that of Laërtes it must have been small. Of its disposition, however, we are informed, which was far from happy. The pot-herbs and fruit-trees were planted in the middle, the latter, in that

hot

hot climate, not requiring walls to force them, and there was not only a grove of cypreſſes, but a row of thoſe trees was alſo ranged along the walls, it being, like the Italian gardens deſcribed by Biſhop Burnet, walled round, and by this double fortification, as it were, completely excluded from a view of the country.

P. 90. l. 1.

" Diogenes," ſays Libanius, " was a native of Synope, " and the uncle of Ariſtophanes." See Vol. I. p. 317.

P. 148. l. 7. ſwallows †.

† In like manner his maſter Libanius (Ep. XLIV.) compares chattering and long letters to ſwallows, birds that are noiſy in the ſummer, and fly to and fro.　　Wolfius.

P. 199. Add to note *.

By the Epiſtles above-mentioned of Libanius, Eutherius appears to have been præfect of Armenia, and to have had a ſon under his tuition.

P. 227. Add to the ſecond paragraph of the note:

In a ſubſequent work Libanius deems both theſe events preſages of the death of Julian. " This," ſays he, " was " predicted by the temple of Apollo deſtroyed by fire. " The God forſook the earth, as it was ſoon to be pol- " luted. This was alſo foretold by the earthquakes con- " vulſing all the ground as harbingers of approaching " diſturbance and confuſion." *In Jul. Imp. Necem*, p. 258.

P. 246. Among the gardens of antiquity to which Milton, b. iv. compares and prefers his " Paradiſe of " Eden," is

　　" That ſweet grove
　　" Of Daphne by Orontes."

P. 247. Add to note *.

Libanius in his Life, p. 47, 8. mentions the Olympics which were celebrated on his 50th birth-day, which muſt have been in the year 364, the year after the death of Julian. " At theſe," ſays he, " I had an ardent deſire to " be preſent ; but on the firſt day was impriſoned, not by " the Prætor, but by a ſevere attack of the gout."

INDEX

TO

VOLUME II.

INDEX.

Page

Bostre-

D.   Page

Dadaſtana, city of, Jovian receives there the deputies
    from the ſenate of Conſtantinople   358
Damaſcus, praiſes of   51
Daniel, a prophecy of, perverted perhaps by Julian 58 (note)
Daphnæan temple of Apollo burnt 243 (note) 250, &c.
    deſcribed   249, &c.
Daphne, its beauty   68. 246
Dead, cuſtom of the Pagans in funerals   309
Delany, Dr.   286 (note)
Democritus, his conſolation of Darius   94
Didymæan oracle, quoted   177
Diodorus, biſhop of Tarſus   205
Diogenes, the philoſopher 90. Julian writes to him   201
Dionyſius, Julian writes to him 158. his cowardice   160
    his drunken abuſe 165. his blunders 169. per-
    haps commander in Greece   210 (note)
Divination of Heathens under Valens 219. inquiſition
    into it   *ib.* (note)
Donatiſts, furious ſchiſmatics   316
Doſitheus, Julian writes to him   79
Dura, city of, Julian loſes four days there 272. igno-
    minious treaty of   280

E.

Ecdicias, præfect of Ægypt, Julian writes to him 11. 17.
        134. 153
Ecebolus, the ſophiſt, Julian writes to him   39
    ———— chief magiſtrate of Edeſſa, Julian writes to
    him   118
Echo, the wife of Pan   151
Edeſſa, city of, perſecuted by Julian 118. zeal of its
    inhabitants for the Chriſtian religion 119 (note)
    Jovian arrives there   310
Edict of Julian relating to phyſicians 63. to profeſſors 110
    forbidding the Chriſtians to teach polite literature 112
    relating to profaners of tombs, and concerning
    funerals   189
Eleuſinian pontiff   50 (note)
Elpidius, the philoſopher, Julian writes to him   154
Ethnarchs, chiefs of the Jews till the beginning of the
    Vth century   58 (note)
Evagrius, Julian writes to him   122

C c 3   *Homer,*

L.

M.

Momus,

Theodorus,

[397]

*** Since this work has been printed off, I am enabled, by the *Nouveau Dictionnaire Historique* *, (*4me edition, 6 tomes, 8vo, à Caen*, 1779), to add the following account of a writer to whom I am much obliged.

BLETERIE (JOHN PHILIP RENE de la), born at Rennes, died in an advanced age, in 1772. He was a man of learning, was much attached to religion, and his morals did not belie his principles. His knowledge, being solid and diversified, rendered his conversation interesting and improving. He published several works, which have been well received by the public. 1. *The History of Julian the Apostate* †, Paris, 1735. 1746. 12mo. a curious performance, well written, and distinguished at once by its impartiality, precision, elegance, and judgement. 2. *The History of the Emperor Jovian*, with translations of some works of the Emperor Julian, Paris, 1748, 2 vols. 12mo. &c. &c.

---

* The work so styled, *ou Histoire abregée de tous les hommes qui se sont fait un nomme par le Genie, les Talens, les Vertus, les Erreurs, &c. depuis le commencement du monde jusqu'à nos jours, par une Societé de Gens de lettres*, is of itself a library.

† This work, it is observable, is not so entitled by the author, but solely *Vie de l'Empereur Julien*.

ERRATA in VOL. II.

Page
17. note † l. 1. r. " Julian
    " was truly"
26. note † l. 6. r. ' χρυσων'
31. note * l. 2. r. " common
    " reading"
65. l. 13. r. ' Chalcis'
66. is mispaged
82. note * l. 3. r. ' ευρει ποιlω'
95. note * l. 7. r. ' δυσωπεισ-
    ' θαι'
97. note † l. 7. ' F. Mar-
    tinius,' &c. belongs to the
    next note
102. note † l. 1. r. ' παιδιων.'
124. l. 13. After ' friends' add
    ‡ and prefix the same re-
    ference to the note be-
    ginning " Julian, it ap-
    pears," &c.

Page
159. l. 5. r. ' Constans'
165. note * l. 3. r. ' Phædon'
169. note * l. 1. r. ' Φαιδον'
206. l. the last, r. ' confectam'
214. l. 4. r. (21)
240. note * l. the last, r.
    ' Chiliades'
259. is mispaged
279. note * l. 3. r. ' to whom'
284. l. 3. fr. the bottom, r.
    ' as were'
291. note † l. 3. r. ' a Latin'
333. note † l. 3. r. ' πασι'
341. l. 17. r. ' Bernicius'
    to note † add   B.
361. note * l. 1. after ' Am-
    mianus', add a comma

F I N I S.